◎Harden's

Theatregoers' Handbook

By Mark Shenton & Roger Foss

Publisher's announcements

Harden's for your PDA
Harden's London Restaurants is now available for use on your PDA (Both Pocket PC and Palm OS).

Other Harden's titles
London Restaurants
UK Restaurants
Hotel Guide
London Party Guide
London Bars & Pubs
Good Cheap Eats in London
London Baby Guide
UK Baby Guide
London for Free

The ideal corporate gift
Harden's London Restaurants, Harden's UK Restaurants, Harden's Hotel Guide and Harden's London Bars & Pubs are available in a range of specially customised corporate gift formats.

For further information on any of the above, please call (020) 7839 4763 or visit www.hardens.com.

© Harden's Limited 2004

Mark Shenton and Roger Foss have asserted their rights under the Copyright, Designs and Patents Act 1988 to be identified as the Authors of this work.

ISBN 1-873721-65-X

British Library Cataloguing-in-Publication data:
a catalogue record for this book is available from
the British Library.

Printed and bound in Italy by Legoprint

Editor: Richard Harden
Production Manager: Elizabeth Warman

Harden's Limited
14 Buckingham Street
London WC2N 6DF

CONTENTS

FROM THE AUTHORS

To hear the West End itself tell it, theatres are falling down and some should even be torn down. Some theatre owners say they don't make (enough) money; others that there are too many theatres, or not enough of the right ones. Meanwhile, performers who actually have to work in them routinely complain about backstage conditions that would "almost have the RSPCA stampeding for the High Court", according to an article by one West End actor, who added, "you needed a tetanus injection if you tripped on the stairs." Audiences are in a no less precarious situation, subject – in an example cited by the same actor – to lumps of plaster falling from the theatre ceiling into the stalls!

Yet simultaneously we're also in a real Golden Age of theatre re-building in London: literally millions of mostly public (and some private) money has been spent on refurbishing the Royal Opera House, the Royal Court, the Almeida, Hackney Empire and the London Coliseum, while an entirely new building has been expensively created for Hampstead Theatre to replace the temporary prefab construction that housed it for more than 40 years. And now, that privately wealthy impresario and theatre owner Cameron Mackintosh, who made his vast fortune in the theatre, is ploughing some of those profits back into a wide-ranging scheme to regenerate the venues in his control, kicking off with the remodelling of the Prince of Wales Theatre, and to be continued with an even bigger scheme embracing the Queen's and Gielgud theatres in Shaftesbury Avenue, and even adding a new studio theatre – The Sondheim – atop them.

Over a decade ago, Mackintosh had not only handsomely but also profitably transformed the Prince Edward Theatre, at a cost of some £4 million, into one of London's most desirable musical houses – the first privately-owned commercial theatre to have had such an extensive refit. "I hope that the money I'm spending will come back in my lifetime," says Mackintosh, "but whatever happens, I will leave for my Foundation, and indeed for the enjoyment of future theatregoers, buildings that are in a much better state than when I got them."

But such altruistic passion has rarely informed theatre ownership, the stock of which has been passed from pillar to post, literally, over the last century. Theatre buildings have famously high overheads – the costs of which, of course, are passed onto the theatre producers who hire them, if they're occupied, but borne by the owner if not, with the result that essential maintenance and refurbishment usually has to work around the shows, rather than in between them.

There is, however, clearly a great deal of money to be made from buying and owning theatres – why else, for example, would Andrew Lloyd Webber's Really Useful Group have shelled out some £85 million to buy the ten theatres in the portfolio of what was then Stoll Moss Theatres?

Now, however, the RU group boldly asserts that four of the prime theatres it bought the leases to at the foot of Shaftesbury Avenue, have returned less combined profit since the Second World War than the cost of refurbishing the Royal Court. In some 54 years, in other words, they are said to have made less than £29 million – allowing for the fact that one of them (the Queen's) was out of commission owing to war damage until the late

1950s, this suggests that something's drastically wrong. Many of the shows that have gone into those same theatres in that time have made a great deal of money for their producers, but if the current landlords and their predecessors fail to have done so they must have been either managing them very badly or striking a lot of poor rental deals... or simply used the profits to maintain the fabric and upkeep of the buildings, which given their decrepit state, can't have been much.

In the same breath that West End theatre owners have cried "foul!" about the lack of Lottery funds available to them to implement improvements to their sometimes foul theatres (since they are commercial enterprises, the Lottery passes them by). It is also they who are trumpeting about how economically important the West End is. According to figures published in 2002, the West End took over £300 million at the box office. With seat prices increasing all the time since then, that figure would be even higher today. Yet a recent report calculates that some £250 million is needed to bring the West End's theatrical fabric up to scratch that government help is being asked to secure.

Money, in short, is being made, but not spent. Someone's making money – in theatre, it is sometimes said, you can't make a living, but you can make a killing – but no one seems to prepared, Mackintosh apart, from taking responsibility for the venues that money is being made in.

It's time that something was done, or the 40 West End theatres that are commercially owned and managed – and account for some 5/6ths of the total attendances in London – will eventually fall into a state of permanent disrepair, and that means they won't be able to function as working theatres anymore. Of course, until the 1880s, theatres would routinely burn down within an average lifetime of around 18 years, so there'd be a natural process of renewal and refurbishment. Better fire protection and better buildings have created their own problems.

Lord Andrew Lloyd-Webber recently called in the House of Lords for a new approach: it's time, he said, to put aside the claims of "heritage" and look to "the demolition and replacement of certain playhouses". Actress Nichola McAuliffe, who has worked in many of them, wrote in response: "He may not have to go to the expense of demolition, if the buildings owned by him and his company, the Really Useful Group – known affectionately as Oxymoron plc – collapse of their own volition. I have played in more than one of them, and remember vividly the dirt and disrepair all around."

These include some of London's most treasured, and treasurable, theatrical houses. But in a world where the short-term gains of immediate profit are put ahead of the ambitions of long-term conservation and respect for what contributes to that cash cow, the situation can only get worse.

This is a depressing spectacle to anticipate for any book that hopes to celebrate visiting these unique venues. But maybe, in pointing out the many pleasures alongside some of the penances of theatregoing, we can contribute to the debate that will ensure it lives on as one of London's defining features.

Mark Shenton   **Roger Foss**

ANOTHER OPENING? DECIDING WHAT TO SEE

The most comprehensive listings for what's playing in all of London's theatres can be found in the weekly magazines *Time Out* and *What's On in London* (new editions hit the streets on Wednesdays), both of which also feature interviews and reviews, and recommendations of West End and fringe productions.

Alternatively, go online for free, to *whatsonstage.com* (with extensive reviews and feature coverage, too, as well as a lively bulletin board on which to post your own comments and questions) and Society of London Theatre's (SOLT) official *londontheatre.co.uk* for news and listings, including resumes of productions. Increasingly, individual West End productions and fringe venues have their own complementary websites, with up-to-date information about the current show and booking details, while theatre critics can be heard mulling over the latest productions on a new website: *www.theatrevoice.com*.

The industry weekly, *The Stage* (published on Thursdays but often available on West End newsstands on Wednesdays), is also worth buying for reviews of new productions and news of forthcoming openings.

The broadsheet UK daily papers (*Times, Telegraph, Guardian* and *Independent*) all have daily arts pages and reviews, while the London morning freesheet, *Metro*, and daily afternoon newspaper, the *Evening Standard*, carry listings, features and reviews. The tabloids have less extensive coverage, though the *Daily Mail* and *Daily Express* are good for theatre roundups on Fridays.

On Sundays, there's extensive theatre coverage in the *Sunday Times* 'Culture' supplement, the *Observer*, *Independent on Sunday* and the *Sunday Telegraph's* 'Review' sections, as well as the *Mail on Sunday* and *Sunday Express*. There are also free listings supplements published with the *Evening Standard* on Thursdays and *The Guardian* and *The Independent* on Saturdays.

For features and interviews with West End stars, the monthly *Theatregoer* magazine comes free with programmes sold at Really Useful Group theatres or £3 where sold separately, while ATG (Ambassador Theatre Group) publishes its own free glossy magazine with features and information about shows and theatres within the West End's second-largest theatre chain.

The Society of London Theatre (SOLT) distributes it's own fortnightly 'official' London Theatre Guide listing the West End shows and major fringe venues. Look out for this handy fold-out brochure displayed in theatre foyers and tourist outlets. *Musical Stages*, published quarterly, is the UK's only magazine devoted to musical theatre. The monthly *Theatre Record*, available by subscription and on sale at the National Theatre bookshop, carries extensive reviews culled from all the main magazines and newspapers.

Apart from the weekly BBC Two *Newsnight* Late Review slot, television is a no man's land for information about current theatre, though Channel Four's Teletext has fairly comprehensive West End and local theatre listings. Similarly, national radio mostly confines itself to theatre reviews on *Front Row* on Radio Four and interviews on Radio Two's Friday night *Arts Programme*. Locally, however, BBC London 94.9FM has regular reviews by Mark Shenton and on LBC97.3 Roger Foss passes judgment on all the latest openings on the late-night *Steve Allen Show*.

BUMS ON SEATS – CHOOSING THE BEST

Where are the best seats in the house? Many West End playhouses, mostly designed by master architects for a social hierarchy long-since vanished, have seating on as many as four levels: the Stalls (level with the stage, known in Broadway as the Orchestra); the Dress Circle (sometimes known as the Royal Circle, an area that in Broadway theatres is known as the Mezzanine); the Upper Circle (sometimes known as the Grand Circle, or on Broadway as the

Balcony); and the Balcony. Many theatres also have seating in boxes. These were designed more to be seen in than to see from, so should mostly be avoided, although in some theatres the side view from a box can be preferable to a restricted view from the back of the Stalls. Balcony seats, often sold at more than the price of a top class cinema seat, are where the paupers used to sit, segregated from the posh lot below. The air high up here is usually so thin it's anorexic and the view is often so poor you might as well be in another theatre.

Always check West End seating plans before you book – either at the theatre itself, online or in this handbook – and remember, expensive front row seats are not always best for sightlines. Also, be extra wary of pillars restricting views and think long and hard before you commit yourself to cheaper seats in the Balcony where you can feel isolated from other theatregoers and distanced from the stage. On the fringe the seats are often unallocated, so just turn up early to grab the seat you want.

Disabled access can vary from the excellent (the National Theatre) to the embarrassingly dire (some West End venues) where staff almost have to carry wheelchair users through side doors. The olde worlde West End buildings are improving although they are often limited by the conditions of their listed status. It's always advisable for disabled theatregoers to contact the box office before booking. The best sources of access information, sound amplification systems such as infra-red or induction loops, guide dogs policy, sign language interpreted, captioned or audio-described performances are from individual theatres or The Society of London Theatres (SOLT) website: *www.theatre-access.co.uk* or the database at *www.artslineonline.com*.

BOX OFFICE BLUES – BOOKING TICKETS WITHOUT THE HASSLE

For the consumer, the bane of the West End is the point-of-entry: how you actually buy your tickets. Unlike most other supply and demand industries, in show business there's only a limited inventory of stock to be sold. There may be upwards of 46,000 seats in the 40 theatres that make up the commercial West End, but once all the tickets are gone, there's no way you can create more space. Selling Just-in-Time tickets to hang from the rafters isn't an option, though you may feel that's already happening in some of the steeper balconies. It's a nice position, of course, for the theatre producer to be in – he's playing to maximum potential – though not so nice for the punter who can't get in to the latest must-see hit.

The other problem is that theatre goods are perishable: like an airline seat, if a Stalls seat goes unoccupied, it's lost revenue. So hit shows have no supply to meet demand, while the weaker ones desperately try to make demand meet supply. The penny has dropped on some managements who, like no-frills airlines, would now rather sell cut-price tickets than have empty seats bringing in no revenue. But you, the potential audience member, are often trapped in the middle, with ready money to spend but no way of spending it if the show's selling out and wary of overspending on something that may not be so good if it's not selling out.

The first rule of the booking theatre tickets used to be to go to the box office in person. It may be the old-fashioned way, but it saves paying credit card booking fees. It also works best on sell-out shows: you may strike lucky with returns, house seats or 'keeps' – tickets held back and only released on the day of the performance. These days, posting your booking by old-fashioned snail-mail along with a cheque and an SAE is probably the most cost-effective booking method of all. Be aware that even telephoning most published theatre box office numbers may not connect you to the theatre's own box office but to a centralised call centre or an online agency; and that most of these add booking and service fees on top of the face value ticket price. A survey by *Which?* magazine revealed that some agencies have been adding up to 28 per cent to the face value of tickets.

The ticket buying landscape has, however, changed dramatically with online bookings enabling you to "visit" the box office remotely from the comfort of your PC. Managements are wising up to the benefits of online booking – the customer does the work, and staffing costs can be cut – and some theatres, like the Royal Court, even recognise this with an internet booking discount!

There's often, however, no need to pay the full price: previews are often sold at reduced prices, and like New York, London has a tkts booth in Leicester Square that sells remaining day-of-performance seats at half price (plus a service charge per ticket) and is open every day except Christmas Day. Additional shows may also be available at a 25 per cent discount. This usually means joining the queue (though unlike its New York counterpart, London's tkts now helpfully accepts credit card payments). Be sure to find the official tkts booth in the clocktower on the south side of Leicester Square, beside the Hampshire Hotel, and don't be scammed by the so-called "Half Price" outfits run by agencies on the approaches to Leicester Square. Ignore any touts lurking around the tkts booth, trying to flog overpriced tickets to hit shows.

Another way to get discounts without queueing, is to search the internet. There are now numerous sites offering access to sometimes quite hefty discounts that can be booked in advance, from the Society of London Theatre's official website (*www.officiallondontheatre.co.uk*, and select the Special Offers button), to *www.whatsonstage.com*, *www.lastminute.com* or *www.theatremonkey.com*. Bookings may be subject to an additional booking fee.

Also, ATG, the Ambassadors Theatre Group, offers generous discounts and special offers to members of its Upstage subscriber discounted ticket scheme (Information Hotline: 020-7369 1789).

Whether booking on-line or in person through an agency it's illegal not to show the face value of a ticket, so always look for agencies displaying the STAR Charter logo. Members of the Society of Ticket Agents and Retailers operate within guidelines supported by, amongst others, the Society of London Theatres and the Office of Fair Trading. Website: *www.s-t-a-r.org.uk*.

Considering the outlay on non-refundable theatre tickets booked in advance, it is possible to buy insurance cover through TicketPlan. For as little as £1 per ticket, this scheme provides cover if you can't attend. Ask about TicketPlan details when booking or see the leaflets in theatre foyers.

On the fringe, the best (and sometimes only) way to book is by ringing the box office direct. With smaller fringe theatres, you may not even speak to a person but will be asked to leave your name on an answerphone, from which a reservations list is compiled. Tickets usually need to be collected just before the performance. Be sure to follow whatever instructions are given, otherwise your tickets may be released.

The Society of London Theatres fortnightly guide (see above) highlights West End theatres offering on-the-day student rates. Some theatres even allow the pre-booking of student tickets by phone. Others, like the Royal Court and the Lyric Hammersmith, also offer special flat rate deals of £5 on Mondays or 'pay what you can' nights.

Finally, ShowPairs offer a chance to see shows at half price. Each month these vouchers offer two top price tickets for the price of one for a selection of West End productions. You'll find them in hotel lobbies and at retail outlets such as Dress Circle.

GETTING THERE – THE UNGLAMOROUS BIT

Parking in central London close to any particular theatre can be a nightmare. Parking meters and single yellow lines mostly apply between 8.30am and 6.30pm from Monday to Saturday throughout most of Theatreland and free meter space after 6.30pm is usually at a premium (be very careful to avoid residents' only bays, or you could find your car ticketed, clamped or, worse, removed!), so public transport is the best bet for any destination in the West End, especially now that London's red bus network has improved. Best off-street car parking deal for theatregoers is the MasterPark Theatreland Parking Scheme run by the City of Westminster and endorsed by the Society of London Theatres. When you visit the theatre you get your parking ticket stamped which entitles you to a reduced parking rate. There are six car parks in the scheme. For a full details pick up at leaflet in theatre foyers, visit: *www.masterpark.com* or phone 0800 243 348.

Beyond the West End, the National Theatre, Barbican Centre and South Bank have dedicated car parks, but beware late night meter charges on the streets around the Hackney Empire where the restrictions apply until 11pm.

Apart from parking fees, the Congestion Charge of £5 per car, per day applies in the central area between 7am and 6.30pm, Monday-Friday evenings (weekends are free). Payment can be made online (*www.cclondon.com*), at selected shops, petrol stations and car parks, by post, by sms from a mobile phone, at BT kiosks within the charging zone, or by phone on 0845 900 1234.

Late night black taxi services in the West End have improved dramatically (but so have the price increases), so there should be no reason for anyone to jump into any illegal minicab touting for trade. For specific information on buses and tubes call London Transport on 020-7222 1234 or National Rail Enquiries on 08457 484950 for London rail services.

BEING THERE – BEST BEHAVIOUR AND THINGS THAT GO WRONG ON THE NIGHT

Theatre Etiquette

In a couch potato age where so many people spend their leisure time interacting with the television set, the PC or the Playstation, some theatre virgins may need a gentle reminder that they're in a theatre surrounded by other people and no longer flicking channels at home!

Despite the routine, and increasingly good-humoured, pre-curtain up announcements to switch off mobiles, pagers and watch alarms, one or more will be sure to go off at every performance, often at a dramatic moment that will destroy the atmosphere and throw the actors. Some cell phone owners have even been known to take the call. Others have been spotted text messaging in the middle of a performance.

If theatregoing is to remain a pleasure for everyone, we suggest the following theatrical no-no's and luvvie do's and don'ts ought to be compulsory:

– Never use mobile phones, pagers, bleepers or wrist watch alarms. Switch them off before you enter the theatre

– Tape recording, photographing or videoing performances is illegal

– Talking during performances or constantly nodding and smiling to your partner is disruptive to those around you. Save up your comments until the interval or after the show

– Never sing-a-long-a your favourite show songs. Unless it's *Mamma Mia!*, leave it to the guys and gals on stage

– Avoid unwrapping sweets or munching crisps from crinkly packets

– Leave babes-in-arms and toddlers at home with a babysitter

– Never arrive late: always double check the performance time before you set out

– Never ever buy tickets from scalpers – the touts who scurry around the entrances to many West End theatres selling dodgy deals

Warning Note: West End theatre managements often need reminding that patrons are not there to be milked of money. With the exorbitant price of add-ons like programmes and drinks, it can often feel as if you are being mugged as soon as you walk through the front door. So here's our luvvie consumer warning list:

— Programmes can cost up to £3 and may contain no more than a cast list, production photos and biographies. Look through the publication first and if it seems a bit thin for the money search out the free cast lists available at many theatres

— Beware of merchandising. While it's tempting to buy the poster and the t-shirt on the night, cast recordings, CDs and videos are often more expensive in theatre gift shops than from the usual record stores. Ask to flick through glossy but often over-priced souvenir brochures before purchasing

— Bar prices often come as a shock to the uninitiated. Some West End theatre bars even insist on selling 'doubles' only, and a bottle of mineral water can cost twice as much as you are used to. Take your own

— Ice creams don't come cheap either. A measly little tub might set you back a couple of quid, so think twice before you buy (pop out instead to a newsagent store nearby, if you can!)

Comfort zones
Smoking is not permitted in the auditoria of any London theatres, but unlike on Broadway it is allowed in most of the public areas, including foyers and bars, with the admirable exception of the Savoy Theatre which is nicotine-free throughout. Some theatres, like the Donmar Warehouse, have now introduced smoke-free bars.

Another legacy of an era when West End theatregoing was a glamorous act of celebration is the loos, which are now mostly cramped curios, often tucked away in awkward corners and almost inaccessible to able-bodied, let alone the disabled.

With London's climate changing, air-conditioning is sadly rare in West End theatres and non-existent on the black box fringe, so be prepared to sweat it out on hot summer nights, or take a fan and litres of bottled water (don't buy them at the bar: the prices are astronomic). Beware the term 'air-cooled'. This usually means someone can open a window somewhere!

Creating a drama
Things that go wrong on the night can include arriving late, forgetting your tickets, finding your seats have been double booked, you can't see, you feel ill, you fall over or are injured, you are disturbed by a constant talker, someone steals your handbag, the star actor is on holiday or off sick, or for some reason the entire show is cancelled. The first port of call for ticketing problems is the Box Office Manager, or if you've bought from an agency get back to them as soon as possible. The House Manager is responsible for all other problems, but if you are not satisfied with his/her solution, get in touch with the theatre management head office next day (the address will be in the programme) and if all else fails contact the Development Office, The Society of London Theatre, 32 Rose Street, London. WC2E 9ET 020-7557 6700/ *enquiries@solttma.co.uk*). SOLT also runs an emergency helpdesk for ticket problems: 08701 535353. And always check when booking to ensure that the star of the show is not off on holiday on the day of your choice.

SHOW BIZ SHOPPING

There are surprisingly few retail outlets dedicated to theatre in London. However here's a selected shopping list:

David Drummond: Pleasures of Past Times
11 Cecil Court, Charing Cross Road WC2
A nostalgic performing arts treasure trove of theatre memorabilia and ephemera, from music hall and variety posters to books and postcards and much more, all presided over by collector David Drummond. Open Monday-Friday 11am-5.45pm (closed lunch 2.30pm-3.30pm), also open first Saturday in the month 11am-2.30pm. Information: 020-7836 1142.

Dress Circle
7-59 Monmouth Street WC2 (near the Cambridge Theatre)
For CDs, videos, DVDs and posters, this star-struck Covent Garden show biz store should be your first port of call. Open Monday to Saturday 10am-6.30pm. Information: 020-7240 2227 or online at www.dresscircle.co.uk.

French's Theatre Bookshop
52 Fitzroy Street, W1 (near Warren Street tube)
World-famous for scripts and theatre books, Samuel French Ltd is the destination of choice, and has been publishing, selling and leasing playscripts for performance since 1830. Open Monday to Friday 9.30am-5.30pm and Saturday 11am-5pm. Information: 020-7255 4300, or online at www.samuelfrench-london.co.uk.

National Theatre Bookshop
Excellent bookshop, also selling cards, videos and CDs, on the ground floor of the National Theatre building (beside the riverside entrance). Open Monday to Saturday, 10am-10.45pm. Information: 020-7452 3456.

Offstage Bookshop
37 Chalk Farm Road, NW1
Second-hand and new theatre and film books, plus posters and old programmes. Open Monday 10am-6.30pm, Tuesday to Saturday 10am-5.30pm, Sunday 11am-6pm. Information: 020-7485 4996.

Royal Court Theatre Bookshop
Sloane Square SW1
Small but useful shop situated downstairs next to the busy bar and restaurant. Good for playscripts. Helpful staff. Open Monday-Friday 3pm-10pm, Saturday 2pm-10pm. Information: 020-7565 5024.

Shakespeare's Globe Shop
21 New Globe Walk, Bankside, SE1
Just the place to brush up your Shakespeare, with texts, books and a vast range of Bard-related merchandising and gifts. Open during season, 10am-5.30pm daily and an after evening performances (not Mondays). Information: 020-7902 1400.

Theatre Museum Shop
Russell Street, Covent Garden, WC2
Sells theatrical books, children's novelties, postcards, posters, souvenirs and stationery featuring images from the museum's collection. Open Tuesday to Sunday 10am-6pm. Information: 020-7943 4700.

THEATRE TOKENS
Gift vouchers in denominations of £1, £5, £10 and £20 (with no expiry date) are exchangeable for tickets at all West End theatres and can be posted direct to homes, hotels and offices anywhere in the UK. Token Line 020-7240 8800, or buy online from www.theatretokens.com or at the tkts ticket booth in Leicester Square and branches of WH Smith, Waterstones, Books etc and Borders.

WALKS AND BACKSTAGE TOURS

Duke of York's Back Stage Tour
St Martin's Lane, WC2
See where Peter Pan first took flight and Puccini was inspired to write *Madame Butterfly*. Check times and prices at 020-7369 1771.

Hackney Empire
Find out what goes on behind the scenes at this refurbished East End theatre. First Saturday of every month at 12.30pm. £5, £4 concs. Phone 020-8985 2424 to book.

London Coliseum
St Martin's Lane, W1
Guided tours of the magnificently refurbished building (not backstage) take place on Saturdays at 11am. Tickets are £5 from 020-7632 8300 or in person at the Box Office.

National Theatre
Upper Ground, SE1
A chance to see all three theatres (Olivier, Lyttelton and Cottesloe), and the backstage areas. The one-hour tours are limited to 30 places. Monday to Saturday at 10.15am, 12.30pm and 5.30pm (these may vary on matinee days). Bookings and ticket prices: 020-7452 3600.

Original London Walks
Long established walking tour company organises a range of theatre-related walks, such as 'Shakespeare's London' and 'Ghosts of the West End'. Visit *www.london.walks.com* for full programme.

Royal Albert Hall
Open to daytime visitors for daily tours, from 10am with the last tour at 3.30pm, Friday to Tuesday inclusive. Tours depart from inside the porch at Door 12 and last for around 45 minutes. Each tour is unique and may include a chance to see rehearsals for a show. The tours do not include a visit to the backstage area. Adults: £6, Child (under 16) £3.50, Under 5s: free, Concs £5.00. Just turn up and go, but tickets are sold on a first come, first served basis, subject to availability.

Royal Court Theatre Building Tours
Occasional behind-the-scenes tour of the redeveloped Sloane Square theatre. Tours take place on Saturdays. Tickets £5/£3 discount Places are limited. Call 020-7565 5000 for dates and times.

Royal Opera House
Visit the backstage and the front of house areas of one of the world's leading opera theatres. Tours take place daily at different times and may include seeing the Royal Ballet in class, the Royal Opera artists in costume or the backstage technology in operation. Bookings, ticket prices and times: 020-7304 4000.

Shakespeare's Globe
21 New Globe Walk, Bankside, SE1
Go back in time to Shakespeare's London on a guided tour of the magnificent replica of Shakespeare's original Theatre. Tours take place daily throughout the performance season. Information: 020-7902 1400.

Theatre Museum
Russell Street, Covent Garden, WC2
National museum of the performing arts situated in the heart of Covent Garden and encompassing permanent displays and changing exhibitions alongside events and activities for children. Also extensive research archives. Admission is free. Open Tuesday to Sunday 10am-6pm. Information: 020-7943 4700.

Theatre Royal Drury Lane
Catherine Street, London, WC2
Through the Stage Door. Tour this venerable playhouse with three professional actors creating characters from its illustrious past, including Nell Gwynne. Monday-Saturday. Phone 020-7494 5094 for times and ticket prices.

Theatreland Walking Tour
In conjunction with the Society of London Theatres, Blue Badge Guide and LBC97.3 broadcaster Diane Burstein leads this theatre district tour on the last Sunday of every month followed by tea at a top London Hotel. The tour starts at 2.30pm outside the Theatre Museum. Bookings: 020-7557 6700.

THEATRELAND RESTAURANTS
Prices shown are typical for a three-course à la carte dinner with wine, coffee and service. Pre-theatre deals will invariably be cheaper. Times shown at the end of reviews are 'last orders'.

SOHO
Ah, the promise of exotic Soho. It may seem sleazy – it is – but it does offer a good variety of pre- and post-theatre dining possibilities, at most price levels.

Aperitivo   £30
41 Beak St, W1   7287 2057
A rather jolly Italian 'tapas' bar on the fringe of Soho. It makes a convivial place for a light pre-theatre meal. / 11 pm

Aurora   £34
49 Lexington St, W1   7494 0514
Romantics looking for a place for a pre-theatre supper with their loved one need look no further. You might need to think to book ahead a bit, though, as this charming low-key restaurant (which even has a garden) is beginning to lose its 'hidden gem' status. / 10.30 pm

Chiang Mai   £31
48 Frith St, W1   7437 7444
If you want a bit of off-stage West End spice, this is one of the very best places to find it. Your smart friends may not appreciate the charms of this heart-of-Soho Thai restaurant, but those prepared to look beyond the tatty décor will find here some of the best-value food in the centre of town. / 11 pm

Chowki   £24
2-3 Denman St, W1   7439 1330
It's not been open for long, but this comfortable modern Indian, a minute's walk from Piccadilly Circus, has made a deserved name as one of the best-value places to eat in the West End. / 11.30 pm

Circus   **£40**
1 Upper James St, W1   7534 4000
If you want to kick off your evening hanging out with the local media dudes, this strikingly understated corner restaurant is one of the best places to do so. Shaftesbury Avenue – via the extraordinarily hidden-away
Golden Square – is surprisingly nearby, too. / midnight

The French House   **£37**
49 Dean St, W1   7437 2477
If you want a bit of 'Old Soho' style to kick off your evening, you're unlikely to do much better than this wonderfully unpretentious, small and friendly dining room above a famous boozer. Book well ahead, as it has
become quite a vogue destination, which some people find quite romantic. / 11 pm

Gopal's of Soho   **£25**
12 Bateman St, W1   7434 1621
Given London's justified reputation as a centre for subcontinental restaurants, it's remarkable how few good,
plain curry-houses there are in the West End. Therefore tt's all the more worth knowing about this stalwart
establishment, which Mr Gopal has presided over for many years. / 11.15 pm

Jimmy's   **£18**
23 Frith St, W1   7437 9521
For an inexpensive supper rather in the style you might have found in the '50s, it's worth seeking out this
jolly basement – a Greek taverna that's occupied its site for over half a century. / 11 pm, Thu-Sat 11.30 pm

Kettners   **£31**
29 Romilly St, W1   7734 6112
The pianist and the champagne bar make this fabulously-housed and once-great institution a pizza house
of more than usual interest. It's moved into the ownership of PizzaExpress in recent times, so let's hope
they're giving the standards the shaking up they clearly needed. / midnight

Masala Zone   **£22**
9 Marshall St, W1   7287 9966
Especially handy for the Palladium, this bright modern canteen specialises in one-plate dishes inspired by the
street-food of the Indian subcontinent. / 11 pm

Melati   **£28**
21 Great Windmill St, W1   7437 2745
A classic pre-theatre pit stop, this long-established Malaysian canteen, a few paces north of Shaftesbury
Avenue, continues to offer tasty and not-too-pricey fare in surroundings offering minimal space or comfort.
/ 11.30 pm, Fri & Sat 12.30 am

Mildred's   **£25**
45 Lexington St, W1   7494 1634
Veggie-dom being so 'normal' in London, there are few specialist restaurants. If you want a real choice of
non-meat dishes, though, you may find it worth seeking out these north-Soho premises. / 11 pm

Pollo   **£16**
20 Old Compton St, W1   7734 5917
Smart it is not, but if you want to sustain yourself before the show with a big bowl of inexpensive pasta, you
won't do so much more cheaply than at this studenty standby of many years' standing. / midnight

Rusticana   **£32**
27 Frith St, W1   7439 8900
This pleasant, young-at-heart, family-run Italian is a handy place for a quick bite. More substantial fare is
also available. / 11.30 pm

16

Shampers £33

4 Kingly St, W1   7437 1692

This congenial wine bar, just off Regent Street, has offered pretty much the same formula of reasonably priced Gallic dishes and decent wines for nearly three decades, and it remains very popular. / 11 pm

Sri Thai Soho £31

16 Old Compton St, W1   7434 3544

This stylish Thai restaurant has long been one of the more civilised central ethnic restaurants. Unsurprisingly, it can get rather busy, but that's just reflecting the fact that it's a good all-purpose central rendezvous – pre- or post-theatre, or at any other time. / 11.15 pm

Tomato £31

54 Frith St, W1   7437 0666

If you just want a quick pleasant pizza before or after a show, these uncompromisingly modern premises offer a good non-chain choice. / 11.30pm

La Trouvaille £42

12a Newburgh St, W1   7287 8488

Just off Carnaby Street, this relatively new bistro is making quite a name by the simple measure of offering a classic old-fashioned Gallic formula. / 11 pm

Yauatcha £45

Broadwick Hs, 15-17 Broadwick St, W1

The original creator of the Wagamama chain (and subsequently of smash-hit oriental Hakkasan) has recently opened this impressive oriental 'tea-house', at the base of a striking new north-Soho building. The excellent dim sum menu is available at dinner time, and is ideal for a pre-theatre supper. / 11pm

Yming £30

35-36 Greek St, W1   7734 2721

It's odd that one of the best Chinese restaurants in central London is just over Chinatown's boundary (Shaftesbury Avenue), and beats its neighbours across the road in pretty much every way. It's a very civilised place, too, with the only possible downside being that it might be a touch quiet for some tastes. / 11.45 pm

CHINATOWN

The 'hard-core' fan of the rich experience which is Chinatown will doubtless have his or her own favourites. We've listed here some of what are generally agreed to be the better and best-established restaurants in the area.

Aaura £32

38 Gerrard St, W1   7287 8033

One of Chinatown's fresher faces, the former China City has been given a facelift in recent times (but it remains under the same ownership). It offers a good range of dishes in quite a smart setting. Service is pleasant too. / 11.30 pm

Café Fish £3536-40

Rupert St, W1   7287 8989

Those with long memories may confuse this no-nonsense fish brasserie with its predecessor, just off the Haymarket. Its successor has never quite achieved the 'golden glow' of the original, but this central spot makes a handy enough place for a light fishy meal before a show. / 11.30 pm

Chuen Cheng Ku   **£24**
17 Wardour St, W1   7437 1398
A Chinatown landmark – if you're looking for the 'classic' local experience, this is one of the very best places to find it. / 11.45 pm

Fung Shing   **£34**
15 Lisle St, WC2   7437 1539
This unpretentious back street spot has long had a reputation as one of the best oriental restaurants in the centre of town (though standards have been a little bit up and down in recent times). The best dishes are the adventurous ones, so don't come here if it's a post-show chicken Chow Mein you're after. / 11.15 pm

Imperial China   **£35**
25a, Lisle St, WC2   7734 3388
A top tip for people who don't like Chinatown. A good all-round performer, it benefits from notably pleasant service. / 11.30 pm

Joy King Lau   **£23**
3 Leicester St, WC2   7437 1132
"Great food, dire surroundings" – that's the deal at this "huge" but "better-than-average" spot just off Leicester Square; it's "always full". / 11.30 pm

Manzi's   **£44**
1 Leicester St, WC2   7734 0224
A traditionalists' heaven in the heart of Theatreland, this jolly, old-style fish and seafood parlour, just off Leicester Square, has been under the ownership of the same family for decades. Simple dishes are best. / 11.45 pm

Mr Kong   **£23**
21 Lisle St, WC2   7437 7341
The chef's specials are the top tip at this old-timer which some aficionados regard as the one of the best Cantonese restaurants in town. It is worth some pains, however, to avoid sitting in the basement. / 2.45 am

New Mayflower   **£26**
68-70 Shaftesbury Ave, W1   7734 9207
It may look a bit rough-and-ready, but if you're still looking for a quality dinner as the witching hour approaches (or has past), it's well worth seeking out this fixture. The food can sometimes be exceptional, too. / 3.45 am

Poons   **£19**
4 Leicester St, WC2   7437 1528
Just north of Leicester Square, a large and pretty basic Chinese restaurant whose location and style make it a 'natural' for pre- or post-theatre dining. / 11.30 pm

Tokyo Diner   **£16**
2 Newport Pl, WC2   7287 8777
It may seem oddly mis-located but this Japanese corner diner has made quite a name for itself as a destination for those in search of cheap and fast West End chow. A place to linger, however, it is not. / 11.30 pm

Wong Kei   **£16**
41-43 Wardour St, W1   7437 8408
If you're looking for the classic no-frills experience, it doesn't come on a larger scale, or at much more modest cost, than at this gaudy behemoth. The service has long been legendary for its rudeness, but there have been unsettling reports recently of staff whose attitude has verged on friendly. / 11.15 pm

COVENT GARDEN

If you want the full 'tourist' experience of dining out, you need only head for the otherwise very pleasant Covent Garden market. Within a few minutes' walk, though, there are some good places – often off the beaten track – from which we've made the following selection. Purists will wish to know that we've included in this section a few north-Covent Garden places which are technically in Bloomsbury.

Abeno £29
47 Museum St, WC1   7405 3211
If you want something a bit 'different' (and quite reasonably priced, too), this café near the British Museum is a place of some charm. It specialises in okonomi-yaki – Japanese omelettes, cooked at your table. / 11 pm

Axis £50
1 Aldwych, WC2   7300 0300
At the smarter end of the restaurants you generally think of as 'pre-theatre', this modernistic Covent Garden-fringe basement is a good-quality all-rounder. Its approach is quite businesslike, perhaps suiting it best to the more formal sort of theatre party. / 11.30 pm

Bank Aldwych £44
1 Kingsway, WC2   7379 9797
If you want a venue your companions are unlikely to be able to miss, this very large modern restaurant on the edge of Covent Garden fits the bill nicely. This is the sort of all-purpose large venue which can deal efficiently with most types of pre- and post-theatre diners. / 11 pm

Banquette £40
Strand, WC2   7420 2392
Wareing's relaunch of the former 'Upstairs' brasserie at the Savoy makes a handy, and surprisingly inexpensive, destination. Well, the food is reasonable – drinks prices are exorbitant. / 10.30 pm

Beotys £36
79 St Martin's Ln, WC2   7836 8768
Traditionalists are particularly likely to enjoy a visit to this long-established restaurant in the heart of Theatreland. It's a comfortable (and quite smart) place, whose old-style Continental menu mixes Greek and French dishes. / 11.30 pm

Boulevard £31
40 Wellington St, WC2   7240 2992
This unpretentious Covent Garden brasserie, not far from the Royal Opera House, has generally been a reliable bastion of value and quality. Even here, though, the odd quality-hiccup is not unknown. / midnight

Brasserie Townhouse £31
24 Coptic St, WC1   7636 2731
Rather hidden away at the north end of Theatreland, this self-descriptive Bloomsbury restaurant makes a handy – and welcoming – place for a pre-theatre dinner. / 11 pm

Café des Amis du Vin £40
11-14 Hanover Pl, WC2   7379 3444
Locations don't come much more theatrical that this cutely located modern brasserie, whose outside tables (in an alley) are almost overshadowed by the bulk of the Royal Opera House. Those in the know tend to ignore the restaurant, and head for the basement wine bar, where the cheese board has quite a reputation. / 11.30 pm

Café du Jardin £38
28 Wellington St, WC2   7836 8769
This nice-looking corner restaurant has got such a name for its pre-theatre dining that it probably has a slightly unfavourable impact on its reputation as a 'proper' restaurant. If you're looking for a no-nonsense 'real' dinner before the show, however, you're unlikely to do much better hereabouts. / midnight

Café in the Crypt £20
Duncannon St, WC2   7839 4342
The atmospheric crypt of Trafalgar Square's great church provides the setting for this rather basic cafeteria but it's especially handy for the theatres of the Strand. It's an intriguing enough place to justify at least one visit, and even critics of the food would probably concede that it is at least inexpensive. / 7.30 pm, Thu-Sat 10.30 pm

Christopher's £47
18 Wellington St, WC2   7240 4222
For grandeur of setting, this townhouse-restaurant, which is one of London's relatively rare American specialists, is hard to beat. The food is nothing to write home about, but the place remains popular: perhaps it's the thrill of mounting that wonderful theatrical staircase, on the way to the airy first-floor dining room. / 11.30pm

Cork & Bottle £29
44-46 Cranbourn St, WC2   7734 7807
If ever there was a place that deserved the tag 'classic pre-theatre rendezvous', this long-established cellar wine bar – by a sex shop, just off Leicester Square – is it. It's probably fair to say that the extensive wine list is more impressive than the food nowadays, but popularity seems unabated. / 10.15 pm

Le Deuxième £39
65a Long Acre, WC2   7379 0033
This sleek modern restaurant near the Royal Opera House is the number two project from the people behind the perennially popular Café du Jardin. It quickly established a name as a similarly reliable destination, and is, of course, especially popular with opera-goers. / midnight

L'Estaminet £40
14 Garrick St, WC2   7379 1432
It's always been a slightly erratic performer, but this low-key, long-established restaurant on the fringe of Covent Garden retains a name as a classic pre-theatre restaurant, especially for those who like to dine in traditional Gallic style. / 11 pm

Exotika £14
7 Villiers St, WC2   7930 6133
The name is frankly a bit misleading – neither the name nor the setting is particularly exotic – but this hard-edged new diner, right by Charing Cross station, is well worth knowing about if you're looking for no more than a pre-show protein-fix at reasonable cost. / 11 pm

Gaby's £23
30 Charing Cross Rd, WC2   7836 4233
It's not going to win any beauty prizes, but this long-established Formica-chic falafel and houmous stop is something of a West End institution, and certainly has one of the most central locations in Theatreland. It also makes a good spot for a salt-beef sandwich on the way home. / 11.15 pm

Gordon's Wine Bar £25
47 Villiers St, WC2   7930 1408
One of the great West End meeting places, this ancient and gloomy wine bar has an immensely handy location, a minute's walk from Embankment tube. The food is plain and simple, but the wine is good value and the crush often considerable. On a sunny evening you might (just) get a place on the terrace. / 10 pm

Hamburger Union **£10**
4-6 Garrick St, WC2   7379 0412
For a quick burger, you won't do very much better than this new diner. The setting isn't designed to encourage you to linger, making it a perfect destination for a quick bite pre-curtain-up. / 10 pm

Hazuki **£26**
43 Chandos Pl, WC2   7240 2530
Value-for-money sushi is the top draw to this new Japanese restaurant at the back of the Coliseum, but it makes a good choice for anyone looking for a reasonably-priced Japanese dinner, a minute's walk from Charing Cross. / 10.30 pm

The Ivy **£48**
1 West St, WC2   7836 4751
What can one say that hasn't already been said about London's most consistently successful restaurant, the Café de la Paix of luvviedom, through which all famous faces of screen and stage at some point pass? Well, book ahead – months ahead – is the only real advice. / midnight

Joe Allen **£39**
13 Exeter St, WC2   7836 0651
This back street basement American restaurant confirms its thespian credentials by having a pretty-much-identical twin just off Broadway. It's resting magnificently on its laurels nowadays, and really only worth knowing about as a post-show place (book well ahead), when you'll often see a few faces from the other side of the curtain. / 12.45 am

Luigi's **£47**
15 Tavistock St, WC2   7240 1795
If you value comfort and traditional style this long-established – and self-consciously theatrical – townhouse-Italian restaurant can be worth seeking out. For the old-style cooking, though, prices are high. / 11.30 pm

Mela **£31**
152-156 Shaftesbury Ave, WC2   7836 8635
Just north of Cambridge Circus, this tacky-but-fun restaurant was in the vanguard of bringing non-hackneyed Indian cooking into the West End. It still makes a very handy rendezvous for a quick and not too pricey meal. / 11.30 pm

Mon Plaisir **£43**
19-21 Monmouth St, WC2   7836 7243
One of London's longest-established and most consistently successful Gallic bistros, this Covent Garden-fringe institution proudly flies an enormous tricolour. It's famous for the value of its all-in pre-theatre special – post-theatre, you'll end up spending a lot more. / 11.15 pm

Orso **£43**
27 Wellington St, WC2   7240 5269
It was such a place in its day – one of the first 'modern' restaurants in '80s London – and this basement Italian quickly became something of a Theatreland institution (especially as an after-opera destination). Perhaps not entirely coincidentally, its current performance can seem rather lackadaisical. / midnight

Le Palais du Jardin **£43**
136 Long Acre, WC2   7379 5353
It never hits the headlines, but this very large restaurant is spiritually London's most authentic Parisian-style brasserie by quite a long way (all the way down to putting quite an emphasis on plâteaux de fruits de mer). It therefore makes a pretty much perfect all-purpose central rendezvous, including before or after a show. / 11.45 pm

Rules £50

35 Maiden Ln, WC2   7836 5314

For 'occasion' pre-theatre dining, London's oldest restaurant (est 1798), with its splendid Victorian interior, is very hard to beat. It has a convenient but quiet location, too, a couple of minutes' walk from the Strand. The food – in the rarely-found English-traditional style – is rather better than you might expect. / 11.30 pm

Sapori £28

43 Drury Ln, WC2   7836 8296

A minute's walk from the Royal Opera House, but slightly off the tourist beat, this friendly and informal pasta stop makes an unusually useful destination in these parts. / 11.30 pm

Sarastro £33

126 Drury Ln, WC2   7836 0101

'The show after the show' – that's the slogan of this madly OTT high-camp-baroque establishment. It's really if you want to make your theatre trip into a party night out that the place is of most interest – both food and service are notably below par. / 11.30 pm

J Sheekey £53

28-32 St Martin's Ct, WC2   7240 2565

Restaurants don't come much more understated than this less-ballyhooed fish-specialist sibling to the Ivy, quietly situated in a quiet courtyard behind the Wyndham and Albery theatres. For a civilised Theatreland experience, though, it's hard to beat. Book well ahead (though parties of two may be able to squeeze in at the bar). / midnight

Thai Pot £28

1 Bedfordbury, WC2   7379 4580

Almost literally wedged into the rear of the Coliseum, this bright and frankly not terribly atmospheric Thai restaurant has become quite a popular theatregoers' standby. It's not really interesting enough to be regarded as anything more. / 11.15 pm

MAYFAIR AND ST JAMES'S

Restaurants in the pukka purlieus of Mayfair and St James's are often quieter (and often more comfortable) than the restaurants of Theatreland proper. Being more sedate, they may be particularly attractive on Thu-Sat nights, when the heart of the West End can seem rather a zoo. (Recognising the fact that the restaurants in this section are a little outside Theatreland, we given walking times to Piccadilly Circus.)

Al Duca £38

4-5 Duke Of York St, SW1   7839 3090

If you're looking for a 'plain vanilla' modern Italian, you won't do very much better than this St James's corner site. (Piccadilly Circus, 5 minutes.) / 10.45 pm

Alloro £46

19-20 Dover St, W1   7495 4768

A bit of a hidden gem, this modern Mayfair Italian is handily located for the west end of Theatreland. It comes complete with a rather smart cocktail bar, which makes an ideal rendezvous for those not too concerned about their budgets. (Piccadilly Circus, 6 minutes.) / 10.30 pm

The Avenue £46

7-9 St James's St, SW1   7321 2111

If you want to put on a bit of style to start (or end) your night, this bright modern restaurant towards the top end of St James's Street may be ideal. The impressive bar makes a great rendezvous, too. (Piccadilly Circus, 8 minutes.) / midnight, Fri & Sat 12.30 am, Sun 10 pm

22

Bentley's **£60**
11-15 Swallow St,W1   7734 4756
Traditionalists looking forward to a night at the theatre are unlikely to do much better than this long-established (1916) and very traditional fish and seafood parlour. Oysters and champagne at the bar, or the full works in the rather quaint restaurant upstairs – the choice is yours. (Piccadilly Circus, one minute) / 11.30 pm

Brasserie Roux **£36**
8 Pall Mall, SW1   7968 2900
Just a few steps from Trafalgar Square, this large brasserie – part of a French chain-hotel – brings a certain 'je ne sais quoi' to the West End dining experience. It would make a good choice for those looking for slightly more formal (but not stuffy) pre-theatre dining. (Piccadilly Circus, 3 minutes) / 11.30 pm

Osia **£53**
11 Haymarket, SW1   7976 1313
This glamorous new Australasian restaurant is a bit pricey for a pre-theatre bite, but the best bit – hidden from the street – is the lofty bar at the back. If a glass of wine and a couple of tapas-style dishes will sustain you, it makes an unusually elegant setting for a light bite (and just opposite 'Phantom', too). (Piccadilly Circus, 2 minutes) / 10.45pm

Veeraswamy **£41**
Victory Hs, 99 Regent St,W1   7734 1401
Restaurant locations don't come much more central than this colourful spot near Piccadilly Circus – the oldest Indian in town, it has been completely revamped in recent times. It makes one of the more civilised and comfortable places, at any sort of reasonable cost, for a pre-theatre dinner. (Piccadilly Circus, 2 minutes) / 11.30 pm

Il Vicolo **£38**
3-4 Crown Passage, SW1   7839 3960
If you like the idea of starting off your evening's theatre going in a classic old-fashioned Italian that's just a little removed from the hurly burly of Theatreland, this long-established back-alley St James's spot may be just the place. (Piccadilly Circus, 8 minutes.) / 10 pm

The Wolseley **£42**
160 Piccadilly,W1   7499 6996
One of the 'biggest' openings of recent times, this opulent former car showroom (and bank) near the Ritz makes an impressive place to kick off a night in the West End, and it's menu is well suited to pre- (or post-) theatre dining. Only problem is it's booked up well ahead, but some tables are held back for 'walk-ins'. (Piccadilly Circus, 5 minutes.) / midnight

Yoshino **£30**
3 Piccadilly Pl,W1   7287 6622
A top sushi and sashimi stop, just 100 yards from Piccadilly Circus. It's an ideal place for a snack before or after a show – beware, though, that it's fairly authentic, and perhaps better if you're not at all timid about Japanese cuisine. (Piccadilly Circus, one minute.) / 10 pm

West End Theatres

Adelphi Theatre

✉ Strand, WC2E 7NA

🏚 www.rutheatres.com

☎ (Box office) 020-7344 0055/0870 899 3338 (24 hours), (Stage door) 020-7836 1166

🖳 020-7379 5709

🕐 Box office open Mon-Sat 10am-8pm

↑ Midway along the Strand, within easy walking distance of Covent Garden, Aldwych and Charing Cross

🚇 Charing Cross

⊖ Embankment/Covent Garden

P Some single yellow line parking on north side of Strand and on streets nearby. NCP car parks in Drury Lane and Upper St Martin's Lane; Masterpark at Spring Gardens, off Trafalgar Square

🚲 Cycle racks in Wellington Street and Southampton Street

♿ To arrange seats in advance call 020-7344 0055. Discounts available for wheelchair users and their companions. No steps from the Foyer to the Stalls, where there are two spaces for wheelchairs at the back with restricted views. Transfer seating available to any of the stalls aisle seats

🎧 Infrared system with seven headsets. £10 deposit payable on collection from box office

👁 No guide dogs are allowed inside the auditorium. Staff will dog sit up to two dogs during the performance

🍸 Four licensed bars

ⓘ Covent Garden Market, Trafalgar Square, Embankment Gardens

There is a memorial plaque to murdered actor William Terris outside the Nell Gwynne pub in Bull Inn Court adjacent to the theatre

Crowded on either side by the Strand's medley of architectural styles, the Adelphi Theatre's distinct cream and black-tiled façade – cleared of the posters that for decades covered the large octagonal Dress Circle bar window – stands out dramatically today as an Art Deco landmark. A ritzy cream, black and silver lobby invites you to enter a buzzing but functional venue, which makes a perfect jazzy setting for the current hit revival (1998) of *Chicago*. There's nothing like arriving at the Adelphi. You stroll off the Strand into the foyer with its geometrical 1930s ceiling, straight past the gleaming row of booking kiosks, and swish through another set of doors into the Stalls where you are greeted by lots of warm red plush. Of the two theatres in the Strand, the Adelphi is unquestionably the more in-yer-face showbiz one than its near neighbour, the intimate Vaudeville. Andrew Lloyd Webber's Really Useful Theatres run it in association with Nederlander International Limited, which will no doubt ensure that the musical comedy connection will remain strong for years to come.

History

Applause for this pre-Odeon-style theatre go to architect Ernest Schaufelberg who designed the 1486-seat building, which opened in 1930 – the fourth time a theatre has emerged on the site since 1806. Originally known as the Sans Pareil Theatre, it was re-named the Adelphi in 1819 and over the decades became a popular home for Victorian extravaganzas and melodrama. No on-stage "Adelphi Drama", however, could compare with the off-stage final act of star tragedian William Terris, who was murdered in 1897 by a crazed actor just outside the stage door. His ghost is said to haunt the building, as does the memory of Jessie Matthews. A huge British stage and film star, Matthews had one of her biggest hits at the Adelphi after it was Deco-fied in 1930, the long-running CB Cochrane revue *Evergreen*. Look out for the memorabilia on the walls of the Stalls bar. Musicals always work wonderfully here. Notable Adelphi productions include Ivor Novello's wartime *The Dancing Years*, Anna Neagle high-kicking in the long-running *Charlie Girl* in the 1960s and the hit '80s revival of *Me and My Girl*, closely followed by Norma Desmond getting ready for her close-up in *Sunset Boulevard*, and the long-running *Chicago*.

Best seat in the house

Despite its clean modernist lines, the Adelphi's air-cooled auditorium contains a few glitches for the uninitiated, with some seats classified as "restricted view" or "side view". Best views – and comfort – are from the centre Stalls from rows D to J. In the Stalls, beware the Dress Circle overhang that means you can't see the top half of the stage from around row R back. The first few aisle seats either side of the main block are to be avoided if you want to see the entire production without craning, as are the first rows of the Dress Circle where the view is great but the leg-room is minimal. Before booking, ask about leg space and sight restrictions in the distant Upper Circle, where safety bars can irritate.

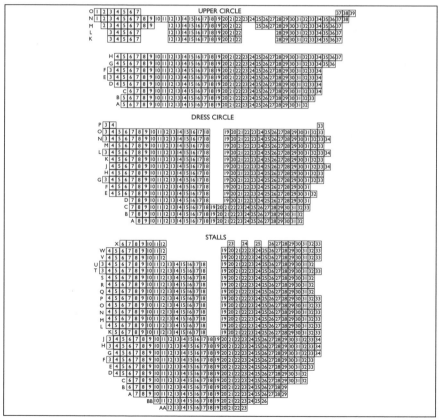

Albery Theatre

✉ St Martin's Lane, WC2N 5AU

🕾 www.theambassadors.com/albery

☎ (Box office) 020-7369 1740, (Stage door) 020-7438 9700

🖷 020-7438 9711

🕐 Box office open from 10am-8pm

↑ Situated opposite New Row south of Cranbourn Street

🚇 Charing Cross.

⊖ Leicester Square (Charing Cross Road East/Cranbourn Street exit), Charing Cross

P MasterPark at Trafalgar Square, NCP at Upper St Martin's Lane and Cambridge Circus. Limited on-street parking on yellow lines and metres in St Martin's Lane and Long Acre

🚲 Racks in Upper St Martin's Lane

♿ Discounts available for disabled theatregoers and their companions. One wheelchair ramp through a side exit door in St Martin's Court. A Royal Circle box has two spaces designated for wheelchair users, or one

wheelchair user and companion. Transfer seating available to any aisle seat in the Royal Circle. No adapted toilets.

🎧 Infrared audio system with 12 headsets to be collected from the centre desk in the foyer. Can be reserved by calling box office, but a deposit is required

👁 No guide dogs inside the auditorium. They are looked after in the 'upstairs office'. Make arrangements when booking

🍹 Three licensed bars

ⓘ The Hippodrome nightclub, Stringfellows, Covent Garden, National Gallery and National Portrait Gallery, Leicester Square, Chinatown, the historic Salisbury public house on St Martin's Lane next door to the theatre, specialist shops in St Martin's Court and Cecil Court

Shares a stage door with Wyndham's Theatre

Back-to-back with the late Victoriana of Wyndham's Theatre, the Edwardian Albery still looks good on paper but is in dire need of a makeover to provide a more people-friendly 21st-century theatregoing experience. In September 2005 ownership reverts from the Ambassadors Theatre Group to Delfont-Mackintosh Theatres, who plan to invest in major improvements to the antiquated public circulation areas and vastly increase capacity in the three unimpressive bars, and in the loos. Hurrah!

History

Framed black and white photographs of Laurence Olivier and Ralph Richardson in the public areas hark back to some of the brightest highlights in the 100-year history of the 879-seat Albery, when it became the wartime base for the blitzed Old Vic and Sadler's Wells companies. The Edwardian opulence of this West End gem – originally named as the New Theatre, after New Row opposite – is a reminder of a rich heritage of dramatic achievements as much as an architectural legacy. Opened in 1902, built by Sir Charles Wyndham and designed by the prolific WGR Sprague, the New fused fashionable Louis XVI style and opulent early Edwardian taste within a large horseshoe auditorium. Through a high proscenium decorated with cupids and angels, generations of theatregoers have watched theatrical fare as diverse as: *Peter Pan* (1915-1919), Noel Coward's first play, *I'll Leave It To You* (1929); the first London production of George Bernard Shaw's *St Joan* (1924); and, after the war, Lionel Bart's *Oliver!*, which packed the New for six years. In 1973 the New Theatre was renamed the Albery in honour of the Sir Bronson Albery, its director for many years. Subsequent hits have included: *Torch Song Trilogy* with Antony Sher; *A Month in the Country* starring Helen Mirren and John Hurt; and, more recently, Dawn French's Bottom in *A Midsummer Night's Dream* and *Endgame* starring Michael Gambon and Lee Evans.

Best seat in the house

Whether it's row AA looking up at the stage or row S watching from the back, the Stalls offer unrestricted views, thanks to the gentlest of rakes (though the ghostly sound of rumbling tube trains can be heard in the front few rows). All seats are comfy, with enough knee room to cross your legs and no problem at the back caused by the Royal Circle overhang. Similarly the Grand Circle overhang is almost unnoticeable from the Royal Circle, although the seats in the two small side blocks either side of the Royal Circle face each other rather than the stage. Higher still, but not much cheaper, the Grand Circle is steep and offers good but distant views, although the safety rail arrangement can be problematic if you are in Row A. Unless you are into extreme sports, avoid the death defying 'slips', a single parapet of seats snaking around the wall. There's an even more vertigo-inducing arrangement in the Balcony. Up an endless Everest of steps, you are so high that the actors look like ants and you'll need an Edwardian ear trumpet to hear the dialogue! From the swishy Stalls you'd never know there were punters in these giddy gods. Unless the seats are sold for a fiver, these four rows for paupers – a legacy of class division long gone – ought to have been abolished long ago.

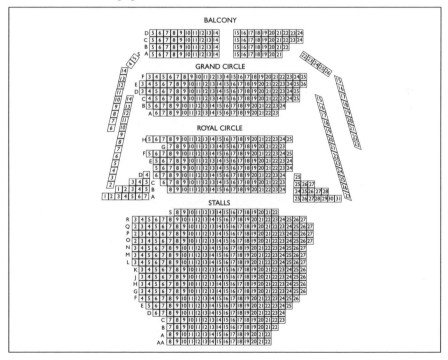

Aldwych Theatre

✉ Aldwych, WC2B 4DF

🖥 www.aldwychtheatre.com

☎ (Box office) 020-7379 3367, (Groups) 020-7930 3000, (Credit card bookings; Ticketmaster) 0870 400 0805, (Corporate Hospitality) 020-7494 5151, (Stage Door) 020-7836 5537

🖴 020-7379 5776

🕐 Box office Mon-Sat from 10am-8pm

↑ On the corner of Aldwych and Drury Lane

🚇 Charing Cross

⊖ Covent Garden, Holborn, Temple

P NCP at Parker Street, Drury Lane, beneath the New London Theatre

🚲 Racks in Wellington Street and Kingsway

♿ Seats are available in the third row of the Dress Circle for wheelchair users who must have an able bodied escort. Access to the Dress Circle is via a side door in Drury Lane, down a ramp inside the door. The theatre has one adapted toilet

🎧 No loop system at present

🔊 Occasional signed performances

👁 Only one guide dog allowed per performance, in Box D

🌟 Four licensed bars, including coffee bar in the rear Stalls and Dress Circle, as well as a champagne and wine bar to the right of the Front Stalls

ⓘ The Meridien Waldorf is next door (good for afternoon tea in the Palm Court, and celebrated tea dances on Saturday and Sunday afternoons), One Aldwych (a modern boutique hotel with an excellent coffee bar facing the Strand Theatre), Covent Garden, The Theatre Museum, Somerset House (including the Courtauld Institute Gallery, and riverside promenade), the Royal Courts of Justice

Built by British actor-manager Seymour Hicks in association with the American impresario Charles Frohman, the Aldwych Theatre approaches its centenary owned by another American, James Nederlander, and operated by Michael Codron Plays. The RSC substantially reshaped the interior of this barn of a place in 1963 and the seating was replaced in 1971. As RSC actress Janet Suzman once wrote, "It was the happiest of choices for the RSC. A real theatre, not a culture bunker." With its Georgian-style 1200-seat interior, this Grade II listed Theatreland monument is always a delight to enter. Nowadays, however, the culture on stage can be bit hit-and-miss and the place often feels more like a heritage bunker than the vibrant theatrical dynamo of yesteryear. But the front-of-house bar staff ladies, some of whom have been serving drinks here for decades, are the jolliest in town.

History

There's nothing new about inner city regeneration. Take the Aldwych. At the turn of the last century the area now bounded by Kingsway, Catherine Street and the Strand was a higgledy-piggledy maze of congested streets and murky alleys lined by notorious timber-built slums. In just five years, the last grandiose Victorian metropolitan improvement scheme swept away all 28-acres of disorder, replacing it with pillared buildings, expansive pavements and wide thoroughfares such as Kingsway (1905). Four rickety theatres were razed, but two brand spanking new ones were built at either end of the centre block of the Aldwych crescent: the Aldwych Theatre, dominating the corner of Drury Lane, and its matching twin, The Waldorf (later renamed The Strand), with the handsome Portland stone Waldorf Hotel in the middle. A novelty of the WGR Sprague-designed Aldwych Theatre in 1905 was a commodious first floor smokers' gallery, from which you could overlook the foyer. In these nicotine-free days it's used as the Circle Bar. Chekhov's *The Cherry Orchard* was given its first performance at the Aldwych, which later became home to Ben Travers's popular Aldwych farces in the '20s and '30s and – after the entire block had escaped threatened demolition – the Royal Shakespeare Company's landmark London tenancy between 1960 and 1982. Other notable productions have been the UK premieres of Tennessee Williams's *A Streetcar Named Desire* and, more recently, Andrew Lloyd Webber's *Whistle Down the Wind* and *Fame: The Musical*.

Best seat in the house

The Aldwych's Edwardian-Georgian décor is priceless, though some of the *Antiques Road Show* seating arrangements do not an enjoyable theatregoing experience make, especially if you've forked out to sit in the three rear Stalls blocks. From here, the mother of all Dress Circle overhangs cuts off the top half of the high proscenium stage for all but a few rows. Between rows T to Z, it's like peeping through a letter-box. You'll get a much clearer peep from the Upper Circle. Similarly, in the steeply raked Dress Circle, the first six rows connect with what's happening on stage but, the further back you go, the more another oppressively low ceiling slices into your enjoyment. The Upper Circle is one of the steepest in town, but low(ish) prices and good(ish) legroom compensate. Apart from the ultra-cramped front row – often only sold on the day of performance at the theatre box office because a safety rail restricts the view – it's just like being up in the old-fashioned 'Gods'.

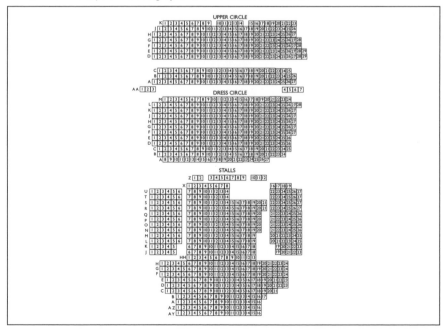

31

Apollo Theatre

✉ Shaftesbury Avenue, W1V 7DH

🖥 www.rutheatres.com

☎ (Box office) 020-7494 5470 or 0870 890 1101 24-hour booking line, (Stage door) 020-7850 8700

📠 020-77494 5154

🕐 Box office open 10am-8pm

↑ At the Piccadilly Circus end of Shaftesbury Avenue, adjoining Rupert Street that leads into the heart of Soho

🚇 Charing Cross

⊖ Piccadilly Circus, Leicester Square

P NCP at Newport Place, Wardour Street or Denman Street. MasterPark at Cambridge Circus

🚲 Racks at junction of Shaftesbury Avenue and Great Windmill Street

♿ Discounts available, but only limited disabled facilities. Wheelchair users must bring a non-disabled companion. There is an awkward wheelchair entrance through a door to the left of the Upper Circle entrance on Shaftesbury Avenue. Transfer seating only, but to any seat. The management will store only two wheelchairs per performance. There are plans to install a chair lift

🎧 Infrared system with six headsets. Not available in front row. Deposit required

👁 Guide dogs allowed into the auditorium or staff will dog sit in the Stalls bar or the manager's office

🍴 Foyer kiosk. Two bars, to the rear of the Stalls and Upper Circle

ⓘ Soho, Chinatown, Piccadilly Circus, London Trocadero shopping centre

Air conditioning

Since 2000, Andrew Lloyd Webber's Really Useful Theatres has been guardian of London's first Edwardian theatre. This is Shaftesbury Avenue theatregoing at its best, and its worst. It is all very well to admire the glorious neo-Renaissance-style interior ornamented with amazing gilded plasterwork and statuary, but the loos and the bars are cramped and awkwardly located, as are some of the sightlines. A management programme note usually urges customers to view the theatre's occasional Edwardian shortcomings "with affection". Easier said than done, perhaps, when you've coughed up top whack for a front row seat and go home with a stiff neck after spending an evening looking up the actors' nostrils, or indeed the actresses' frocks. Maybe for opulent Edwardians these were secret joys of the West End?

History

The dramatic quartet of Art Nouveau angels looking down from the top of the Apollo façade have witnessed countless first-night comings and goings since the smallest theatre on Shaftesbury Avenue opened its doors in 1901 – a month after the death of Queen Victoria – to a musical flop called *The Belle of New York*. Owner-manager Henry Lowenfeld was originally going to name his 775-seat theatre The Mascot, but eventually settled on the Apollo as more fitting for light musicals and operetta. By the Great War this gorgeous-looking theatre had turned to plays, including the 1916 premier of *Hobson's Choice*. From then on it has been very much a jobbing West End venue, with star names as varied as Ivor Novello, Jack Hulbert, Cicely Courtneidge, Terrence Rattigan, Noel Coward, John Geilgud, Vanessa Redgrave, Ben Elton, Donald Sinden and Felicity Kendal appearing on the big posters perching above the ornate iron and glass canopy and just below those four ever-watchful Apollo angels.

Best seat in the house

The Balcony at the Apollo is appalling. If it's open, avoid. Even if you are desperate and can only afford the knock-down ticket price it's hardly worth the effort of climbing all the stairs to this showbiz stratosphere. If you must experience the thrill of thin air, safety rails and fisheye views, take up paragliding. Elsewhere, the auditorium was nattily designed without pillars. Even so, unacceptable sightlines proliferate and the management is perfectly straightforward about this. "Due to the nature of the auditorium, some seats are classified as 'restricted view' or 'side view' – please check with our operators when booking your tickets," they advise. The Stalls front rows are too close to the high-ish stage. Far better to choose centre aisle seats, or better still the front row of the rear Stalls block, set back in a kind of cozy alcove, which has loads of legroom. Seats O7 and O8 in front of the aisle provide a clearer view of the stage than from the Dress Circle, where there are too many "side view" seats for comfort.

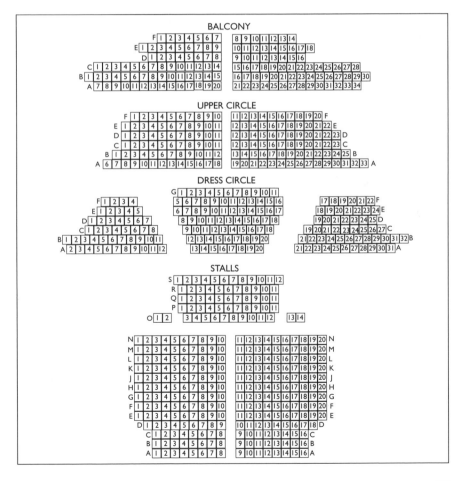

Apollo Victoria Theatre

✉ 17 Wilton Road, SW1V 1LG

🖰 www.cclive.co.uk

☎ (Box office) 020-7834 6318/0870 4000 650 (24-hour Ticketmaster), (Stage door) 020-7834 7231

↑ Immediately opposite the Wilton Road exit of Victoria main line station

🚇 Victoria

🚌 Victoria

P MasterPark at Rochester Row, NCP at Semley Place, off Buckingham Palace Road

🚲 Racks outside Victoria station

♿ Discounts available for disabled customers and their companions. Phone 020-7828 7074 for access information. Wheelchair entrance to the Dress Circle is via an exit door on Wilton Road leading to four allocated seats in Row A. Transfer seating to row B. Up to 10 wheelchairs can stored per performance. One adapted toilet

🎧 No infrared system at present

👁 Guide dogs allowed into the auditorium. Aisle seats are recommended. Staff will also dog sit

🍸 Large bar in entrance foyer, two more in Dress Circle

ⓘ Westminster Cathedral (Roman Catholic), St James's Park, Buckingham Palace

It's nowhere near the original picture house concept of a 'mermaid's dream of heaven', yet after too many years serving as a giant skating bowl for *Starlight Express*, the Apollo Victoria has regained an identity. If you don't get too disoriented by the twin entrances, or lost in the vast acreage of carpeted corridors, this is a place which is definitely helping to bring back a real sense of occasion to theatregoing.

History

Considering it was one of the first cinemas to be "listed" and is generally regarded as the most important piece of cinema design in the UK, it is rather odd that the streamlined Apollo Victoria (or The New Victoria as it was called when it opened by the Gaumont-British chain in 1930) has spent around half its working life as a venue for live shows, concerts and musicals. Indeed, since the mid-1970s, it has housed *Starlight Express* for 18 years and before that longish runs of *Camelot* with Richard Harris, *The Sound of Music* with Petula Clark, Wayne Sleep in *Dash* and Topol in *Fiddler on the Roof* and, more recently, *Bombay Dreams*. But even as a 2860-seat cathedral of the movies – with identical neon-lit entrances in Wilton Road and Vauxhall Bridge Road – it often staged cine-variety, and even hosted one Royal Command performance. The Apollo survived attempts to carve it up into smaller cinema segments, and even a ballroom, but the rising Compton cinema organ sadly vanished long ago, along with the stalactite-shaped light fittings. Over the years much more of the original sub-aquatic décor has been removed, though thanks to recent sympathetic renovations, bronzed Deco mermaids and vast shell-like structures remind today's theatregoers of the watery wonderland that once plunged picture-goers into a fantasy world. Post-*Starlight*, the 684 seats removed for the skate tracks were put back, thus enlarging the theatre's capacity to 2208 seats and making it the third largest in the West End after the Theatre Royal, Drury Lane and the Palladium.

Best seat in the house

It goes without saying that the further you are away from the stage in this mammoth auditorium the less likely you are to get caught up in the show. Don't get too close though. Inevitably, when the stage is as high as an elephant's eye, the first half-dozen rows are best ignored. The view from the front section of the two side blocks of the stalls is also restricted. The entire length of Row Q has an extremely wide gangway in front, so sit back here, stretch those legs and enjoy. You are probably better off anywhere in the two middle Circle blocks than at the back of the Stalls, where powerful field glasses are essential handbag accessories alongside the Maltesers.

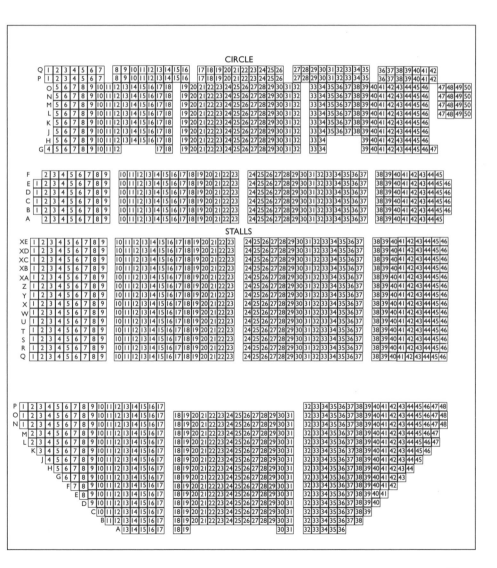

Arts Theatre

✉ 6/7 Great Newport Street, WC1E 7HF

⌂ www.artstheatre.com

☎ (Box office) 020-7836 3334, (Stage door) 020-7836 2132, (Information desk) 020-7836 3334

✉ info@artstheatre.com

① Box office open from 10am-8pm

↑ Within yards of Leicester Square Underground station (Charing Cross Road East & Cranbourn Street exit)

🚇 Charing Cross

⊖ Leicester Square, Covent Garden

P Upper St Martin's Lane, NCP Swiss

Centre Car Park, Wardour Street. Masterpark Chinatown, Newport Place

🚲 Racks in Upper St Martin's Lane

♿ Eight wheelchair spaces, with access via a side exit door

◠ Sound amplification induction hearing loop headsets

👁 Guide dogs allowed

🍴 New licensed cafe/bar in the foyer serving snacks. Small bar downstairs to the rear of the Stalls

① Photographer's Gallery is next door, Covent Garden, Leicester Square

Apart from the signage outside, you'd easily could walk past the Arts and think it's just another part of London's ever-expanding bar scene. The new look Arts Café with its big windows opening on to Great Newport Street has already attracted a younger crowd looking for a bit more than cappuccino culture, and the range of limited season productions seems to have turned this 340-seat theatre into one of the most attractive and interesting venues in Theatreland. Not so über-hip as the equally dinky Donmar maybe, and not yet a producing house, but this is now one of the most audience friendly places in town. 'Cool' would be the word, if only they had air-conditioning!

History

During the 1940s and '50s, under the directorship of actor Alec Clunes, the Arts Theatre Club provided one of the few alternatives to mainstream West End fare, offering acclaimed seasons of classics and new plays which earned it the title of the 'Pocket National'. But ever since it was built in 1927, next door to where Sir Joshua Reynolds once lived in what is now the Photographer's Gallery, membership club status enabled this tiny venue to circumvent the censorious Lord Chamberlain. By 1955 the artistic directorship had fallen into the lap of a young Peter Hall who was soon staging the UK premier of *Waiting For Godot*. The rest is history. Pinter's *The Caretaker*, Orton's *Entertaining Mr Sloane*, O'Neill's *The Iceman Cometh* and Tennessee Williams' *Suddenly Last Summer* all received their English or world premieres here. For a short time the Royal Shakespeare Company even set up its London base at the Arts. State censorship was abolished in 1966 and the 'club' attachment was dropped, but by then the Arts Theatre's star was waning. For 22 years the Unicorn Children's Theatre took up residence, producing children's shows in the daytimes while the evenings were given over to a mixed bag of plays. Eclipsed by the growth of the fringe, the Arts became something of and afterthought and even went totally "dark" for a time. But in 2000 producers Paddy Wilson and Edward Snape and a group of American producers, bought the lease and refurbished the dreary front of house. They also joined the Society of London Theatres, making this an 'official' West End theatre presenting highly successful revivals of *Another Country* and *Entertaining Mr Sloane*, the Pet Shop Boys' musical *Closer to Heaven* and *Happy Days*, directed by Sir Peter Hall.

Best seat in the house

Once you've pushed your way through the front-of-house buzz, it's a bit of a shock to discover that the Arts has a rather dated looking black shoe box auditorium with an old-fashioned proscenium stage at one end and some very creaky, very narrow seats. So steer well clear of the front few rows in the Stalls, as the stage height could leave you with an osteopath's bill. Anywhere else in the slightly raked Stalls will do fine, except perhaps for the end seats in rows G, H and J which are wedged close to the pillars supporting the Circle. Upstairs, seating extends around the side walls of the auditorium (not shown below) and it feels a bit cramped, although the view is mostly clear enough.

DRESS CIRCLE

	1	2	3	4	5	6	7	8	9	10	11	12	13	14	15	16	17
F	1	2	3	4	5	6	7	8	9	10	11	12	13				
E	1	2	3	4	5	6	7	8	9	10	11	12	13	14	15	16	17
D	1	2	3	4	5	6	7	8	9	10	11	12	13	14	15	16	17
C	1	2	3	4	5	6	7	8	9	10	11	12	13	14	15	16	17
B	1	2	3	4	5	6	7	8	9	10	11	12	13	14	15	16	
A	1	2	3	4	5	6	6	7	8	9	10	11	12	13	14		

STALLS

	1	2	3	4	5	6	7	8	9	10	11	12	13	14	15	16	17	18
N	1	2	3	4	5	6	7	8	9	10	11	12	13	14				
M	1	2	3	4	5	6	7	8	9	10	11	12	13	14	15	16		
L	1	2	3	4	5	6	7	8	9	10	11	12	13	14	15	16	17	18
K	1	2	3	4	5	6	7	8	9	10	11	12	13	14	15	16	17	18
J	1	2	3	4	5	6	7	8	9	10	11	12	13	14	15	16	17	18
H		1	2	3	4	5	6	7	8	9	10	11	12	13	14	15	16	
G		1	2	3	4	5	6	7	8	9	10	11	12	13	14	15		
F	1	2	3	4	5	6	7	8	9	10	11	12	13	14	15	16	17	18
E	1	2	3	4	5	6	7	8	9	10	11	12	13	14	15	16	17	18
D	1	2	3	4	5	6	7	8	9	10	11	12	13	14	15	16	17	18
C	1	2	3	4	5	6	7	8	9	10	11	12	13	14	15	16	17	18
B	1	2	3	4	5	6	7	8	9	10	11	12	13	14	15	16	17	
A	1	2	3	4	5	6	7	8	9	10	11	12	13	14				
BB	1	2	3	4	5	6	7	8	9	10	11	12						
AA	1	2	3	4	5	6	7	8										

Barbican Theatre and Pit Theatre

✉ Barbican Centre, Silk Street, EC2Y 8DS

✈ www.barbican.org.uk

☎ (Box office) 020-7638 8891, (Stage door) 020-7628 3351

🖳 020-7382 7270

🕐 Box office open 9am-8pm daily

↑ The most direct route is from Barbican station. Just walk along the Beech Street tunnel facing the station exit and Silk Street is on your right. From Moorgate, follow the signs and hope for the best

🚇 Liverpool Street

⊖ Barbican, Moorgate, Liverpool Street

P Barbican Centre underground car parks serve both theatres, with free parking for orange badge holders. Limited free on-street parking nearby

🚲 Cycle racks in Silk Street opposite main entrance of Barbican Centre

♿ Half-price discounts for both disabled customer and their companion. Wheelchair users must bring a non-disabled companion. Wheelchair available to loan from the Operational Services Department: 020-7638 4141 x 7348. Lifts to all levels. Barbican Theatre: Four wheelchair spaces at Stalls level and at Upper Circle level. Transfer seating available to back row of Stalls. Pit Theatre: Wheelchair space at front of side block

🎧 Sound amplification infrared system with 30 headsets. Returnable deposit of £5

👁 Limited space for guide dogs but staff will dog sit for up to four dogs per performance. Large parties should contact the theatre manager on 020-7628 3351 x 7124

🍴 Both theatres share a wide choice of eating and drinking facilities located around the Barbican Centre. The Pit shares a bar with Cinema I

ⓘ Museum of London, Smithfield market (an increasingly trendy area for restaurants)

Air-conditioned

One of the wonders of the modern world – that's how HM The Queen described the Barbican when she officially opened the complex in March 1982, perhaps forgetting that most visitors simply wondered how to find the place. It has also been compared with New York's Lincoln Center and the Pompidou in Paris. Theatrewise the main 1156 seat auditorium is mostly audience-friendly, with long and spacious rows of comfortable Stalls and Circle seats, and projecting blocks either side (locked in at each end by electromagnetically operated doors). The Pit, seating just 175 people, offers no-frills theatregoing. Without the RSC's financial and artistic clout, the future for these important performance spaces is very much an open book. However, under John Tusa's Managing Directorship and with Graham Sheffield as Artistic Director, quality is assured. A £12.5million scheme to comprehensively overhaul the Barbican Centre's vast foyers and often bewildering public spaces has now begun, with a completion date due in 2006. Rather than make the kind of superficial changes that have blighted the unloved space since it was opened, the new scheme has been designed to adopt a fully integrated approach that (it is hoped) will solve the navigation difficulties once and for all. Major changes have already taken place, such as the removal of the staircase that led from the main Silk Street entrance down to the mezzanine level – instead, visitors now have to cross the existing bridge (which will itself be replaced during the implementation of the scheme) to the main foyer on the other side, adjoining the Lakeside, and make their way to all other front-of-house levels that are served by lifts and stairs from there. Future plans include the construction of a new bridge, as well as new direct access routes into the foyer from one of the car parks for the first time, a new cafe, shop and bar, and new box office, information point and cloakrooms. During construction, the Barbican's arts programme will be unaffected.

History

Londoners have the Luftwaffe to thank for two theatres at the heart of Europe's largest multi-arts and conference venue. The multifunctional, 35-acre Corbusier-influenced residential estate known as the Barbican was once a bit like Clerkenwell, a maze of small streets and warehouses, until the entire area was blitzed to smithereens in December 1940. Only St Giles', Cripplegate – where Oliver Cromwell was married and John Milton is buried – has survived intact. Joint LCC and Corporation of London plans for wholesale redevelopment were submitted in 1955, incorporating a theatre, although construction work didn't begin until 1971. Meanwhile, the RSC became involved in the planning of the main auditorium and the smaller Pit, buried below ground level. The company took up residency from 1982 (when the Barbican opened) until 2002, when it inexplicably abandoned the idea of a permanent London base. Since then both theatres seem to be occupied by productions programmed as part of the annual, year-round BITE festival (Barbican International Theatre Event), comprising local and visiting theatre and dance companies from abroad.

Best seat in the house

Most Stalls seats offer fine views, the only exception being the front rows either side of the stage where you can feel too close and too sideways-on, and towards the rear where you are constantly reminded of the sheer size of the auditorium. Upstairs in Circle 1, the side seats, or slips, provide great vantage points, possible better value than the central seating which can feel remote from the performers. Circles 2 and 3 should be chosen only if you are on a tight budget, the latter being more like a top shelf dangling above lighting gantries with bench seats designed for anorexics. The Barbican Pit is a completely flexible space, with the seating layout changed from production to production.

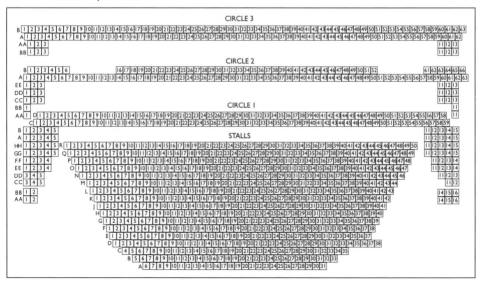

Cambridge Theatre

✉ Earlham Street, WC2 9HU

⌨ www.rutheatres.com

☎ (Box office) 020-7494 5080/0870 890 1102, (Stage door) 020-7850 8710

⏱ Box office open 10am-8pm

↑ Faces Seven Dials monument in Covent Garden, where Monmouth Street and Endell Street meet and branch off from each other

🚉 Charing Cross

⊖ Covent Garden/Leicester Square

P MasterPark at China Town Car Park, Newport Place; NCP at Upper St Martin's Lane

🚲 Racks in Monmouth Street

♿ To arrange seats for the disabled call

0870 895 5505. Discounts available. Entrance into the Stalls is via an exit door in Earlham Street. The theatre can accommodate six wheelchair users (two using spaces provided, four transferring). Wheelchair users must bring a non-disabled companion

🎧 Sound amplification infrared system with eight headsets

👁 No guide dogs inside the auditorium. Staff will dog sit for two dogs per performance, in the manager's office

🍸 Three licensed bars

ⓘ Covent Garden, Dress Circle specialist cast recording and theatrical memorabilia shop is less than a minute away on Monmouth Street

One of six West End theatres built in the 1930s, the Cambridge now serves London well as a home for crowd-pleasing musical theatre, although its description by the management as one of the 'most attractive theatres in the West End' always seemed a tad fanciful when you looked at the front of house detail in daylight. But after a facelift for *Jerry Springer* the place is smarter than ever, and by night, when it really counts, any blemishes are concealed by the low lighting, and the happy crush in the mirrored Stalls bar corridor running around the back of the Stalls always adds to an air of expectation. The auditorium now looks almost like new.

History

Imagine Covent Garden in 1930 when it was still very much the same flower, fruit and veg market Eliza Doolittle would have recognised. Then imagine the Cambridge Theatre suddenly arising out of the triangle of rough and tumble facing the junction at Seven Dials. It must have looked as if tomorrow had arrived. There's no Edwardian opulence or neo-classical ornamentation here. This was futuristic, functional theatre design created out of steel and concrete with a slate-grey Portland Stone frontage and an impeccable moderne interior created by Russian-born designer Serge Chernayeff (who later worked on the supremely Deco-styled De La Warr Pavilion at Bexhill-on-Sea). Today you can still get a flavour of his original Jazz Age décor, thanks to a significant facelift in 1986 supervised by theatre designer Carl Toms. Under the management of Stoll Moss Theatres and, since 2000, Really Useful Theatres, the Cambridge has come out of the cold and staged popular musicals, like *Fame – The Musical*, *Grease*, *The Beautiful Game*, *Our House* and *Jerry Springer – The Opera*. For years before that, the Cambridge was perceived as remote from Theatreland proper, despite successes like *Half A Sixpence*, *Little Me* and the original London production of *Chicago*, and even screened films before closing down and going dark from 1984-87. But that grim,

Germanic thirties frown that seemed to engulf the entire exterior has lifted and the Cambridge is looking chipper once more in the midst of a rejuvenated Covent Garden.

Best seat in the house

The main pitfall of the wide 1283-seat fan-shaped auditorium is the side seating, from where you are likely to miss some of the on-stage action (depending on the layout of the set). Centre aisle seats, especially from around Row F back, are by far the best to go for down here. But the best view of the Cambridge stage is from the steepish Royal Circle centre block, where leg-room is ample too. Avoid if possible the back rows, from where the Grand Circle overhang can feel unduly oppressive. High up in the dim and distant Grand Circle you can almost reach out and touch the elliptical Deco ceiling. Steer clear of Row J seats next to stairwells here and look out for the safety barriers. Still, the lower ticket price compensates for the distress of feeling disconnected.

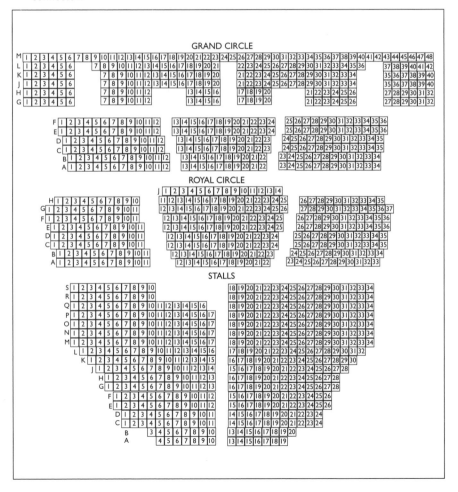

Comedy Theatre

✉ Panton Street, SW1 4DN

🖰 www.theambassadors.com

☎ (Box office) 020-7369 1731, (Stage door) 020-7321 5300

🕘 Box office open 10am-8pm

↑ Panton Street is a side street south of Piccadilly Circus extending between Haymarket and Leicester Square

🚇 Charing Cross

⊖ Piccadilly, Leicester Square

P The streets around the Haymarket are no-go zones for parking. There is a Masterpark car park in nearby Whitcomb Street where you can get reduced fees if you show your theatre ticket beforehand (details 020-7839 5858)

♿ Wheelchair access is obtained through a side door in Oxendon Street which takes you straight to the Dress Circle via a temporary ramp where there is limited space for just one wheelchair with restricted leg room next to seat E17. A few end of row seats are also available in the Dress Circle for transfer seating. The severely disabled must be accompanied by an able bodied person. No wheelchair accessible toilets, but if the Royal Room is not in use, the private toilet there can by used, though you'll have to negotiate six

steps to reach it

🎧 Sennheiser infrared system with 12 headsets. You will be asked to leave a security deposit at the box office

👁 Guide dogs are not allowed into the auditorium but staff will dog sit up to two pooches per performance, in the manager's office

🍸 Three bars: one stand-up bar squeezed into a corner of the already crowded foyer, the other two are in the Upper Circle and at the rear of the Stalls

ⓘ Piccadilly Circus, Regent Street shops, and Leicester Square cinemas. Apart from the grim-looking Odeon Cinema, both sides of Panton Street are lined with inviting eateries, ranging from a Pizza Express at one end of the block to the Woodlands Vegetarian Restaurant at the other. In between there's the cheapo duo of West End Kitchen and Stockpot for cheerful low-budget fillers (often frequented by actors appearing at the surrounding theatres, especially on matinee days) and le Piaf and Cocoma for pre- or apre-show special deals. The Tom Cribb pub opposite the theatre is handy for interval drinks if you want to avoid paying through the nose in one of the theatre's three bars

The lack of air-conditioning is particularly noticeable in this theatre!

M idweek matinee or glitzy first night, there's invariably a before-the-show frisson about attending the 780-seat Comedy. This is mostly because the chandeliered foyer is so petite that the posh Stalls, elegant Dress Circle and impoverished Gods are all forced to rub shoulders and spill out onto Panton Street – much to the annoyance of passing taxis and cyclists – which creates a community of anticipation rare in London's Theatreland. Cramped bars, inaccessible loos (none at Dress Circle level), creaky seats and restricted views and legroom are the downside.

History

It may have been designed by the *eminence gris* of high Victorian architecture Thomas Verity, but Queen Victoria was probably not amused when the 'Royal Comedy Theatre' opened its doors on 15 October 1881 in a newly rebuilt West End district that had been notorious for dubious dives and naughty nightlife. The aim was to rival the swanky Savoy Theatre which opened just a few days before, but, with no official warrant, the cheeky use of the Royal moniker had to be dropped. The strait-faced Queen might well have cracked a dim smile at the diet of revue and musical comedy eventually presented here during the First World War by CB Cochrane and Andre Charlot – popular fare of a type which continued until the 1950s – but she most certainly wouldn't have approved of the name change in 1956 to the New Watergate Theatre Club. The formation of a subscription club theatre cocked a snook at the Lord Chamberlain and for a short time transformed the Comedy into one of the few West End playhouses presenting experimental work. Without this club, there was no way *Cat on a Hot Tin Roof*, *Tea and Sympathy* and *A View From the Bridge* could have been staged at that time. Later the Comedy become famous as the West End home of the musicals *The Rocky Horror Show* and *Little Shop of Horrors*. It has seen so many productions of Harold Pinter plays that some have suggested a name change to the Pinter Theatre. Look out for the display of Pinter posters on the stairs leading down to the Stalls. Despite refurbishments in the 1930s and 1950s and the galaxy of Hollywood stars who have graced the Comedy's stage of late, you can't ignore this theatre's Victorian heritage. Theatre legends like Sarah Bernhardt and Herbert Beerbohm Tree had big success here. The framed programme for the opening production in 1881 is on display next to the little booking kiosks in the foyer – an English translation of *The Mascotte*, an operetta by Edmond Audran.

Best seat in the house

Unless you enjoy looking up, steer clear of the Stalls front row. Best views are probably from seats A6 to A7 in the front row of the Dress Circle (though leg-room is short) or from the middle of rows C to L in the Stalls. The Dress Circle overhang cuts off some sightlines from the back of the Stalls. Similarly there's an Upper Circle overhang above

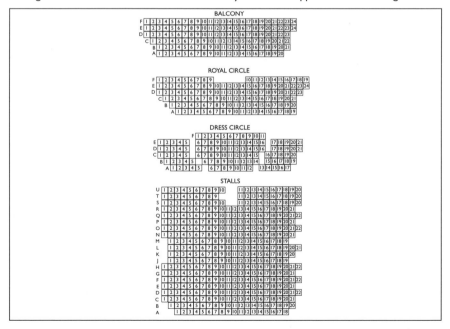

the Dress Circle rear seats. Beware adjusting your posture during quiet moments when sitting in creaky Stalls seats and avoid the restricted views created by the padded iron pillars in the Stalls (from row M back), the Dress Circle (from row C back) and the Royal Circle (from row B back). Tickets for some restricted view seats are cut-price. Depending on the production, the view from the ends of the first four rows in the Stalls misses some of the on-stage action. Only book Royal Circle and nosebleed-inducing Balcony seats if you have double-jointed knees and don't mind safety barriers blocking a chunk of what you've paid to watch.

Criterion Theatre

✉ Piccadilly Circus, W1V 9LB

☎ (Box office) 0870 060 2313, (Stage door) 020-7839 8811

🖨 020-925 0596

↑ Opposite the statue of Eros at the junction of Shaftesbury Avenue and Piccadilly

🚇 Charing Cross

⊖ Piccadilly Circus (Eros exit)

P MasterPark at Whitcomb Street, NCPs in Denman Street and Leicester Place

🚲 Racks in Lower Regent Street and at the southern end of Shaftesbury Avenue

♿ Wheelchair users enter from an entrance in Jermyn Street, next to the stage door leading to the street-level Upper Circle where there are two spaces (with slightly restricted views) for wheelchair users. Transfer seating is available to aisle seats. Wheelchair users must bring a non-disabled companion. One adapted toilet

🎧 Sound amplification loop system in all parts of the auditorium

👁 No guide dogs inside the auditorium. Staff will dog sit for two dogs per performance

🍸 Two licensed bars at Dress Circle level

ⓘ Eros, Marco Pierre White's Criterion Restaurant next door, Harry Ramsden's fish and chip restaurant

Air conditioned

The Criterion is not only a visual design classic, it was the first West End theatre to be run by a trust. Formed in 1992, it sets out to operate the theatre and to "promote, maintain, improve and advance education by the encouragement of the arts." After a major refurbishment that brought the building back to its full Victorian glow, the Criterion re-opened in the same year and although the freehold was subsequently sold to a property company the theatre's ability to both inspire and amuse seems secure, as the Trust's lease doesn't expire until the 2050s.

History

Of all the West End theatres, the 590-seat Criterion always demands that you wear your best going out finery. It is such a Victorian chocolate box that you almost want to give the auditorium a standing ovation when you arrive. To reach it, however, you have to go through a fairly unassuming canopied entrance and wend your way down numerous flights of stairs lined with original painted tiles (which some say give this theatre the appearance of a Victorian public lavatory), huge plate glass mirrors and ceilings covered with crotchety cherubs. For the Criterion (or 'Cri' as it is affectionately known) was built in the 1870s by eminent Victorian architect Thomas Verity entirely underground. Cleverly designed to be part of an arts complex, with a restaurant, ballroom and a gallery, it later became one of the first public buildings in London to have air conditioning, no doubt installed to prevent the toffs in the Stalls from passing out while watching the light comedies and French farces that suited the 'Cri' down to the ground. Much later, during the Blitz, the hit radio show ITMA (It's that Man Again) was broadcast from here by the BBC. Notable 20th-century successes include Terrence Rattigan's French Without Tears, Joe Orton's Loot and the transfer from the Arts of Beckett's Waiting For Godot, while the genial Reduced Shakespeare Company looks likely to become a permanent Criterion fixture well into the 21st-century.

Best seat in the house

Apart from Dickens, children and Christmas, one thing the Victorians loved was cast iron pillars. There are five in the Stalls and three whoppers in the Dress Circle and although the octagonal shape of the big ones is aesthetically pleasing and others have been softened with foam padding, they do lead to a lot of craning of necks. Stalls rows A to J are pillar-free, but those sitting in Rows N to S suffer the most, as well as getting a dose of Dress Circle overhang syndrome. The Dress Circle itself can feel like pillar city, unless you go mid-pillars. Try the three-row Upper Circle instead, which is like a street level shelf and is entirely pillar-less. Consult your seating plan carefully.

UPPER CIRCLE

```
C    6 7 8 9 10 11 12 13 14 15 16 17 18 19 20
B  5 6 7 8 9 10 11 12 13 14 15 16 17 18 19 20 21 22 23 24 25 26 27 28 29 30
A  6 7 8 9 10 11 12 13 14 15 16 17 18 19 20 21 22 23 24 25 26 27 28 29
```

DRESS CIRCLE

```
G        6 7 8 9
F      4 5 6 7 8 9 10                              21 22 23 24 25 26 27
E  1 2 3 4 5 6 7 8 9 10 11 12 13 14 15 16 17 18 19 20 21 22 23 24 25 26 27 28 29
D  1 2 3 4 5 6 7 8 9 10 11 12 13 14 15 16 17 18 19 20 21 22 23 24 25 26 27 28
C  1 2   3 4 5 6 7 8 9 10 11 12 13 14 15 16 17 18 19 20 21 22 23 24 25 26   27 28
B        6 7 8 9 10 11 12 13 14 15 16 17 18 19 20 21 22 23 24 25
A  1 2 3   5 6 7 8 9 10 11 12 13 14 15 16 17 18 19 20 21 22 23 24 25 26 27   28 29
```

STALLS

```
S  4 5 6 7 8 9 10 11 12 13 14 15 16 17 18 19 20 21
R  3 4 5 6 7 8 9 10 11 12 13 14 15 16 17 18 19 20 21 22 23
Q  2 3 4 5 6 7 8 9 10 11 12 13 14 15 16 17 18 19 20 21 22 23 24
P  1 2 3 4 5 6 7 8 9 10 11 12 13 14 15 16 17 18 19 20 21 22
N  1 2 3 4 5 6 7 8 9 10 11 12 13 14 15 16 17 18 19 20 21
M  2 3 4 5 6 7 8 9 10 11 12 13 14 15 16 17 18 19 20 21 22
L  2 3 4 5 6 7 8 9 10 11 12 13 14 15 16 17 18 19 20 21
K  1   3 4 5 6 7 8 9 10 11 12 13 14 15 16 17 18 19 20 21

G  2 3 4 5 6 7 8 9 10 11 12 13 14 15 16 17 18 19 20 21 22 23 24
F  2 3 4 5 6 7 8 9 10 11 12 13 14 15 16 17 18 19 20 21 22 23 24
E  2 3 4 5 6 7 8 9 10 11 12 13 14 15 16 17 18 19 20 21 22 23 24
D  2 3 4 5 6 7 8 9 10 11 12 13 14 15 16 17 18 19 20 21 22 23 24
C  2 3 4 5 6 7 8 9 10 11 12 13 14 15 16 17 18 19 20 21 22 23 24
B  3 4 5 6 7 8 9 10 11 12 13 14 15 16 17 18 19 20 21 22 23
A  8 9 10 11 12 13 14 15 16 17
```

Dominion Theatre

✉ 268-269 Tottenham Court Road,
WIT 7AQ

🏛 www.ccLive.co.uk

☎ (Box office) 020-7413 1713/
0870 169 0116 (connects to 24-hour
Ticketmaster), (Stage door) 020-7927
0900

🖷 020-7580 0246

↑ The corner of Tottenham Court
Road and New Oxford Street

🚇 Charing Cross

🚇 Tottenham Court Road (Exit 3
emerges right in front of the theatre)

P NCP at Great Russell Street

🚲 Racks outside entrance

♿ Wheelchair users must bring a non-
disabled companion, but discounts
are available for disabled customers

and their companions. There are
three spaces for wheelchair users at
the ends of the back three rows, two
of which are on a slight slope.
Motorised wheelchairs are offered a
restricted view from one of the circle boxes, reached through an
entrance at the side of the premises.
Access enquiries: 020-7636 2296

🎧 Infrared audio system

👁 One of the few London theatres
where guide dogs are allowed into
the auditorium, though staff will also
dog sit

🍴 Four bars at stalls and circle level, big
on confectionary and merchandising,
too

ⓘ West End shopping on Oxford
Street, The British Museum, the
bookshops in Charing Cross Road

Situated on the eastern-most edge of Theatreland, the Dominion is in many respects like its cinematic twin up West, the Apollo Victoria – best at spectacle and song. Some may find its sheer vastness too much of a throwback to the days of mass pic-ture houses, but sightlines are mostly fine and from around Row G in the Circle you can even look down and imagine a smaller scale Radio City Music Hall. When full, The Dominion rivals the London Palladium for communal atmospherics; half empty it can feel mighty lonely out there.

History

For over two centuries the crossroads where Tottenham Court Road, Charing Cross Road and Oxford Street now meet has maintained an entertainment link. Back in 1764 a brewery covered the site now occupied by the Dominion Theatre. A fun-fair tem-porarily filled the space when Meux's Horseshoe Brewery was demolished in 1922, before the mighty Dominion opened its doors in 1929 for the staging of spectacular musical revues, rather like it does today. But, as *The Stage* newspaper observed, "At first sight the interior of the house gives one the impression it was really meant to be a super cinema." And for much of its life, that's what this Gaumont-style people's palace became – a massive movie house, showing silents, then talkies and eventually widescreen blockbusters like *South Pacific* and *The Sound of Music*. Fortunately for Londoners, various changes in ownership and a listed building status granted in 1982 have prevented the 2174-seat auditorium with its classical-Deco lines and atmospheric Wurlitzer-style details being turned into a bland multiplex, so the theatre has reverted back to becoming a home of big live shows, ballet, pop concerts and more recently mega-scale musicals like *Notre-Dame de Paris*, Disney's *Beauty and The Beast* and *We Will Rock You*.

Best seat in the house

With a noticeable rake in the Stalls, most seats on this wide acreage have good legroom and are fine for sightlines, even if the Circle overhang does tend to snip off a sliver of the top of the stage the further back you get from around Row S. Centre block seats offer best all-round value. Try to avoid the end seats in the first few rows of the side blocks, unless you don't mind missing out on some of the stage setting. The Circle is divided into two sections. The block nearest the stage offers excellent views and good legroom. But the high-up rear section, divided into five separate mini-blocks, feels distant from the stage and disconnected from the rest of the audience, especially if you find yourself in limbo watching from the end seats in the back rows. It's like being confined in the isolation wing. Generally though, whatever the price range, always aim for central block seats in the Dominion and you won't go wrong.

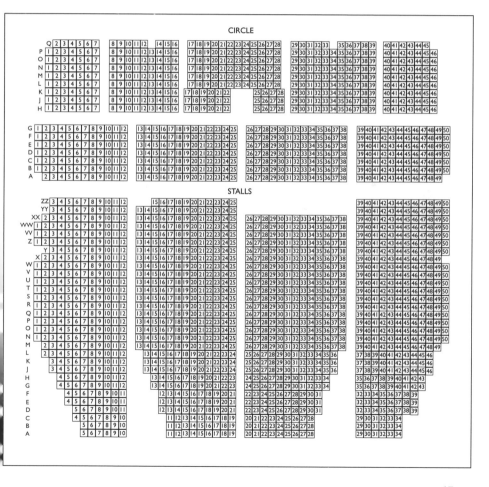

Donmar Warehouse

✉ 41 Earlham Street, WC2H 9LX

🖰 www.donmarwharehouse.com

☎ (Box office) 020-7369 1732 connects to Ambassador Theatre Group (no booking fee), 0870 534 4444 (24-hour Ticketmaster), (Group Booking) 020-7369 1717

🖨 020-7438 9211

↑ Face the Cambridge Theatre, make for Earlham Street towards the left and look out for the Donmar neon sign, opposite Belgo restaurant. Next door to Quicksilver, there is also access to the box office through Thomas Neal's shopping centre during the day until 6.30pm

🚇 Charing Cross

⊖ Covent Garden, Leicester Square, Holborn

P MasterPark at Cambridge Circus, NCP at Drury Lane

🚲 Cycle racks in Monmouth Street

♿ A lift takes you up to all levels of the auditorium, shared with the Thomas Neal's shopping centre. There is a slope up from the lift to the back of the Stalls where there is one space for a wheelchair user at D31. Each wheelchair user must bring a non-disabled companion who can sit at D32. Transfer seating available to row C. Wheelchairs can be stored

🎧 Sound amplification infrared system with four headsets. Returnable deposit required

🖐 Regular signed and audio described performances

👁 Guide dogs cannot be brought into the auditorium. Staff look after dogs in the bar area

🍸 There are two bars; the stalls bar is non-smoking

ⓘ Covent Garden Market and shops, Neal's Yard, Antonio Carluccio's Neal Street Restaurant

If David Beckham were a theatre, it would surely be the Donmar. Ever youthful, sexy, always in the news and rather fashionable too, this is the premiere division place to be seen in as much as watching the latest production. But it's nowhere near as well off. With only 250 seats, even if it's packed every night, the Donmar is not economically viable enough to remain standing on its own legs, so it still depends on sponsorship and the support of the Friends of the Donmar, dubbed rather jokily the "Backstage Crew". For details contact the Development Department on 020-7845 5815.

History

In just a decade the Donmar has become probably the most globally known modern London theatre, famous for starry actors in strong home-grown productions (who will ever forget Nicole Kidman's brief nude appearance in *The Blue Room*, which had one critic salivating that it was "pure theatrical Viagra"?), and for Sam Mendes, who was Artistic Director from 1990 to 2002. But the Donmar is located in a building with a long non-theatre past. In the1870s it was used as a vast hop warehouse for a Covent Garden brewery. It was also a film studio and a banana-ripening depot before 1961 when theatre impresario Donald Albery converted it into a rehearsal studio for the London Festival Ballet, a company he formed with Margot Fonteyn. Thus the Donmar was born – glueing Don and Mar together to give the space its name. Between 1977 and 1981 it was the RSC's London studio theatre. After the RSC vacated it for the Barbican, it became a London receiving theatre for small-scale studio productions, until it was closed and refurbished as part of the new shopping mall development, Thomas Neal's, next door. Re-opening in 1992 as a producing powerhouse, the bare brick industrial look of the former warehouse and the thrust stage with seating on three sides was maintained, but it now came handsomely equipped with new bars, a spiral staircase leading to each level, and a smart new foyer. Now owned by the Ambassador Theatre Group and with Michael Grandage succeeding Mendes, this influential but pint-sized powerhouse looks set to ensure that the awards and the audiences will still keep coming, maintaining its position as the West End's top "fringe" theatre.

Best seat in the house

Turn up early. Ignore the hubbub in the bars. Take your seat before the rest of the crowd. You'll find the Donmar is pin-drop silent. Rather like going into a church. But then the long rows of dull-coloured bench seating placed around three sides of an open stage are reminiscent of a place of worship, except that you should choose your personal pew here extremely carefully, in a descending order of preference. First, all the seats facing the stage offer grandstand close-up views from where you feel part of the action. Next, go for the Stalls side seating. It's sideways on but still works. Finally, if all else fails, go upstairs to the Circle and choose the ends of rows facing the stage, otherwise you'll find yourself crammed into some of the worst seating arrangements in any London theatre apart from the King's Head in Islington. Just pray that you don't have a panic attack. The Donmar might be hip, but you may well need a hip replacement after a hot night up in the narrow back row.

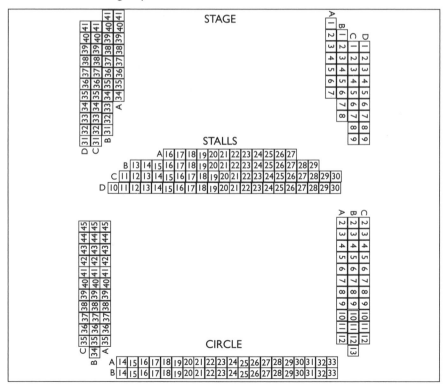

Drury Lane (Theatre Royal)

✉ Catherine Street, WC2B 5JF

🕯 www.rutheatres.com

☎ (Box office) 020-7494 5000/0870 899 3338 (24 hour), (Stage door) 020-7850 8791

↑ The entrance to one of the most famous theatres in the world is not actually in Drury Lane but in Catherine Street, reached either from the Aldwych off the Strand, or go to Covent Garden Piazza and walk along Russell Street with the Theatre Museum on your right. The grand portico entrance will suddenly loom before you

🚇 Charing Cross, Waterloo (and a ten-minute walk across Waterloo Bridge)

⊖ Covent Garden, Holborn

P NCP in Drury Lane

🚲 Cycle racks in Southampton Street, Wellington Street and Kingsway

♿ Discounts for each disabled theatre-goer and companion. Book on 020-7494 5470. Wheelchair entrance is through a fire exit door on Russell Street that leads into the left of the Stalls. Four parking spaces for wheel-chairs users; companions can sit in the same row. Transfer seating to aisle seats. Each wheelchair user must bring a non-disabled compan-ion. One adapted toilet

🎧 Sound amplification infrared system with 10 headsets. Best reception is in the centre of the Stalls and Circle. Headsets obtained from duty manag-er in main foyer

👁 No guide dogs allowed in the audito-rium. Staff look after them in an office

🍸 Six licensed bars, including Theatreland's biggest, prestigious and most beautiful one located in the Dress Circle

ⓘ Covent Garden, Royal Opera House, Theatre Museum, and the public houses Nell of Old Drury and Opera Tavern across the street

Grand staircases. A spectacular rotunda. Bars the size of the Ritz. Glittering chande-liers that would have made Liberace look plain. Imposing statues. Busts of revered thespians. Massive Doric and Ionic columns. Is London's oldest theatre a museum piece? Pop in and wander round the enormous vestibule during the daytime hours when the front-of-house staff creep silently around, or look bored stiff. There is defi-nitely a whiff of heritage beeswax about the place. But when the audience arrives *en masse*, often by the coach load, you couldn't imagine a livelier and more exciting the-atre to watch a show in anywhere on the planet. For despite its Royal tag, Drury Lane is very much a workaday people's palace – a home for populist big-scale musicals, the statues of the past and liveried footmen looking on with a snobby disdain.

History

Whether it's King Charles II granting letters patent to open a theatre building in 1662, Nell Gwynne flogging oranges, David Garrick barnstorming audiences in *Macbeth*, Paul Robeson's amazing vocals in *Show Boat*, Rodgers and Hammerstein wowing post-war austerity-struck London with *Oklahoma!*, *Miss Saigon* pulling in the crowds for years, or Miss Martine McCutcheon missing yet another performance of *My Fair Lady*, or swing-ing Gershwin tunes in *Anything Goes*, the Theatre Royal Drury Lane continues to makes waves in Theatreland and still provides the economic dynamo for the Covent Garden wing of the West End. The building may be haunted by its own history and by the ghosts that roam the huge auditorium, with its beautiful Wedgwood-style detailing, but the present internal décor really dates from a substantial rebuild in 1922, which retained much of the early 18th century work, with some major alterations made after wartime bombing destroyed some of the structure. Architectural add-ons over the centuries include the magnificent portico in 1820 and the grand colonnade along the Russell Street side of the building a decade later.

Best seat in the house

Just "being there" is the ultimate Theatre Royal high. Stalls row K, with a wide gangway in front of it, gives you a view and luxury legroom fit for a Queen. Some seats, however, let you down with a bump. Those at the back of the stalls centre block can be blighted by the sound box and four pillars. The Dress Circle has sight and Upper Circle overhang problems, especially at the far ends of rows. The Upper Circle feels distant and has a couple of pillars at the back. In the Balcony, you'll pay cheaper prices for an even more distant view restricted by safety rails. Apart from that, anything goes in this show biz heaven.

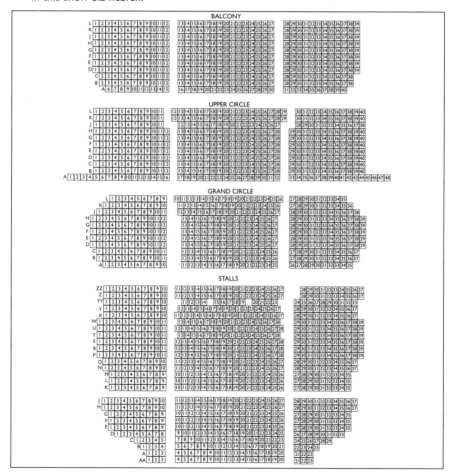

Duchess Theatre

✉ Catherine Street, WC2B 5LA

✆ www.rutheatres.com

☎ (Box office) 020-7494 5070/
0870 899 3338

🖷 020-7494 5154

↑ Catherine Street runs off the
Aldwych, near the Strand

🚇 Charing Cross

⊖ Covent Garden, Temple, Holborn

P NCP at Drury Lane

🚲 Racks in Wellington Street and
Covent Garden Piazza

♿ Limited access. Call 0870 895 5505
to arrange seats

🎧 Infrared system with 10 headsets

👁 Guide dogs are allowed into the
auditorium but you must be seated
in an aisle seat or a box. Staff will
dog sit two guide dogs per performance

★ Two small bars, a tiny one next to
the foyer at Dress Circle level, the
other at the back of the Stalls

ⓘ Covent Garden, The Theatre
Museum, Somerset House and
Collection, The Waldorf Meridien

Once you're inside the auditorium it's like snuggling up inside a sort of cozy theatrical cocoon. Apart from the striking stylised gilded reliefs, inset either side of
the compact proscenium stage (and painted over for recent productions), the 1930s
décor feels muted, dull even. Don't miss the miniscule foyer bar, no bigger than a
broom cupboard. The veneered semi-circular foyer is similarly of its time, though beige
wallpaper, a modernised box office and drab job lot floral carpet add an air of faded
functionality. From the outside, the 1930s Tudorbethan Duchess sometimes looks like
the filling between two sandwich bars; at others a dismayed dowager, smelling of stale
scent and just about keeping up appearances in the shadow of its two stately older
sisters, the Strand and the Theatre Royal Drury Lane.

History

With the benefit of its ingenious 1929 design solution to the knotty problem of building a theatre on an awkward sliver of Covent Garden real estate, the Duchess was
soon at the cutting edge of West End drama. By the mid-1930s, time play experi-
menter JB Priestley became associated with the management. Three of his plays were
premiered here and his wife Mary Wyndham Lewis even redecorated the place. After
playing in the theatre's opening production, *Tunnel Trench*, in 1929, young theatrical
blade Emlyn Williams became another Duchess star. He had his first play produced
here, *Night Must Fall*, headlining in both it and in *The Corn Is Green*. Noël Coward's
Blithe Spirit packed the place during the war years. Terrence Rattigan's *The Deep Blue
Sea* was a main attraction in the 1950s, and by 1960 new boy Harold Pinter's *The
Caretaker* was attracting a different crowd. Later, when London had learned to swing,
you could have easily mistaken the Duchess for a Soho knocking shop. *The Dirtiest
Show In Town*, *Oh Calcutta!* and *No Sex Please – We're British* all kept the punters coming.
Since then, despite Pinter returning twice, the theatre has often gone 'dark'. Simon
Callow lit the place up by appearing naked in *Through The Leaves*. But the Duchess,
now owned by Lord Lloyd Webber's Really Useful Theatres, no doubt blushes most
when reminded that she holds the record for the shortest West End Run ever. In 1930
the curtain was rung down on *The Intimate Revue* midway through the opening night.

Apparently the show was so bad, even the usherettes walked out.

Best seat in the house

Because of its clever design, most of the 476 seats in the two-level Duchess provide uninterrupted views. Exceptions are where a taller-than-average person plonks in front of you and the sight problems in the side seats of the first four or five rows of the Stalls, which are angled too acutely to see all of the stage. Central aisle seats are worth choosing first. Upstairs in the Dress Circle claustrophobics might feel a bit cramped in the middle of Row A, where leg-room is tight, even if the sightlines are superb. Considering the intimacy of this theatre, the rear Dress Circle block feels kilometers away from the stage initially, but you soon adjust.

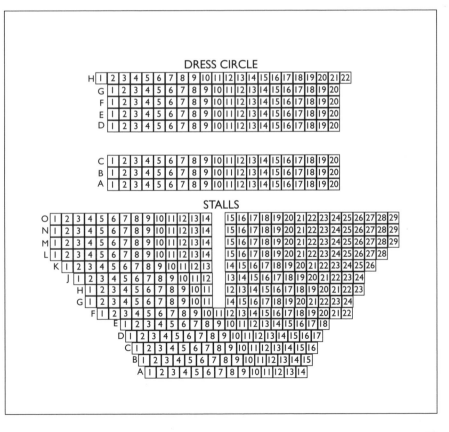

Duke of York's Theatre

✉ St Martin's Lane, WCN 4BG

🖰 www.theambassadors.com/dukeofy-orks

☎ (Box office) 020-7369 1791/0870 534 4444 (24 hour), (Stage door) 020-7836 4615

🖨 020-7565 6485

↑ Walk down St Martin's Lane towards St Martin's in the Fields. The theatre is on your right, just along from the Salisbury pub

🚇 Charing Cross

⊖ Leicester Square, Charing Cross, Embankment

P MasterPark Spring Gardens, off Trafalgar Square; NCP at St Martin's Lane

♿ Two spaces for wheelchair users in the back row of the Royal Circle, with slightly restricted view. Transfer seating available. Maximum of two wheelchair users per performance. One adapted toilet

🎧 Sound amplification infrared system with 20 headsets, available from box office

👁 Two guide dogs allowed per perfor-mance. Guide dog sitting available

🍸 Two licensed bars

ⓘ Leicester Square, Trafalgar Square, St Martin's in the Fields, National Portrait Gallery, National Gallery, Covent Garden, The Salisbury pub

Over the years, numerous mainstream musicals and plays have come and gone, one of the most recent being the long-running, award-winning *Stones In His Pocket*. But the Ambassador Theatre Group bought the Duke of York's in 1992 and raised the artistic stakes by hosting Royal Court productions while its Sloane Square home was being refurbished. A co-production of *The Weir* ran for over two years and won the 1999 Olivier Award for Best New Play. So it looks as if the grand old Duke of York's has got its face set firmly on the future, by attracting the younger audiences the West End needs to thrive.

History

A West End warhorse, the Duke of York's is steeped in theatre history. It was the first theatre to be built in this part of Theatreland, and one of the earliest productions was the English premiere of Ibsen's *The Master Builder*. Whenever you watch a show here, it's worth looking at the ornamented neo-18th century interior and thinking back to 1904 when Peter and Wendy flew for the first time in JM Barrie's *Peter Pan* – and returned every Christmas until World War I broke out. Later, a 14-year-old Charlie Chaplin walked on to this very stage in *Sherlock Holmes*. If you ever feel a tingle down your neck, you've probably felt the ghost. Not Ibsen's, but a woman dressed in black, said to be Violette Melotte, the wife of the first manager, who roams the Dress Circle whenever the mood takes her. Ladies and gentlemen of the stage met here in 1929 to form Equity, the actors' union. David Belasco's *Madame Butterfly*, was seen here by Puccini, who later turned it into his famous opera. But despite the period atmospher-ics, this interior is not all original. It's had two recent refurbishments: a major one in 1980 when Capital Radio owned it, the other in 1999.

Best seat in the house

The arrangement of the boxes either side of the stage, extending in to the Stalls, Royal

Circle and Circle, might have pleased Victorians requiring a bit of class decorum in a 650-seat auditorium, but this can seem like a design fault today. The exterior walls of these boxes face you like modesty panels, cutting off sight of anyone in them but also slightly obscuring the view of the stage from the end Stalls seats around rows C, D, E and F. Further forward you are fine: much further back you feel slightly isolated from everyone else. For the same reason, in the Royal Circle avoid the end seats in rows B and C, and in the Circle rows B to F, even if they are sold at a 'restricted view' knock-down price. Go central anywhere in this slimline auditorium and you won't miss much.

UPPER CIRCLE

```
 H                              8  7  6  5  4  3  2  1
 G                              7  6  5  4  3  2  1
 F  21 20 19 18 17 16 15 14 13 12 11 10  9  8  7  6  5  4  3  2  1
 E 22 21 20 19 18 17 16 15 14 13 12 11 10  9  8  7  6  5  4  3  2  1
 D 23 22 21 20 19 18 17 16 15 14 13 12 11 10  9  8  7  6  5  4  3  2  1
 C       22 21 20 19 18 17 16 15 14 13 12 11 10  9  8  7  6  5  4  3  2  1
 B       21 20 19 18 17 16 15 14 13 12 11 10  9  8  7  6  5  4  3  2  1
 A  20 19 18 17 16 15 14 13 12 11 10  9  8  7  6  5  4  3  2  1
```

ROYAL CIRCLE

```
 F  19 18 17 16 15 14 13 12 11 10  9  8  7  6  5  4  3  2  1
 E  18 17 16 15 14 13 12 11 10  9  8  7  6  5  4  3  2  1
 D  18 17 16 15 14 13 12 11 10  9  8  7  6  5  4  3  2  1
 C 23 22 21 20 19 18 17 16 15 14 13 12 11 10  9  8  7  6  5  4  3  2  1
 B 22 21 20 19 18 17 16 15 14 13 12 11 10  9  8  7  6  5  4  3  2  1
 A  18 17 16 15 14 13 12 11 10  9  8  7  6  5  4  3  2  1
```

STALLS

```
 U              11 10  9  8  7  6  5  4  3  2  1
 T           14 13 12 11 10  9  8  7  6  5  4  3  2  1
 S           13 12 11 10  9  8  7  6  5  4  3  2  1
 R           14 13 12 11 10  9  8  7  6  5  4  3  2  1
 Q           13 12 11 10  9  8  7  6  5  4  3  2  1
 P              10  9  8  7  6  5  4  3  2  1
 O           17 16 15 14 13 12 11 10  9  8  7  6  5  4  3  2  1
 N 21 20 19 18 17 16 15 14 13 12 11 10  9  8  7  6  5  4  3  2  1
 M 21 20 19 18 17 16 15 14 13 12 11 10  9  8  7  6  5  4  3  2  1
 L 21 20 19 18 17 16 15 14 13 12 11 10  9  8  7  6  5  4  3  2  1
 K 21 20 19 18 17 16 15 14 13 12 11 10  9  8  7  6  5  4  3  2  1
 J 21 20 19 18 17 16 15 14 13 12 11 10  9  8  7  6  5  4  3  2  1
 H 21 20 19 18 17 16 15 14 13 12 11 10  9  8  7  6  5  4  3  2  1
 G    19 18 17 16 15 14 13 12 11 10  9  8  7  6  5  4  3  2  1
 F 21 20 19 18 17 16 15 14 13 12 11 10  9  8  7  6  5  4  3  2  1
 E 21 20 19 18 17 16 15 14 13 12 11 10  9  8  7  6  5  4  3  2  1
 D    19 18 17 16 15 14 13 12 11 10  9  8  7  6  5  4  3  2  1
 C       16 15 14 13 12 11 10  9  8  7  6  5  4  3  2  1
 B          12 11 10  9  8  7  6  5  4  3  2  1
 A           10  9  8  7  6  5  4  3  2  1
BB           10  9  8  7  6  5  4  3  2  1
AA           10  9  8  7  6  5  4  3  2  1
```

Fortune Theatre

✉ Russell Street, WC2B 5HH

⌖ www.theambassadors.com/fortune

☎ (Box office) 020-7369 1737, (Stage door) 020-7836 0441

🖨 020-7379 7493

↑ Russell Street runs along the north side of the Theatre Royal Drury Lane

🚇 Charing Cross, Waterloo

⊖ Covent Garden, Holborn

P NCP at Drury Lane

♿ Racks in Covent Garden Market and Wellington Street

♿ Entrance is via a side exit in Crown Court with five steps to the Dress Circle where transfer seating is available to seat F17 at one end of the back row. Must be accompanied by a non-disabled person. The view is restricted. No adapted toilets

🎧 No facilities at present

👁 Guide dogs are allowed into Box A

📶 Two small bars, in the Stalls and Upper Circle

ⓘ Covent Garden, The Theatre Museum, the Strand, Somerset House

A Schools' Resource Pack is available to accompany The Woman in Black, downloadable from www.pwprods.co.uk. A Teachers' Club offers a regular newsletter with information on forthcoming events and ticket deals. Details: 020-7734 7184

Perched high up on this theatre's modest-looking façade there's a lovely gilded statue of a goddess, possibly either Terpsichore, the Greek muse of dance, or Fortuna, the Roman goddess. Entering through the Art Deco front doors you are greeted by a pretty little gift box of a foyer done out in beaten copper and marble. But the illusion of 1920s chic (the exposed concrete façade was revolutionary in its day) soon evaporates once you wend your way downstairs to the stalls to be greeted by a ugly carpeting, uncomfortable old seating and uninspired white, grey and gold décor that gives the auditorium's original 1920s mouldings a veneer of faded fustiness. Not much Theatreland magic here. The loos are archaic, the downstairs ladies' next to the cramped gloss-painted stalls bar being so miniscule that a long queue of females usually ends up mingling with customers trying to order a drink while avoiding the pong of Toilet Duck. Some say that the dust-cloth ambience adds to the ghostliness of the long-running The Woman in Black. Others paying for top price tickets, may look at the tardy A4 photocopied signage on the walls or visit the glum bars that feel as if they exist in a parallel luvvie universe and wonder why some of the small fortune made from this cheap-to-run show hasn't been ploughed back into the infrastructure.

History

Small and perfectly formed? You could probably squeeze the entire Fortune through the stage door of the Theatre Royal Drury Lane (opposite) with room to spare. In the tiny foyer notice the brass plaque stating: "There is a tide in the affairs of men, which taken at the flood, leads on to fortune." Constructed on the site of the Albion Tavern, this was famously the first West End theatre to be built after World War I, but it has probably staged more misfortunes than box office hits since it opened in 1924. Ingeniously designed by Ernest Schaufelberg to share a site with Church of Scotland premises, the pre-Modernist building was financed by wannabe impresario Laurence

Cowan who opened the theatre with one of his own plays, *Sinners* – an instant flop. Despite some notable productions, the Fortune became a home to amateur companies until the World War II when ENSA, the forces' entertainment unit, took it over. Later, one budding actor who suffered the Fortune's fate was an unknown Dirk Bogarde who appeared in *Power Without Glory* in 1947. It closed within a few weeks – because of a lack of star name! By the late 1950s, revue was making the Fortune a fortune. Flanders and Swann's *At the Drop Of A Hat* was followed by the ground-breaking *Beyond the Fringe*, setting a trend for small cast shows which has continued with the astonishing 15-year (and counting!) run of the spooky two-hander *The Woman in Black*. In 2001 The Fortune became part of the Ambassador Theatre Group.

Best seat in the house

With just 432 seats to choose from in such an intimate theatre – only 11 rows in the Orchestra Stalls and seven in the Dress Circle – you'd imagine that any place will do. Think again. Sit too close to the stage and you'll come out with an unfortunate neckache, while the side seating at the end of the aisles is positioned at an angle. Best seats down here are towards the centre back. Upstairs in the Dress Circle legroom is at a premium and 1920s brass safety rails, though evoking another age, block most views of the stage today. The steep Upper Circle is really remote from the stage and most rows have been arranged for stumpy-legged folk only. The back three rows might as well be in another theatre altogether and the thicket of safety rails can be distracting. Try the middle rows to avoid eye fatigue – and vertigo.

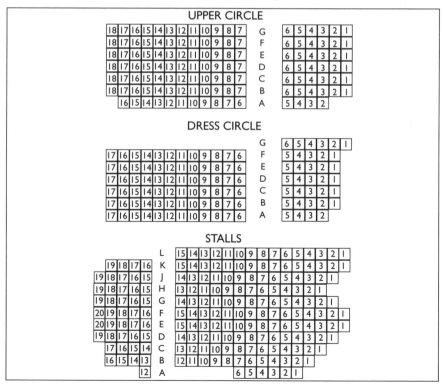

Garrick Theatre

✉ Charing Cross Road, WC2 0HH

⌁ www.rutheatres.com

☎ (Box office) 0870 890 1104 (24 hours by phone; in person, open Mon-Sat 10am-8pm), (Stage door) 020-7850 8730

↑ In the West End, just off the north east side of Trafalgar Square (diagonally opposite entrance to National Portrait Gallery) and the east side of Leicester Square

🚇 Charing Cross

⊖ Leicester Square; Charing Cross; Piccadilly Circus

P nearest car park is in Whitcomb Street (off Leicester Square)

♿ Almost level access to the Dress Circle level via the foyer or rear courtyard. Call Customer Services Department, 020-7494 5470 to make arrangements

🎧 Sennheiser Infrared system. Ask Manager for headsets

🍦 Usual bar service; ice-creams served by ushers in interval

ⓘ National Portrait Gallery is diagonally across the street and the National Gallery is around the corner

This four-level, 656-seat Victorian house (though the top gallery is no longer in use) is a slightly musty, traditional playhouse, with a highly distinctive feature that it shares with Sloane Square's Royal Court: the deep rumble of tube trains underneath can be heard at regular, reassuring intervals. The original construction of the theatre, however, was delayed owing to a different underground obstruction: the discovery of a river running below it!

History

Built for WS Gilbert, of Gilbert and Sullivan fame, the theatre was named after the famous 17th-century actor David Garrick and opened on April 24, 1889. A copy of a Gainsborough portrait of Garrick (the original of which has been lost) hangs in the crowded foyer, welcoming audiences with the expectation of seeing great actors in great performances once again. In recent years, productions have tended to move here after runs in other theatres first to prolong their lives, including *Side by Side* by Sondheim (from Wyndham's), *No Sex Please We're British* (from the Strand), *Our Country's Good* (from the Royal Court), *Bent* (from the National), *The Rehearsal* (from the Almeida), *An Inspector Calls* (from the National and Aldwych), and *Feelgood* (from Hampstead Theatre). But shows new and old thrive thanks to the theatre's central position on the major thoroughfare of Charing Cross Road, just off Leicester Square, and a warm auditorium (in every sense of the word) that cosily embraces the audience in its grasp.

Best seat in the house

The Garrick Stalls stretches a long way back in this auditorium, so go for the centre seats of the front Stalls blocks or either of the shallow five rows only circles – Dress and Upper – in which case its worth avoiding the seats at the ends of rows as views can be restricted. Also, bear in mind that the leg-room is not good up here. Because of intrusive boxes, these end seats are sometimes sold at a lower price as "restricted view", but we still don't think it's worth it. In the Stalls, look out for the pillars the ends of rows G, N, R and S that can obstruct views – and because of the heavy Dress Circle overhang, you won't see much of the the top of the stage set from around row P back either. One special little feature of the Garrick worth noting, especially during the hot summer months, is the outdoor balcony of the Upper Circle bar. Pop up here for a drink and a breather when it gets stifling inside. Why does the air cooling never seems to cope with hot weather?

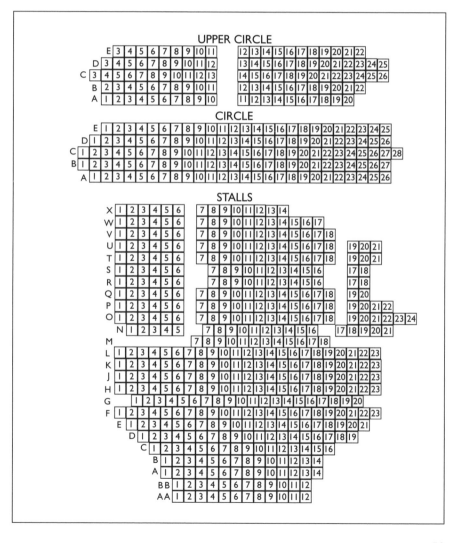

Gielgud Theatre

✉ Shaftesbury Avenue, W1V 8AR

⌂ www.rutheatres.com

☎ (Box office) 0870 899 3338, (Stage door) 020-7850 8740, (Information desk) 0870 899 3338

🖩 020-7494 5154

↑ From Piccadilly Circus walk up the tacky end of Shaftesbury Avenue and the Gielgud is the third theatre on your left, past the Lyric and Apollo, on the corner of Rupert Street

🚇 Charing Cross

⊖ Piccadilly Circus, Leicester Square

P NCPs at Wardour Street, Newport Place, Denman Street, Lexington Street, MasterPark at Poland Street

🚲 Cycle racks at south end of Shaftesbury Avenue

♿ Wheelchair entrance to the auditorium is through and exit door on Rupert Street, leading to the front of the Dress Circle. Seats B1 and 21 can be removed to provide two slightly restricted view spaces. Book on 0870 895 5505. Transfer seating available to row B, or up or down two steep steps to A or C. No disabled toilet

🎧 Sound amplification infrared system with 14 headsets collected from the foyer kiosk. Best reception is in the front area of all levels of the auditorium

👁 Guide dogs cannot be brought into the auditorium. Staff will look after up to two dogs per performance

🍸 Three licensed bars, with a particularly pleasant Dress Circle bar that overlooks the main foyer – though don't get too close to the railings if you suffer from vertigo!

ⓘ Soho, Chinatown, Leicester Square, Piccadilly Circus

Sir Cameron Mackintosh has big plans for the 889-seat Gielgud. When the current lease reverts to Delfont Mackintosh Theatres in 2006, the theatre will become part of a £20 million refurbishment aiming for a complete reinvention of the Gielgud and Queen's island site on Shaftesbury Avenue. Plans include a communal foyer linking the two theatres, improved public spaces – and a brand new 500-seat studio theatre above the Queen's, called the Sondheim Theatre. After all that, who knows, shoddy Shaftesbury Avenue might become a place for glamorous nights again.

History

Sir John Gielgud, David Garrick and Lord Olivier are the only great classical actors to have a London theatre named after them. For Sir John, the honour came late in life in 1994 but seemed appropriate at the time since he'd appeared and directed plays at the Globe, as it was previously called, many times, including his famous sell-out 1939 production of *The Importance of Being Earnest* with Edith Evans as Lady Bracknell, her performance immortalising the line: "A haaandbaaag?" Besides, Shakespeare's Globe had just opened on Bankside so then owners Stoll Moss decided that two Globes in London would confuse the public. The Gielgud originally opened in 1906 as The Hicks Theatre, named after actor-manager Seymour Hicks, and was designed by the great WGR Sprague to match the Queen's, at the Wardour Street end of the block. Hicks, also co-owner of the Aldwych, pulled out in 1909 and for more than 70 years the Globe, as it became known, staged typical West End fare, ranging from Somerset

Maugham and Noël Coward to Alan Ayckbourn. For decades the Globe was also the centre of operations for the HM Tennent company, run by the now forgotten but then all-powerful producer Hugh "Binkie" Beaumont from a tiny office at the back of the balcony. For now, the Gielgud is being run by another West End powerhouse, Andrew Lloyd Webber's Really Useful Theatres.

Best seat in the house

Don't let those "How may I help you" box office clerks tell you otherwise. Ultimate views at the Gielgud are to be found from Stalls Row J. There are 14 seats here with a gangway in front of them and they are all just far enough from the stage top give you an uninterrupted all-round view. In the two side blocks go for aisle seats or you'll lose too much of the stage. Further back, the Dress Circle overhang cuts off the top of the proscenium. Second choice should be the Dress Circle centre block, though it's comparatively cramped and there's another overhang to make life difficult for anyone sitting in the back three rows. End seats in Row A are invariably sold as "restricted view" because the boxes get in the way. In the steep Upper Circle you'll have to put up with reduced legroom and lots of safety barriers. Apart from that, the view's not bad and the acoustics here were good enough to hear Edith Evans's "haaandbaaag", so you ought to catch some of what's going on down there.

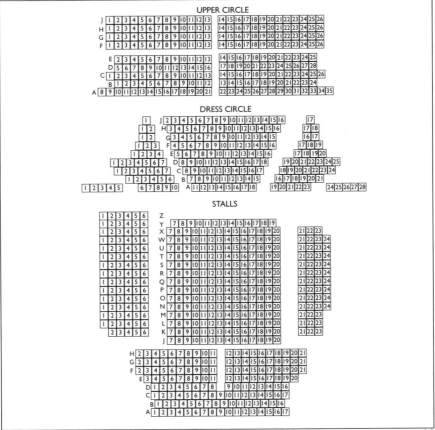

Haymarket Theatre (Theatre Royal)

✉ Haymarket, SW1Y 4HT

🖥 www.trh.co.uk

☎ (Box office) 0870 901 3356, (Stage door) 020-7930 8890

↑ Located near the bottom of the Haymarket on the left hand side heading from Piccadilly Circus, across the street from the Her Majesty's Theatre. There is a wonderful head-on view of the theatre, perfectly framed at the end of Charles II Street as you approach the theatre from Lower Regent Street

🚇 Charing Cross

🚍 Piccadilly Circus, Charing Cross

P MasterPark at Whitcomb Street

♿ There is level access to the auditorium via exit doors to the left and right-hand side of the main entrance. There is space for one wheelchair at the rear of the Stalls, or transfer seating is available to any seat. Wheelchair users must be accompanied by a non-disabled companion

🎧 No facilities at present

👁 Guide dogs are not allowed in the auditorium, but can be looked after by staff

🍸 Usual bar service; look out for the beautiful bar that hides below the entrance to the stalls seating

ⓘ New Zealand House with the beautiful Royal Opera Arcade tucked behind it, Trafalgar Square, Regent Street, Piccadilly Circus

The Haymarket, as it is universally known though it is properly called the Theatre Royal, is one of London's most beautiful and imposing traditional playhouses, with its golden auditorium and most traditional of prosceniums topped by a royal coat of arms. There is always a sense of occasion to visiting this theatre that has come to be associated with star actors giving star performances in classical plays, though that is not necessarily all that it houses.

History

One of London's most historic theatre sites, there has been a theatre here since 1720. The current theatre dates from exactly a century later, when Court architect John Nash created the imposing white-faced building with six imposing Corinthian columns topped by a row of rose windows. In 1837, the use of gaslight was introduced, and the centre chandelier converted from oil and candle. More recent improvements – in 1994 at a cost of £1.5million – saw the theatre re-gilded, using 1200 "books" (layers of 24 carat English gold leaf) to give it the sparkling appearance it has today. At the same time, the stage roof trusses, originally installed in 1821, were overhauled and reinforced, and 2000 lead crystals in the central chandelier were cleaned.

Best seat in the house

Though the rear Stalls are affected by the overhang of the Dress Circle, views elsewhere in the Stalls are excellent, though be warned that the seats are arranged in long continuous rows from one end to the other, with not much passing room, so that if you are seated in the middle and arrive late you will have to clamour over lots of people to get to your seats. Likewise, if you are on the ends, you will have to keep getting up to let people pass. The Dress and Upper Circles are arranged in a more civilized way with two central aisles dividing the seating into three sections in each case, though beware side seats in the Upper Circle that lose visibility around the horseshoe. The Balcony that begins behind the upper circle rather than above it is a very long way from the stage.

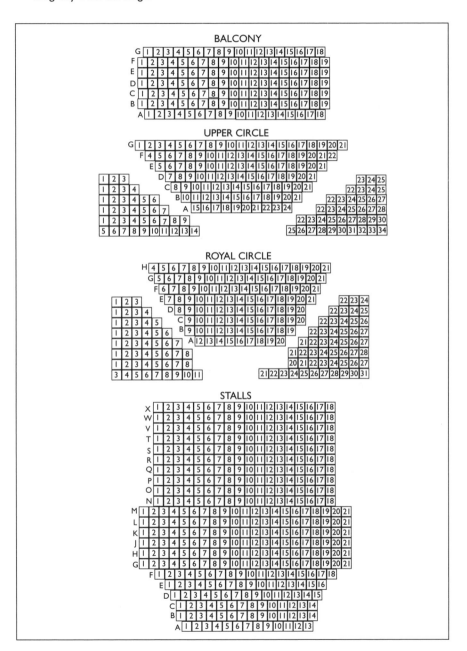

Her Majesty's Theatre

✉ Haymarket, SW1Y 4QR

🖰 www.rutheatres.com

☎ (Box office) 020-7494 5400/0870 899 3338, (Stage door) 020-7850 8750

🖷 020-7930 8467

↑ With the Trocadero behind you, walk south down the wide one-way Haymarket on the right hand pavement, and just past the UGC cinema you'll see Her Majesty's on the right, opposite the Theatre Royal, Haymarket

🚇 Charing Cross

🚇 Piccadilly Circus

P MasterPark at Whitcomb Street

♿ Call 0870 895 5505 to arrange seats for the disabled. Discounts are available. Wheelchair use a side exit door in Charles II Street, leading to two spaces for wheelchair users next to back row Stalls seat S12. Transfer seating available to any aisle seat in the Stalls. An usher will be assigned to disabled theatregoers, but each wheelchair user must bring a non-disabled companion. One adapted toilet

🎧 Sound amplification infrared system with six headsets, available from cloakroom or any member of staff

👁 Guide dog sitting available

🎫 Three licensed bars

ⓘ New Zealand House with the beautiful Royal Opera Arcade tucked behind it, Trafalgar Square, Regent Street, Piccadilly Circus

When it's spectacularly lit up at night and haunting shadows fall over its palatial façade, it's as if Her Majesty's and *The Phantom of the Opera* were made for each other, especially if you start humming "Music of the Night" to yourself. Even the production's false proscenium and crashing chandelier work so beautifully within this grandiose ambience. Backstage it's fairly cramped, with *Phantom's* scenery and high-tech mechanics packed in alongside original wooden Victorian stage machinery, including an amazing Thunder Run that zig-zags downwards from fly-floor level. But nothing lasts forever and when the day arrives when the final curtain comes down on the last of Andrew Lloyd Webber's long-running blockbusters, it's hard to know what else could possibly provide the same theatrical synergy.

History

The crowds queuing to see *The Phantom of the Opera* since 1986 probably never give the commemoration stone dedicated to Sir Herbert Beerbohm Tree a second glance. Yet Tree was one of the pre-eminent Edwardian actor-managers who epitomised the West End for an entire generation of theatregoers. Between 1897 and 1917 he ran His Majesty's (as it was called until the present Queen's accession in 1952). He acted in plays there and lavishly mounted umpteen ultra-realistic productions of Shakespeare (with real rabbits in Arden and a real horse for *Richard II*). He put on *Chu Chin Chow*, which – until *The Mousetrap* caught on – was the longest running West End show ever (it ran for 2,235 performances from 1916). He even lived in the dome above the theatre until he died, and founded the Royal Academy of Dramatic Art there. Tree's spectacular dynamism perfectly suited such a spanking new theatre, the fourth to be built on this spot in the Haymarket, with its ornate frontage and fabulously theatrical interior, ideally suited for big musicals like *West Side Story* and *Fiddler on the Roof*. Maybe some of Tree's energy still lights this brightest lamp in the Haymarket, where the operatic *Phantom* continues to play to capacity.

Best seat in the house

Some seats are sold at reduced prices as the production of *The Phantom Of The Opera* is not fully visible from all sections of the auditorium. So choose carefully to get the full dramatic effect and *never* buy from ticket touts. Anywhere centre Stalls is fine, remembering not to go too close to the stage and bearing in mind that there are four pillars to negotiate from Row O back. The seats located behind these are often on sale only on the day of performance. Best of all, go for the centre of the Royal Circle. Ends of rows don't quite give you the full *Phantom* picture either, and the quartet of pillars up here should be noted. The higher you go, the cheaper the seats, the more you have to stretch to see and hear what's going on downstairs.

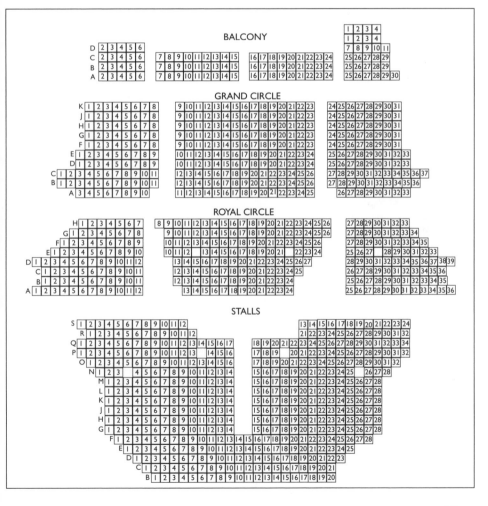

London Palladium

✉ Argyll Street, W1V 1AD

🖰 www.rutheatres.com

☎ (Box office) 020-7494 5572/0870 890 1108, (Stage door) 020-7850 8770

↑ The Palladium frontage dominates Argyll Street, between Oxford Street and Marlborough Street

⊖ Oxford Circus is a minute away

P NCP car park, Kingly Street

🚇 Oxford Circus is a minute away

♿ Call 0870 895 5505 to arrange seats for the disabled. Wheelchair access is through nearby Ramillies Place through to the Stalls where four wheelchairs per performance can 'park' in rows L, O, Q and S. Each wheelchair user must be accompanied by a helper. One adapted toilet

🎧 Sound amplification infrared system with 30 headsets

👁 Guide dog sitting available

🌟 Three licensed bars including the spacious 'Cinderella' dress circle bar

ⓘ Dickens & Jones department store and Liberty's are across the street, Oxford Circus, Regent Street, Carnaby Street

It looks like Greek temple on the outside, but however many times you've been to the London Palladium there's nothing in the world quite like giving yourself the red carpet treatment, walking up those foyer stairs and discovering the riot of white, gold and marble in the lobby before you settle down to watch the show in the magical warmth of the Matcham-designed auditorium. There are nostalgic posters and photos everywhere, the bars are huge, the vast advance booking hall makes you want to linger and look, but this is, and always was, very much a living theatre, although it still reeks of old-fashioned Saturday nights out in the West End.

History

If you ask any Londoner to name a West End theatre, it's a sure bet they'll instantly come back with London Palladium, even if they've never set foot in the place. A true national treasure, this Edwardian masterpiece designed by that inspired genius of theatres Frank Matcham truly entered the popular DNA in 1955 when the powerful impresario Val Parnell broadcast *Sunday Night At The London Palladium* live on the new ITV network. If you remember the Beat the Clock sequence with Tommy Trinder and sweeping shots of the audience eagerly anticipating the entertainment to come, you're old enough to know that the Palladium itself always was the real star. Ever since this elegant 2298-seat palace opened on Boxing Day 1910 it was all about all big names, big audiences, stellar variety bills, spectacular annual pantomimes and mile-long queues winding around the block, hence the "Variety Bar" and "Cinderella Bar". After the war, Parnell turned it into the "Ace variety theatre of the world", and anyone who's anyone in show biz topped the bill, making it the UK equivalent of New York's Palace. With the collapse of variety and revue, large-scale family musicals have fitted in perfectly with the Palladium ethos.

Best seat in the house

The back half-dozen or so rows in the Stalls suffer from oppressive Dress Circle overhang and the end seats in the two Stalls side blocks, especially those close to the stage, are less than good value for money. Go for the centre block in the Royal Circle first for truly magnificent views, even if the seating feels surprisingly cramped. It's to be expected that the vast Upper Circle blocks are going to feel distant, but the back few rows are so dire that you get none of the Palladium magic, so why bother, unless of course your budget really can't be stretched to anything better.

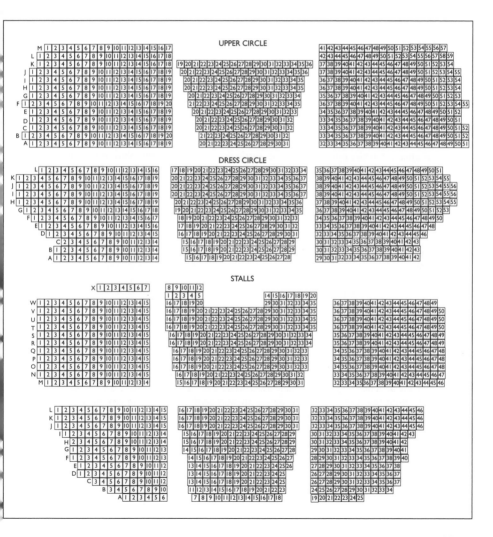

Lyceum Theatre

✉ 21 Wellington Street, WC2E 7DA

🖰 www.ccLive.co.uk

☎ (Box office) 0870 243 9000, (Stage door) 020-7420 8100

↑ Located just off the Strand diagonally opposite the end of Waterloo Bridge, this historic theatre has been reclaimed as a major West End musical house after years of neglect

🚇 Charing Cross

⊖ Charing Cross, Embankment, Covent Garden, Temple

P Some single yellow line parking on north side of Strand and around the Aldwych. NCP car parks in Drury Lane and Upper St Martin's Lane; Masterpark at Spring Gardens, off Trafalgar Square

🚲 Cycle racks in Wellington Street and Southampton Street

♿ There are spaces for 8 wheelchairs in the rear stalls, accessible via a double exit door to the left-hand side facing the theatre. Wheelchair users must be accompanied by a non-disabled companion. There are adapted toilets by the stalls entrance

🎧 Infrared system with 25 headsets, to be collected (deposit required) form the confectionary kiosk beside the main entrance. Reception is best in the royal circle and stalls

👁 Guide dogs allowed in the auditorium, provided box office informed at time of booking

🍸 Usual bar service in crowded area in front of entrances to the stalls, but a more commodious bar is available in the royal (dress) circle. There is also a bar in the grand (upper) circle

ⓘ Orso's Restaurant in Wellington Street and Joe Allen's in Exeter Street are two theatrical legends, both from the same American owner. One Aldwych (a modern boutique hotel, with an excellent coffee bar facing the entrance to the Strand Theatre), the Meriden Waldorf Hotel (good for afternoon tea in the Palm Court, and celebrated tea dances on Saturday and Sunday afternoons), Covent Garden, the Theatre Museum, Somerset House (including the Courtauld Institute Gallery, and riverside promenade), the Royal Courts of Justice

Though the wallpaper used to adorn the Lyceum's '90s refurbishment manage to make it look a bit like an Indian restaurant, it's nevertheless wonderful to have the Lyceum back at all and in such demand as a home for major musicals that require a large seating capacity (the Lyceum has nearly 2100 seats, making it one of the largest in the capital).

History

The Lyceum has undergone many incarnations since the foundations were first laid in 1771 for a building on this site, and it opened originally as "Exhibition Rooms with Paintings and Sculptures" as the headquarters of the Society of Artists in Great Britain. When the society became insolvent, some of its members went to Somerset House and founded the Royal Academy, while the premises variously became a place for boxing and fencing displays, panoramas and an unlicensed theatre where out-of-work actors could play for their own benefit. When the Theatre Royal, Drury Lane burnt down in 1809, arrangements were made for its company to play down the road at the Lyceum until their own theatre was re-built, so it acquired a proper license for the first time for the presentation of plays; and when Drury Lane re-opened in 1812, the Lyceum retained its license for the summer months, and was completely rebuilt in 1815 as London's first theatre to be lit by gas. Now it was the Lyceum's turn to burn down. The theatre was lost to fire in 1830, and its replacement – which opened in 1834 – would later prove hospitality to another theatre, Covent Garden, when that venue went up in flames in 1856. In 1871, Henry Irving would become a huge star here, and by 1878 had taken over the management of the theatre, and remained solely in control until 1899. A fire in the scenery store that destroyed most of his assets, however, saw him sell control to a syndicate, and he would make his last appearance here in 1902, writing to his co-star Ellen Terry: "The place is now given up to the rats – all light cut off, and only Barry and a fireman left. Everything of mine I've moved away, even the cat." The syndicate demolished and rebuilt it as a music hall that re-opened in 1904, designed by Bertie Crewe who was also responsible for the Phoenix, Piccadilly and Shaftesbury theatres. It became a home to melodrama, pantomime and variety, up to 1939. After the Second World War, it re-opened as a dance ballroom, and would remain as such for the next 40 years, also housing occasional pop concerts. After another period of closure and neglect, it was finally returned to theatrical use in 1994 when Apollo Leisure – then Britain's largest theatre owning company – acquired the lease and restored it as a musical house.

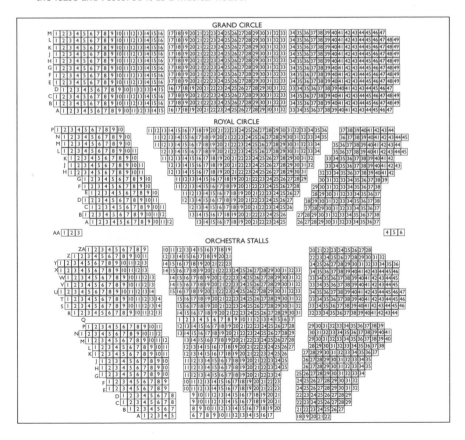

Best seat in the house

As always with a large house, the further back you go the more remote everything becomes. Rear stalls and the rear Royal (Dress) Circle suffer from the overhang of the circles above them. But central Stalls and Royal Circle offer fine, uninterrupted views. The Grand (Upper) Circle is high and steeply raked.

Lyric Theatre

✉ Shaftesbury Avenue,, W1D 7ES

🖰 www.rutheatres.com

☎ (Box office) 0870 890 1107 (24 hours by phone; in person, open Mon-Sat 10am-8pm), (Stage door) 020-7850 8760

↑ At the Piccadilly Circus end of Shaftesbury Avenue, the Lyric is the first theatre you come to in the stretch of four that mark out this area of London as the heart of Theatreland

🚇 Charing Cross

🚇 Piccadilly Circus

P NCP car parks at Wardour Street, Newport Place and Denman Street

🚲 Racks at junction of Shaftesbury Avenue and Great Windmill Street

♿ There is level access through the 'Royal Entrance' on Shaftesbury Avenue to the Dress Circle, with transfer seating available in the boxes at Dress Circle level, or a maximum of two wheelchairs per performance can 'park' in box D or E. Each wheelchair user must be accompanied by a helper. There is an adapted toilet inside the 'Royal Entrance'

🎧 Sennheiser Infrared system with headsets, available from cloakroom in dress circle bar

👁 Guide dogs are allowed in the boxes but not elsewhere in the auditorium. Staff can dog sit if necessary

🍴 Usual bar service in four licensed bars; a small crowded room as you enter through the foyer serves as the dress circle bar, but a more spacious bar beneath the stalls area takes care of customers seated there

ⓘ Soho, Chinatown, Piccadilly Circus, London Trocadero shopping centre across the street, Rain Forest Café

One of the West End's most perfectly proportioned intimate houses, the Lyric remains a historic gem that continues to entice theatregoers today. But the auditorium is slightly musty now, with a smearing of brown paint and dull carpeting that make it look gloomier than it should be.

History

The oldest theatre on Shaftesbury Avenue, the Lyric opened at the end of 1888. Designed by CJ Phipps as a home for operetta, this charming playhouse for over 900 theatregoers is surprisingly intimate, staging plays and smaller-scale musicals with equal facility. Its prime location on Shaftesbury Avenue makes it a very popular choice with producers, not to mention audiences, looking for the quintessential West End theatregoing experience. Amongst recent long-running successes here, the musical *Five Guys Named Moe* enjoyed a five-year run; Jessica Lange starred in a revival of *Long Day's Journey into Night*; while Brendan Fraser starred in *Cat on a Hot Tin Roof*.

Best seat in the house

Some seats in the rear Stalls suffer from supporting pillar syndrome, but further forward views are excellent, though the removal of the central aisle means that seats are now arranged in continuous, inconveniently long rows. The two circles are relatively intimate, with pillars again affecting the rear seats, and poor side seats in the Upper Circle. The Balcony is high and remote.

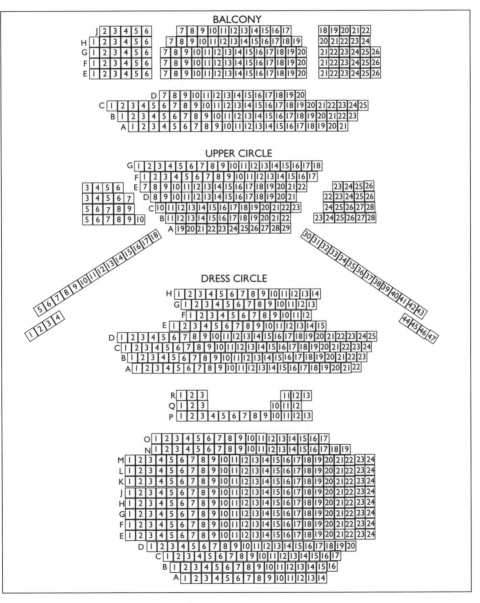

New Ambassadors Theatre

✉ West Street,, WC2H 9ND

🏠 www.newambassadors.com

☎ (Box office) 020-7369 1761 (24 hours by phone; in person, open Mon-Sat 10am-8pm)

↑ Tucked away off Charing Cross Road, walking north from Leicester Square turn right onto Lichfield Street (or walking south from Tottenham Court Road, turn left onto Lichfield Street) and the theatre is next door to the St Martin's Theatre (home of The Mousetrap), straight ahead of you

🚇 Charing Cross

⊖ Leicester Square, Tottenham Court Road, Piccadilly Circus, Covent Garden

P MasterPark at Cambridge Circus, NCP at Upper St Martin's Lane and Bedfordbury

♿ Box Office and foyer are situated at street level, but the stalls area is down a flight of 30 steps and the dress circle up a flight of seven steps. There is no room for wheelchairs to 'park', but patrons who are able to can transfer into an aisle seat

🎧 Sennheiser Infrared sound amplification system available; two devices available from the box office

👁 Guide dogs are welcome in the auditorium, but be sure to be booked into an aisle seat. Alternatively, staff will dog sit

🍸 Usual bar service in two tiny bars, off the rear of the stalls and beside the dress circle entrance

ⓘ The Ivy (probably the most fashionable theatrical restaurant) is across the street, as will be witnessed by the inevitable posse of photographers outside

One of the West End's most intimate theatre with less than 450 seats (only the Fortune has a few fewer), this is a friendly and welcoming place that feels very clubby. There's not much public space to speak of, so audiences tend to spill out onto the pavement outside before the show and during intervals – all the better to see the comings and goings at the Ivy across the street. It could also be because the theatre gets notoriously hot, whatever the weather.

History

Originally known as the Ambassadors, this theatre was conceived by architect WGR Sprague as a companion to the St Martin's Theatre next door which he also designed. But the Ambassadors opened first in 1913 when the First World War interrupted construction of the St Martin's. Decorated in an elegant Louis XVI style, this intimate theatre on two levels is probably best known as the original home to The Mousetrap, which opened here in 1952 and ran for 22 years before transferring to the St Martin's next door. Subsequent hits included the long-running 1980s RSC transfer of Les Liaisons Dangereuses, and for three years from 1996 the theatre became the home of the Royal Court's Theatre Upstairs programme. This adventurous spirit continued when, in 1999, it was re-branded the New Ambassadors Theatre and became the West End's only commercial theatre implementing an in-house artistic policy that concentrated on providing a home for limited seasons of new work. This has, however, lately given way to extended runs for established hits, like The Vagina Monologues and Stones in His Pockets that both originated here, transferred elsewhere, and returned here to complete their London runs.

Best seat in the house

The rear Stalls strangely dip in the middle and rake downwards rather than upwards, so avoid them; legroom in the small Circle is miniscule except for row F where there's a terrific break between the front seating and the rear. So really, except for Row F upstairs, the only place to be is downstairs towards the front.

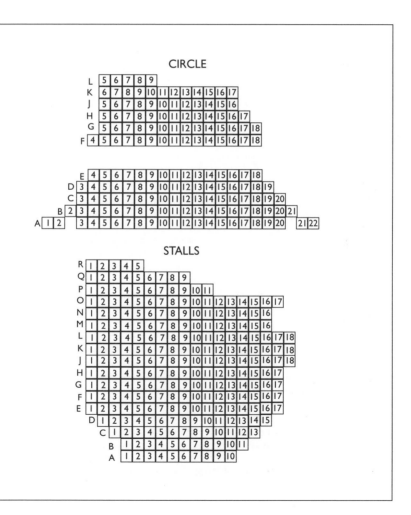

New London Theatre

✉ Drury Lane (entrance in Parker Street), WC2B 5PW

🖥 www.rutheatres.com

☎ (Box office) 0870 890 0141 (24 hours by phone; in person, open Mon-Sat 10am-8pm), (Stage door) 020-7242 9802

↑ A little 'forgotten' to the east of Covent Garden, this modern theatre is actually very accessible, in every sense

⊖ Holborn or Covent Garden

P nearest car park is an NCP car park in Parker Mews, directly below the theatre

🚇 Holborn or Covent Garden

♿ There is level access into Stalls row S via lift at Stage Door, transfer seating if available to Stalls S1. If patrons can manage one step, they can transfer into Stalls R5 or T1. A maximum of one wheelchair per performance can 'park' in Stalls S1. Call Customer Services Department, 0870 895 5505 to make arrangements

🎧 Sennheiser Infrared system. Ask Manager for headsets

👁 Guide dogs can be looked after in the Manager's office during the performance

🍸 Usual bar service to left and right of main foyer as you enter from the stairs or escalator

ⓘ Covent Garden with its host of pre- and post-theatre restaurants and bars, as well as the Theatre Museum and the London Transport Museum for a complete day out

From the outside this glass-fronted building may resemble a conference centre more readily than a theatre, an impression reinforced inside by the utilitarian ground floor foyer with an escalator providing the main entrance for traffic up to the theatre. But upstairs are some refreshingly spacious bar areas, leading into an unusually wide but surprisingly intimate, well-raked amphitheatre-like auditorium of 1100 seats on two levels. Originally intended to be a "theatre for the future", the theatre's design incorporates a 60-feet wide revolve which includes the stage, orchestra pit and part of the seating – all of which were sent into movement in the opening minutes of *Cats*, leading the ads to declare that latecomers would not be admitted while the auditorium was in motion. As well as an underground car park, the building also contains a cabaret room, the Talk of London that is occasionally also pressed into theatrical use.

History

Between 1973 when this modern venue (built on a site that has seen theatres built here since Elizabethan times) first opened and 1981, it was considered to be the "white elephant" of Theatreland that no one wanted to book, and after a series of flops became used as television studio from 1977 to 1980. Amongst the attractions during its prior theatrical use were a production of *Grease* in 1973, starring a then-unknown Richard Gere as Danny Zuko, and a season of plays by Steven Berkoff including *Metamorphosis*, *East* and *The Fall of the House of Usher*, in 1977 and 1978. But then *Cats* arrived in 1981, and put the theatre on the map, literally, to prove that it's not the theatre that counts but the show. *Cats* eventually became the longest running musical in the history of the British theatre, finally closing on May 11, 2002 – its 21st birthday – to be followed by a revival of *Joseph & His Amazing Technicolor Dreamcoat*.

Best seat in the house

Go for the central seating in the nicely raked second section of the Stalls. Side seats may offer a distorted view, depending on the production, and in the front section of the Stalls you are too close.

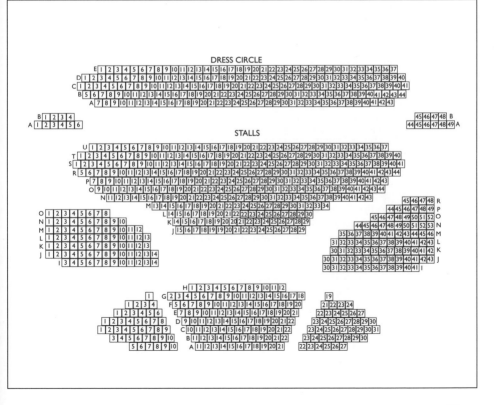

Old Vic Theatre

✉ The Cut, SE1 8NB

🖰 www.oldvictheatre.com

☎ (Box office) 020-7928 7616, (Stage door) 020-7928 2651

📠 info@oldvictheatre.com

↑ Located two minutes from Waterloo Station (rail, underground and Eurostar; follow signs for the Waterloo Road exit and turn right), this celebrated classical theatre may be 'on the wrong side of the tracks' but it's an area that is fast becoming more fashionable, with several interesting restaurants in The Cut and down the other end of the Cut on Blackfriars Road

🚇 Waterloo

🚌 Waterloo; or Southwark

P Free on-street parking available after 6.30pm on weekdays and after 1pm on Saturdays; there are also paid car parks available in and around the National Theatre, a five-minute walk away

♿ Level access via an exit door on Webber Street, with spaces for four wheelchairs in the row D of the stalls, and transfer seating available also to aisle seats. There is an adapted WC inside the side entrance. For details, contact 020-7928 2975

🎧 No facilities at present

👁 Guide dogs are not allowed into the auditorium, but staff can dog sit

🍴 The newly refurbished basement Pit Bar, accessible either via the theatre entrance on the Cut or a side door on Waterloo Road, offers a full menu and wine list daily from 12 noon till late; there are also drinks bars on the two circles levels. Ice-creams are served by ushers in interval

ⓘ The South Bank cultural complex that includes the National Theatre and Royal Festival Hall and other assorted attractions, including the London Eye near Westminster Bridge and the Tate Modern and Shakespeare's Globe, between Blackfriars and Southwark Bridges, are all nearby

With Sir Elton John now Chairman of the Board of Trustees, and Kevin Spacey having accepted the title of Artistic Director of a theatre at which he appeared in a transfer of O'Neill's *The Iceman Cometh* from the Almeida, the Old Vic's future is now more secure than it has been for some time. This beautiful theatre, steeped in both history and atmosphere, has lacked an artistic soul since the departures of the National, Jonathan Miller and Sir Peter Hall, and acting as a receiving house for commercial productions that can't find a more mainstream address across the river hasn't done it any favours. But Spacey may yet restore its theatrical vision.

History

Originally opened in 1818 as the Royal Coburg Theatre, the Old Vic is one of the most famous theatres in the world and one of the oldest working theatres in London. Renamed the Royal Victoria Hall in 1833 in honour of the then Princess Victoria, it would eventually affectionately become known as the Old Vic in her honour. Its theatrical legacy as a classical theatre was established under the management of the legendary Lilian Baylis, who ran it from 1914 and produced the whole of Shakespeare's first folio in sequence. In 1950, the Old Vic Company, with Laurence Olivier and Ralph Richardson at the helm, was established here. This company became the genesis of the

National Theatre that was formally established here in 1963 and continued to call the Old Vic home until, in 1976, it moved to its nearby purpose-built theatre complex on the South Bank. After a few years of erratic programming, including a now legendarily terrible 1980 production of *Macbeth* starring Peter O'Toole in the title role, Canadian theatrical impresario Ed Mirvish acquired the theatre, restored and renovated it extensively, and funded artistic regimes with Jonathan Miller and later Sir Peter Hall at the helm. When Mirvish decided to sell up and the theatre put on the open market in 1998, a new charitable trust was established to acquire it and prevent it from becoming, as was mooted at the time, a themed pub or a lap-dancing club!

Best seat in the house

With just over 1000 seats in all, this medium-sized, three-level playhouse is arranged with the two horseshoe circles (the Upper Circle is named the Lilian Baylis Circle, in honour of the legendary former manager) beginning a long way back over the Stalls, so if you want to be close to the action, the Stalls is the only place to be. The rows are better raked the further back you go, however, so you may want to avoid the front stalls, too. There is also no centre aisle, so if you're in the middle of one of the very long rows downstairs, you may feel a little trapped.

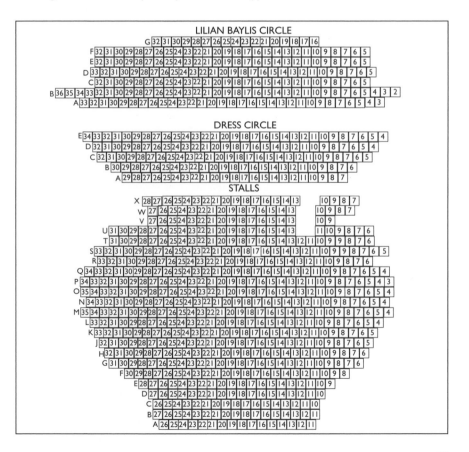

Open Air Theatre

✉ The Ironworks, Inner Circle, Regent's Park, NW1 4NR

⚲ www.openairtheatre.org

☎ (Box office) 020-7486 2431, (Stage door) 020-7935 5756

📠 info@openairtheatre.org

↑ A pleasant stroll through Regent's Park brings you to the Inner Circle, in which the Open Air Theatre is located. Be warned that after the show, the park itself is shut, so follow the crowds along the roadways to bring you back to Marylebone Road

🚉 Marylebone

⊖ Baker Street/Regent's Park

P free on-street parking in the Inner Circle after 6.30pm

♿ Fully accessible to people with reduced mobility. Spaces in the auditorium for wheelchair users and their companions can be booked in advance at the box office

∩ There are sign-interpreted performances for each main show, and an FM Assisted listening system is also available. Request a headset when booking

👁 Guide dogs welcome

🌟 The theatre opens at 6.45pm (with performances starting at 8pm) to allow audiences plenty of time to either avail themselves of the excellent on-site catering or eat their own picnics on the lovely picnic lawn. The restaurant offers traditional home-made dishes, with daily specials such as poached salmon, salads and desserts, as well as a barbeque that cooks hamburgers and bratwurst in front of you. The long bar also offers coffee and mulled wine in the intervals, as well as the usual full bar service, and stays open after the show, too. For matinee performances, drinks and snacks are available from 2pm

ⓘ Beautifully situated in the Inner Circle of Regent's Park, the theatre is a stone's throw from such features as the gorgeous and fragrant Rose Garden. London Zoo, on the Outer Circle, is also nearby, as is Madame Tussaud's and the London Planetarium on Marylebone Road

You know the British summer has arrived, in spirit if not body, when the Open Air Theatre opens for business in Regent's Park. The annual season runs for three months from the beginning of June to the beginning of September, usually presenting two Shakespeares in repertoire with a popular musical. A Midsummer Night's Dream is a virtually annual staple here – the policy now is to do a new production every three years and take a year off between them. On a nice summer's night, you can't beat the experience (despite occasional disruptions from the overhead roar of metallic flying birds or the chirping of real ones!). On a more inclement evening, watch the Dunkirk spirit at its best. Performances are never cancelled before the advertised starting time, and then only in the event of very bad weather. If cancellation is unavoidable, ticket holders will be entitled to seats for any other performance, subject to availability, in the current or future years. Refunds are not given.

History

Located in a high, wide amphitheatre auditorium that is open to the skies, the Open Air Theatre offers one of London's longest-established celebrations of al fresco theatre. In 2002, it celebrated its 70th birthday, though it hasn't always enjoyed the high reputation it now deservedly has for top-class professional productions of classic Shakespeare and modern musicals. Its origins were far more modest: an old tennis court was dug out in 1932 to create it, with a rising slope upon which deck chairs of various shapes and sizes were scattered. It operated successfully until the Second World War intervened, when only matinees were possible because of the blackout. Co-founder Robert Atkins went on to run the Shakespeare Memorial Theatre in Stratford-upon-Avon for two seasons after the end of the war – this was long before the RSC was founded – and returned to direct in the Park. But in 1960, he finally ran out of money, and there was even talk of turning it back into parkland. Fortunately, however, David Conville took over (initially jointly with another director, David William), and continued to run it up to 1987, when he handed the artistic reigns over to an actor-turned-director, Ian Talbot, who has been at the helm ever since.

Best seat in the house

Seating for nearly 1200 people is in two main areas: a fan-shaped area in front of the stage, and a wider, more steeply raked section on a wooden grandstand further back after a gangway break between the two. The front offers the more close-up experience, but you get a better sense of the scale of the place further back, especially as darkness falls, the stage lighting gradually takes over, and the rest of the audience are lost in darkness.

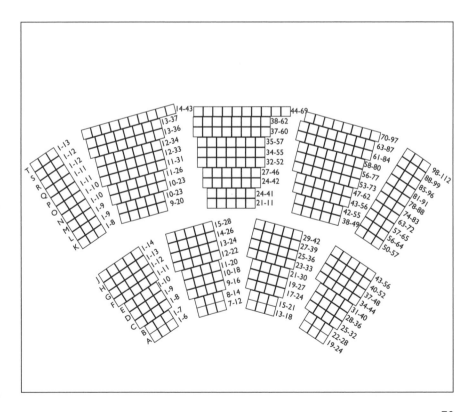

Palace Theatre

✉ Shaftesbury Avenue, WIV 8AY

🏵 www.rutheatres.com

☎ (Box office) 0870 899 3338 (24 hours by phone; in person, open Mon-Sat 10am-8pm), (Stage door) 020-7434 0088

↑ Located at Cambridge Circus where Shaftesbury Avenue and Charing Cross Road meet, the Palace is a beautiful London landmark

🚇 Charing Cross

⊖ Piccadilly Circus (walk up Shaftesbury Avenue); Leicester Square (walk north on Charing Cross Road); Tottenham Court Road (walk south on Charing Cross Road)

P NCP at Upper St Martin's Lane, MasterPark at Cambridge Circus

♿ There is access via a side exit on Shaftesbury Avenue, from which there is one step to negotiate and then a slight incline to the stalls. Transfer seating is available to any stalls aisle seat, and a maximum of one wheelchair per performance can park near the rear of the stalls. Each wheelchair user must be accompanied by a non-disabled companion. There is an adapted toilet near the wheelchair users' entrance

🎧 Sennheiser Infrared system with headsets

👁 Guide dogs not allowed inside the auditorium but staff can dog sit

🌠 Usual bar service in spacious bars on all levels – particularly impressive is the stalls bar area, with lots of nooks and crannies for private assignations

ⓘ Soho; Covent Garden

With the exterior of this beautiful theatre stunningly revealed anew after years of grime were sandblasted off it in the '80s, the interior of this 1400 seater theatre still awaits a comprehensive restoration scheme. Some improvements have been made on the foyer and its imposing staircase that goes from the entrance to all levels of the theatre. Night-time spotlighting makes the exterior a real London landmark; now the interior needs to catch up!

History

Originally opened in 1891 as the Royal English Opera House by the producer Richard D'Oyly Carte (who would later go on to establish the Savoy Theatre, as well), his lofty ambitions to provide a home here for English operetta soon floundered and by the following year the theatre was re-branded the Palace Theatre of Variety. It was here that the first Royal Command Variety Performance took place in 1912, prompting the comment by Sir Oswald Stoll, "The Cinderella of the Arts at last went to the ball". Later the theatre would become best known for its musicals, giving the original London runs to such shows as *No No Nanette* (which ran 655 performances from 1925), *On Your Toes* (in 1937) and *The Sound of Music* (2385 performances). But it was Andrew Lloyd Webber and Tim Rice's *Jesus Christ Superstar* (3358 performances) that smashed the record books in the '70s, and led indirectly to Lloyd Webber himself buying the theatre... though it's his one-time co-producing partner and friendly rival Cameron Mackintosh who, since 1985, has been paying him rent to house *Les Miserables* there! That show has finally left the building (to move to the smaller Queen's Theatre on Shaftesbury Avenue), with Lloyd Webber finally free to put another of his own musicals on there at last – *The Woman in White*.

Best seat in the house

The Stalls is wide and deep, and with the Dress Circle overhanging the Stalls quite far forward, the top of the stage is lost from rear seats, with the circles in turn overhanging each other towards the front, bringing them closer to the stage but causing restrictions further back. Front Dress Circle offers the best uninterrupted views. After the generously proportioned ten- and eight-row Dress and Upper circles, the real surprise in this theatre is the massive balcony, which offers 15 rows of vertigo-inducing terror at one of the steepest, most distant and cramped angles in the West End.

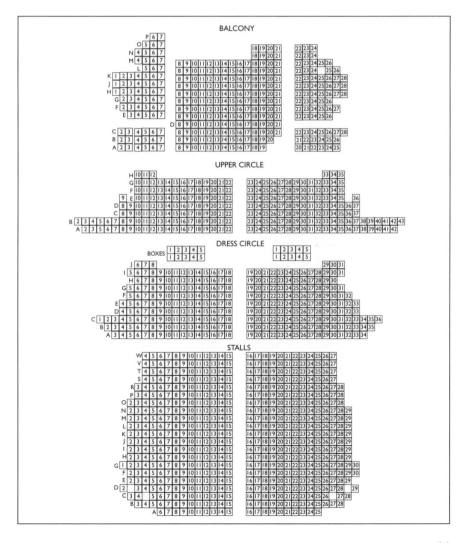

Phoenix Theatre

✉ 110 Charing Cross Road, WC2H 0JP

⌂ www.theambassadors.com/phoenix

☎ (Box office) 020-7369 1733

🚇 Charing Cross

🚇 Tottenham Court Road, Leicester Square, Piccadilly Circus

P NCP at Great Russell Street

🚇 Tottenham Court Road, Leicester Square, Piccadilly Circus

♿ From a side entrance on Flitcroft Street, to the left of the box office, there is a parallel ramp up to the left-hand side of the Dress Circle where there is space for one wheelchair user and a companion in a box. There is alternatively transfer seating available to seats on the front row of the dress circle. A non-disabled companion must accompany each wheelchair user. There is an adapted toilet behind the box

🎧 No facilities at present

👁 Guide dogs not allowed inside the auditorium but staff can dog sit

🍸 Usual bar service in several locations, including the Noël Coward bar inside foyer to the main Phoenix Street entrance to the theatre, opened by Coward himself in 1969

ⓘ In the traditional heart of the West End's bookselling trade, with Foyles across the road and a big branch of Borders next door, plus other specialist bookshops on Charing Cross Road

This Italianate theatre has a highly distinctive feature: it actually has two entrances, though the one on the corner of Charing Cross Road and Flitcroft Street is actually used as an exit instead, but is situated on a striking corner site of four columns with a canopy topped by an attic of square windows. The main entrance on Phoenix Street is wider and more spacious, and leads into a smart, intimate auditorium full of glass, curtains, sculpted wooden doors and decorated ceilings. Mirrors are everywhere in the foyers leading into the auditorium, giving this theatre a real sense of occasion inside to helpfully offset the functional strip of shops (including the theatre's own advance box office) and apartment block above it on Charing Cross Road.

History

The theatre opened in 1930 with the premiere of Noël Coward's *Private Lives*. Starring the playwright and Gertrude Lawrence as well as the young Laurence Olivier, the Phoenix would become closely associated with Coward who returned six years later with Lawrence to present *Tonight at 8.30* and again, in 1952, with *Quadrille*, starring the premiere American theatrical couple, the Lunts. The Coward connection is now marked by the foyer bar being named in his honour. Other leading figures who regularly graced its stage during the '40s and '50s included John Gielgud and Paul Scofield, until the musical version of *The Canterbury Tales* set up shop in 1968 for a record-breaking five-year-run. But that record has in turn long been broken by the ongoing run of another musical *Blood Brothers* that transferred from the Albery in 1991 and is still going strong.

Best seat in the house

This medium-sized theatre of just over 1000 seats, comfortably arranged over three levels, offers surprising intimacy in the Stalls (though rear seats lose a little of the top of the stage), excellent sightlines from the front Dress Circle, and an Upper Circle that, for once, doesn't feel too far away.

UPPER CIRCLE

Row	Left block	Right block
J	1 2 3 4 5 6 7 8 9 10 11 12 13 14	15 16 17 18 19 20 21 22 23 24 25 26 27 28
H	1 2 3 4 5 6 7 8 9 10 11 12 13 14	15 16 17 18 19 20 21 22 23 24 25 26 27 28
G	1 2 3 4 5 6 7 8 9 10 11 12 13 14	15 16 17 18 19 20 21 22 23 24 25 26 27 28
F	1 2 3 4 5 6 7 8 9 10 11 12 13 14	15 16 17 18 19 20 21 22 23 24 25 26 27 28
E	1 2 3 4 5 6 7 8 9 10 11 12 13 14	15 16 17 18 19 20 21 22 23 24 25 26 27 28
D	1 2 3 4 5 6 7 8 9 10 11 12 13 14	15 16 17 18 19 20 21 22 23 24 25 26 27 28
C	1 2 3 4 5 6 7 8 9 10 11 12 13 14	15 16 17 18 19 20 21 22 23 24 25 26 27 28
B	1 2 3 4 5 6 7 8 9 10 11 12 13 14	15 16 17 18 19 20 21 22 23 24 25 26 27 28
A	1 2 3 4 5 6 7 8 9 10 11 12 13 14 15	16 17 18 19 20 21 22 23 24 25 26 27 28 29 30

DRESS CIRCLE

Row	Left block	Right block
K	1 2 3 4 5 6 7 8 9 10 11 12 13 14	15 16 17 18 19 20 21 22 23 24 25 26 27 28
J	1 2 3 4 5 6 7 8 9 10 11 12 13 14	15 16 17 18 19 20 21 22 23 24 25 26 27 28
H	1 2 3 4 5 6 7 8 9 10 11 12 13 14	15 16 17 18 19 20 21 22 23 24 25 26 27 28
G	1 2 3 4 5 6 7 8 9 10 11 12 13 14	15 16 17 18 19 20 21 22 23 24 25 26 27 28
F	1 2 3 4 5 6 7 8 9 10 11 12 13 14	15 16 17 18 19 20 21 22 23 24 25 26 27 28
E	1 2 3 4 5 6 7 8 9 10 11 12 13 14	15 16 17 18 19 20 21 22 23 24 25 26 27 28
D	1 2 3 4 5 6 7 8 9 10 11 12 13 14	15 16 17 18 19 20 21 22 23 24 25 26 27 28
C	1 2 3 4 5 6 7 8 9 10 11 12 13 14	15 16 17 18 19 20 21 22 23 24 25 26 27 28
B	1 2 3 4 5 6 7 8 9 10 11 12 13 14	15 16 17 18 19 20 21 22 23 24 25 26 27 28
A	1 2 3 4 5 6 7 8 9 10 11 12 13 14	15 16 17 18 19 20 21 22 23 24 25 26 27 28

STALLS

Row	Left block	Right block
	1 2 3 4	13 14 15 16 17 18 19 20 21 22 23 24
R	1 2 3 4 5 6	15 16 17 18 19 20 21 22 23 24 25 26 27 28
Q	1 2 3 4 5 6 7 8 9 10 11 12 13 14	15 16 17 18 19 20 21 22 23 24 25 26 27 28
P	1 2 3 4 5 6 7 8 9 10 11 12 13 14	15 16 17 18 19 20 21 22 23 24 25 26 27 28
O	1 2 3 4 5 6 7 8 9 10 11 12 13 14	15 16 17 18 19 20 21 22 23 24 25 26 27 28
N	1 2 3 4 5 6 7 8 9 10 11 12 13 14	15 16 17 18 19 20 21 22 23 24 25 26 27 28
M	1 2 3 4 5 6 7 8 9 10 11 12 13 14	15 16 17 18 19 20 21 22 23 24 25 26 27 28
L	1 2 3 4 5 6 7 8 9 10 11 12 13 14	15 16 17 18 19 20 21 22 23 24 25 26 27 28
K	1 2 3 4 5 6 7 8 9 10 11 12 13 14	15 16 17 18 19 20 21 22 23 24 25 26 27 28
J	1 2 3 4 5 6 7 8 9 10 11 12 13	14 15 16 17 18 19 20 21 22 23 24 25 26
H	1 2 3 4 5 6 7 8 9 10 11 12 13 14	15 16 17 18 19 20 21 22 23 24 25 26 27 28
G	1 2 3 4 5 6 7 8 9 10 11 12 13 14	15 16 17 18 19 20 21 22 23 24 25 26 27 28
F	1 2 3 4 5 6 7 8 9 10 11 12 13 14	15 16 17 18 19 20 21 22 23 24 25 26 27 28
E	1 2 3 4 5 6 7 8 9 10 11 12 13 14	15 16 17 18 19 20 21 22 23 24 25 26 27 28
D	1 2 3 4 5 6 7 8 9 10 11 12 13	14 15 16 17 18 19 20 21 22 23 24 25 26
C	1 2 3 4 5 6 7 8 9 10 11 12	13 14 15 16 17 18 19 20 21 22 23 24
B	3 4 5 6 7 8 9 10 11	12 13 14 15 16 17 18 19 20 21 22
A	4 5 6 7 8 9 10	11 12 13 14 15 16 17 18 19 20

Piccadilly Theatre

✉ Denman Street, W1V 8DY

🏛 www.theambassadors.com/piccadilly/

☎ (Box office) 020-7369 1734 (24 hours by phone; in person, open Mon-Sat 10am-8pm), (Stage door) 020-6468 8800, 020-7867 1128

↑ Tucked just behind Piccadilly Circus, on the north west side nearest to the start of Regent's Street, it's hidden from view but easily found by locating Burger King and walking beyond to the corner, where you will see the Regent Palace Hotel. Walk towards the hotel, and the theatre will appear on the right

🚇 Charing Cross

⊖ Piccadilly Circus

P There are car parks in Denman Street (adjoining the theatre), and Brewer Street (two minutes away). Street parking in the area is very scarce

♿ Is available into the theatre through a side exit door on Sherwood Street, with space for people available to transfer into a seat in the front row of the Royal Circle. There is also a box on the left hand side with room for two wheelchair users and their companions, although this is sometimes used for technical equipment and the view of the left-hand side of the stage is slightly restricted. The theatre has no adapted toilet available, however

🎧 There are no Infrared facilities at present

👁 Guide dogs not allowed inside the auditorium but staff will give dogs the royal treatment in the Royal Room

🍸 Usual bar service on all three levels, with two bars available in the stalls (one at the rear of the auditorium, and another smaller side bar on the left hand side of the auditorium)

ⓘ Piccadilly Circus and Soho are on the doorstep

This red-plush velvet auditorium, within which an inexplicable smell of cooking sometimes pervades, is a superb but often unlucky house with seating for just over 1,200 on whose stage musical flops have played with unfortunately regularity in recent years, from *Metropolis*, *Mutiny!* and *Moby Dick* to *Which Witch* and a French musical version of *Romeo and Juliet*.

History

After opening as a theatre in 1928 – with a Jerome Kern musical, *Blue Eyes* – the Piccadilly soon operated as a cinema instead, having offered the premiere of the first talking picture to be shown in Britain, *The Singing Fool* with Al Jolson. *The Jazz Singer* also opened here, and at the end of the film, Jolson came out on stage and sang 'Mammie'. When it returned to theatrical use in 1941, with Noël Coward's supernatural comedy *Blithe Spirit*, the theatre soon became blighted with possibly supernatural activities all of its own: the unluckiest production of the theatre's unluckiest play, *Macbeth*, with John Gielgud in the title role, saw four of its cast die during its run and the designer later committing suicide. The theatre has since been used for plays and musicals of all kinds, as well as the most successful commercial ballet season ever seen in the West End when Adventures in Motion Pictures presented their production of *Swan Lake*, featuring an all-male corps of swans in the late 1990s.

Best seat in the house

There are good sightlines from most seats in the Stalls, though it does go back quite deep so stick to the front if you want to feel close to the action. The seats are, however, desperately uncomfortable! There are also good views from the front of the Dress Circle (here called the Royal Circle), though the overhang of the Upper Circle will affect views further back.

UPPER CIRCLE

M	1	2	3	4	5	6	7	8	9	10	11	12	13	14	15	16	17	18	19	20	21	22	23	24	25	26	27	28
L	1	2	3	4	5	6	7	8	9	10	11	12	13	14	15	16	17	18	19	20	21	22	23	24	25	26	27	28
K	1	2	3	4	5	6	7	8	9	10	11	12	13	14	15	16	17	18	19	20	21	22	23	24	25	26	27	28
J	1	2	3	4	5	6	7	8	9	10	11	12	13	14	15	16	17	18	19	20	21	22	23	24	25	26	27	28
H	1	2	3	4	5	6	7	8	9	10	11	12	13	14	15	16	17	18	19	20	21	22	23	24	25	26	27	28
G	1	2	3	4	5	6	7	8	9	10	11	12	13	14	15	16	17	18	19	20	21	22	23	24	25	26	27	28
F	1	2	3	4	5	6	7	8	9	10	11	12	13	14	15	16	17	18	19	20	21	22	23	24	25	26	27	28
E	1	2	3	4	5	6	7	8	9	10	11	12	13	14	15	16	17	18	19	20	21	22	23	24	25	26	27	28
D	1	2	3	4	5	6	7	8	9	10	11	12	13	14	15	16	17	18	19	20	21	22	23	24	25	26	27	28
C	1	2	3	4	5	6	7	8	9	10	11	12	13	14	15	16	17	18	19	20	21	22	23	24	25	26	27	28
B	1	2	3	4	5	6	7	8	9	10	11	12	13	14	15	16	17	18	19	20	21	22	23	24	25	26	27	28
A	1	2	3	4	5	6	7	8	9	10	11	12	13	14	15	16	17	18	19	20	21	22	23	24	25	26	27	28

ROYAL CIRCLE

L	1	2	3	4	5	6	7	8	9	10	11	12	13	14	15	16	17	18	19	20	21	22	23	24	25	26	27	28
K	1	2	3	4	5	6	7	8	9	10	11	12	13	14	15	16	17	18	19	20	21	22	23	24	25	26	27	28
J	1	2	3	4	5	6	7	8	9	10	11	12	13	14	15	16	17	18	19	20	21	22	23	24	25	26	27	28
H	1	2	3	4	5	6	7	8	9	10	11	12	13	14	15	16	17	18	19	20	21	22	23	24	25	26	27	28
G	1	2	3	4	5	6	7	8	9	10	11	12	13	14	15	16	17	18	19	20	21	22	23	24	25	26	27	28
F	1	2	3	4	5	6	7	8	9	10	11	12	13	14	15	16	17	18	19	20	21	22	23	24	25	26	27	28
E	1	2	3	4	5	6	7	8	9	10	11	12	13	14	15	16	17	18	19	20	21	22	23	24	25	26	27	28
D	1	2	3	4	5	6	7	8	9	10	11	12	13	14	15	16	17	18	19	20	21	22	23	24	25	26	27	28
C	1	2	3	4	5	6	7	8	9	10	11	12	13	14	15	16	17	18	19	20	21	22	23	24	25	26	27	28
B	1	2	3	4	5	6	7	8	9	10	11	12	13	14	15	16	17	18	19	20	21	22	23	24	25	26	27	28
A	1	2	3	4	5	6	7	8	9	10	11	12	13	14	15	16	17	18	19	20	21	22	23	24	25	26	27	28

STALLS

T	3 4 5 6 7 8 9 10 11 21 22 23 24 25 26 27 28 29 30
S	3 4 5 6 7 8 9 10 11 21 22 23 24 25 26 27 28 29 30
R	2 3 4 5 6 7 8 9 10 11 12 13 14 15 16 17 18 19 20 21 22 23 24 25 26 27 28 29 30
Q	1 2 3 4 5 6 7 8 9 10 11 12 13 14 15 16 17 18 19 20 21 22 23 24 25 26 27 28 29 30
P	1 2 3 4 5 6 7 8 9 10 11 12 13 14 15 16 17 18 19 20 21 22 23 24 25 26 27 28 29 30
O	1 2 3 4 5 6 7 8 9 10 11 12 13 14 15 16 17 18 19 20 21 22 23 24 25 26 27 28 29 30
N	1 2 3 4 5 6 7 8 9 10 11 12 13 14 15 16 17 18 19 20 21 22 23 24 25 26 27 28 29 30
M	1 2 3 4 5 6 7 8 9 10 11 12 13 14 15 16 17 18 19 20 21 22 23 24 25 26 27 28 29 30
L	1 2 3 4 5 6 7 8 9 10 11 12 13 14 15 16 17 18 19 20 21 22 23 24 25 26 27 28 29 30
K	1 2 3 4 5 6 7 8 9 10 11 12 13 14 15 16 17 18 19 20 21 22 23 24 25 26 27 28 29 30
J	2 3 4 5 6 7 8 9 10 11 12 13 14 15 16 17 18 19 20 21 22 23 24 25 26 27 28 29
H	3 4 5 6 7 8 9 10 11 12 13 14 15 16 17 18 19 20 21 22 23 24 25 26 27 28
G	3 4 5 6 7 8 9 10 11 12 13 14 15 16 17 18 19 20 21 22 23 24 25 26 27
F	3 4 5 6 7 8 9 10 11 12 13 14 15 16 17 18 19 20 21 22 23 24 25 26 27 28
E	2 3 4 5 6 7 8 9 10 11 12 13 14 15 16 17 18 19 20 21 22 23 24 25 26 27
D	3 4 5 6 7 8 9 10 11 12 13 14 15 16 17 18 19 20 21 22 23 24 25 26
C	3 4 5 6 7 8 9 10 11 12 13 14 15 16 17 18 19 20 21 22 23 24 25 26
B	5 6 7 8 9 10 11 12 13 14 15 16 17 18 19 20 21 22 23 24 25 26
A	7 8 9 10 11 12 13 14 15 16 17 18 19 20 21 22 23 24
BB	7 8 9 10 11 12 13 14 15 16 17 18 19 20 21 22

Playhouse Theatre

✉ Northumberland Avenue, WC2N 5DE

⌗ www.theambassadors.com/playhouse/

☎ (Box office) 020-7369 1785, (Stage door) 020-7839 4292

↑ Located just off the Embankment, at the foot of Northumberland Avenue beside the new western (Westminster facing) side of the new Hungerford Foot Bridges

🚊 Charing Cross or Waterloo (via walk across Hungerford Bridge)

⊖ Embankment; Charing Cross; or Waterloo (walk across Hungerford Bridge)

P There is a MasterPark in Spring Gardens, off Trafalgar Square), and a NCP car park at Bedfordbury

♿ Arrangements need to be made in advance so that a ramp can be placed over the three steps inside the main entrance. But once there, there are no further steps to the stalls. There are two places for wheelchair users, and transfer seating is available to any Stalls aisle seat. Wheelchair users must be accompanied by able-bodied companions. An adapted WC is available to the right of the stalls entrance

∩ An induction loop system is available in the stalls, with best reception in the centre

👁 Guide dogs are allowed inside the auditorium, and staff can also dog sit

🍴 A basement restaurant offers food, plus there are bars at the rear of each of the three levels of the theatre

ⓘ The western branch of the Hungerford Footbridge (facing Westminster) begins steps away from the Playhouse to take you to the South Bank in a pleasant walk across the river; it's a three-minute walk the other way up Northumberland Avenue to the revamped Trafalgar Square and then on to the heart of the West End

With the opening of the new Hungerford footbridges that takes pedestrian traffic between the West End and the South Bank, what used to be a hidden gem of a theatre is now on a route with much passing trade. That should help revive its fortunes, and deservedly so, for this is an intimate yet deliciously ornate theatre seating almost 800, with wonderful curved wooden balustrades at the front of the two circles.

History

Originally called the Royal Avenue Theatre when it opened in 1882, the Playhouse has had a chequered but impressive theatrical history that has seen such notable landmarks as offering the premiere of George Bernard Shaw's first West End play, *Arms and the Man* in 1894, a period from 1917 to 1933 when it was managed by the famous West End actress Gladys Cooper, and then another period, between 1988 and 1996, when it came under the ownership of the now infamous novelist, sometime playwright and politician Jeffrey Archer. But for a 25-year period, from 1950 to 1975, it had ceased to be used as a theatre at all when the BBC took it over and ran it as a studio to record radio shows at in front of a live audience. After they left the Playhouse lay dark for over a decade until a property developer, Robin Gonshaw, restored it beautifully and re-opened it, before selling it on to Archer. Other owners have come and gone since, but it is now independently owned by Maidstone Productions, belonging to

American theatre producers Ted and Norman Tulchin, with the Ambassadors Theatre Group charged with the day-to-day running and programming of the theatre on their behalf.

Best seat in the house

The Stalls is intimate and the Dress Circle overhangs them at a sufficient height not to impede any views, so it's safe to sit anywhere – though the rear of the Stalls can suffer from front-of-house noise from staff setting up interval drinks during the performance if this isn't kept in check by the management. The central block of the front Dress Circle is also good for unimpeded views; further back, the overhang of the Upper Circle can interrupt them.

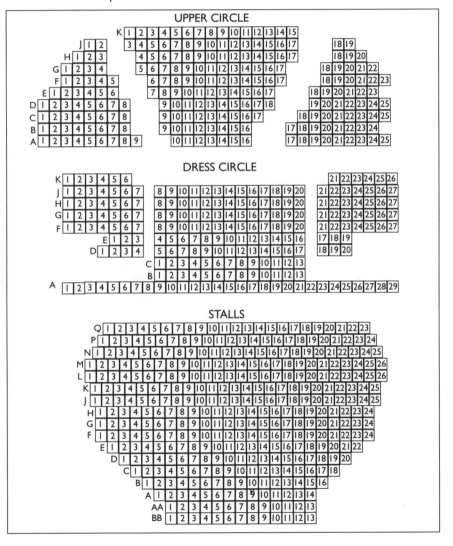

Prince Edward Theatre

✉ 30 Old Compton Street, W1V 6HS

🖥 www.delfont-mackintosh.com

☎ (Box office) 0870 850 0393 (in person or by phone direct to the box office from Mon-Sat 10am-7pm; outside of these hours, calls are transferred to Ticketmaster, where an additional service charge is applied), (Stage door) 020-7439 3041

↑ Located in the heart of Soho on Old Compton Street, that runs parallel a block northwards of Shaftesbury Avenue

🚇 Charing Cross

⊖ Equidistant from Piccadilly Circus, Tottenham Court Road and Leicester Square

P There is a MasterPark car park at Cambridge Circus

♿ For wheelchair users who cannot transfer from a wheelchair, a box is available in the Dress Circle with direct level access from Greek Street, which can accommodate a maximum of two regular sized wheelchairs. Each one must be accompanied by an able bodied person in the adjacent seat. These must be booked in advance, and a member of the front-of-house staff must be contacted on arrival in the foyer. For wheelchair users who are able to occupy a theatre seat, there are total of four seats available in the front row of the Dress Circle, again with direct level access from Greek Street. Each wheelchair transfer patron must be accompanied by an able bodied person. There is an adapted toilet available on the right hand side of the main foyer

🎧 Infrared receivers are available from the foyer kiosk upon receipt of a refundable £5 deposit

👁 Guide dogs allowed inside the auditorium, and staff can also dog sit by prior arrangement

⭐ Usual bar service

ⓘ Old Compton Street is nowadays the heart of gay London, with numerous bars, shops and restaurants that are available to all; also nearby is Chinatown

This previously unloved West End theatre has been transformed into a lushly luxurious musical house that is a treat to visit. Even its previously bland brick exterior has revealed some attractive recessed surprises that were formerly hidden by hoardings.

History

One of four new theatres to open in 1930 (the other three were the nearby Phoenix, Cambridge and Whitehall), the Prince Edward took the longest of all to find its theatrical feet. Its first production, *Ric Rita*, imported from Broadway, ran for just 59 performances, and subsequent shows didn't fare too much better. In 1936, the theatre was re-branded the London Casino to stage cabaret floorshows, until closed by the Blitz in 1940. During the war years it became the Queensbury All Services Club. Afterwards it reverted to its original intended use as a musical house, until in 1954 was turned into the London home for Cinerama, a technology that featured an extralarge, curved screen on which to project films specially made for the format (a precursor to IMAX). This lasted for 20 years, until the building was re-established as a theatre, reverting to its original name and finally having a run of successes from 1978 with

Evita, Chess and *Anything Goes* – all, coincidentally, originally starring Elaine Paige. But then came a return to the flops it had been previously known for, until in 1992, with Cameron Mackintosh now partnering the then sole owner Lord Bernard Delfont, it was extensively remodelled at a cost of over £3million. As well as a completely restructured auditorium, the stage – amongst the largest in London – was enlarged, and the acoustics improved. Previous ill-fortunes have now been entirely reversed, with hit following hit into the theatre from *Crazy for You* to *Mamma Mia!* and *Mary Poppins* to follow.

Best seat in the house

This is a large theatre containing over 1600 seats, and though there are no obstructions in the new layout, the further back or higher you go might make you feel some distance from the stage. An interesting feature of the Dress Circle are loge boxes located on either side of it (not shown below), more often seen in Broadway houses than over here, that bring you closer to the stage than the Dress Circle itself, though at a side angle. For more central views, go for the centre of the front of the Dress Circle instead. The front Stalls (to Row K) don't have a centre aisle but are arranged in very long rows; Row L has an aisle in front of it, so is to be recommended for those requiring more legroom. Otherwise, aisle seats from row L backwards in the well-raked Stalls are recommended.

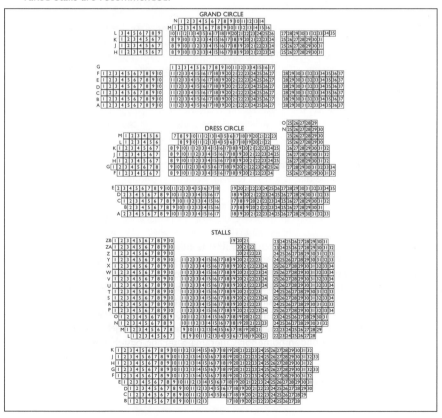

Prince Of Wales Theatre

✉ 31 Coventry Street, W1D 6AS

⌂ www.delfont-mackintosh.com

☎ (Box office) currently closed for refurbishment, (Stage door) 020-7930 1432

↑ Located on Coventry Street, directly across the street from the Trocadero Centre and a stone's throw from Piccadilly Circus (from where it is clearly visible), it is on a major thoroughfare, halfway to Leicester Square

🚇 Charing Cross

⊖ Piccadilly Circus, Leicester Square

P MasterPark car park in Whitcomb Street around the corner

♿ To be advised after refurbishment

🎧 To be advised after refurbishment

👁 Guide dogs not allowed inside the auditorium but staff can dog sit

🌟 Once the theatre re-opens, the Stalls Bar (to be re-named the Delfont Bar) and the American Bar will become two of the largest theatre bars in the West End, capable of accommodating over two-thirds of the audience

ⓘ Piccadilly Circus and Leicester Square are both a stone's throw away

This popular musical theatre has recently undergone a total transformation, budgeted at some £7million. The façade of the building has been improved, to allow people to see in as well as out and offers views from Piccadilly to Leicester Square that the theatre is located between; while the auditorium has been entirely rebuilt using a colour palette of gold, bronze and copper. With its unbeatable location on Coventry Street, across the street from the modern monstrosity of the Trocadero Centre, it probably has the most passing trade of any theatre in London; but more than that, it's a theatre that now deserves the audiences it can attract. With the audience seated on only two levels in long, wide rows, this is a London theatre that most resembles a Broadway house, which are typically laid out in the same way. It also has one of the best and most spacious stalls bars of any theatre in London.

History

The current building dates from 1937, though the first theatre on this site originally opened in January 1884. That theatre closed on 16 January 1937; the foundation stone for the new theatre was laid on June 17, and was opened just four months later, on October 27: an amazingly fast schedule! The Prince of Wales has forever been associated with musicals, revues and solo shows, with appearances here by everyone from Sid Field and Sammy Davis Jr to Max Bygraves, Tommy Steele and Paul Daniels. Notable musicals have included the original West End run of Barbra Streisand in *Funny Girl* and Juliet Prowse in *Sweet Charity*, both in the '60s, while more recent tenants have included the National Theatre's production of *Guys and Dolls*, Andrew Lloyd Webber's *Aspects of Love*, and imports from Broadway including *City of Angels*, *Smokey Joe's Café* and *The Full Monty*, while *Mamma Mia!* has re-opened the refurbished theatre.

Best seat in the house

Pre-refurbishment, there were 1133 seats; the refurbished theatre promises both more leg-room and more comfortable seats!

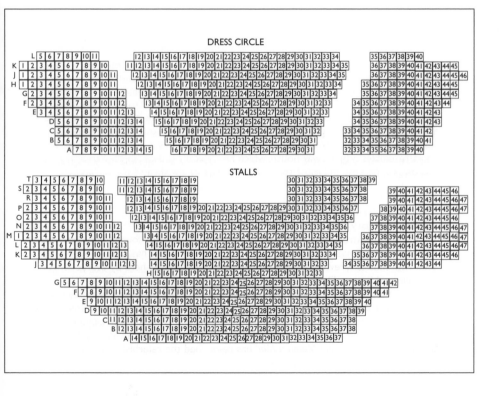

Queen's Theatre

✉ Shaftesbury Avenue, W1D 6BA

⌖ www.rutheatres.com

☎ (Box office) 0870 890 1110 (24 hours by phone; in person, open Mon-Sat 10am-8pm), (Stage door) 020-7850 8780

↑ Located in the heart of London's main theatrical strip, Shaftesbury Avenue, a stone's throw from Piccadilly Circus

🚇 Charing Cross

⊖ Piccadilly Circus

P Several car parks in vicinity: NCP in Wardour Street, Newport Place, Denman Street and Lexington Street; MasterPark at Poland Street

♿ Level access to the Dress Circle from theatre exit on Wardour Street, with adapted toilet available in foyer corridor. Call customer services to arrange visit – 020-7850 8530

🎧 Sennheiser Infrared system – headsets available from manager

👁 Guide dogs allowed in the theatre boxes, or staff can dog sit

★ Usual bar service on all three levels – note that the airless, subterranean Stalls bar is now a no-smoking zone, with smoking only permitted in the Dress Circle bar (with good views onto Shaftesbury Avenue occasionally disrupted, depending on the theatre's advertising hoardings) and Upper Circle bar

ⓘ The heart of Soho and Chinatown are a stone's throw walk up or down Wardour Street

Though the modern, curved frontage put up in 1958 is not unattractive (and neither is the comfortable three-level theatre behind it), producer/theatre owner Cameron Mackintosh has plans to completely overhaul the theatre. In a scheme that will cost approximately £20 million, the Queen's will be linked to the Gielgud via a spacious communal foyer area, and seating in the Queen's increased from 990 over three levels to 1213 over two – a size that will make it ideal for all but the largest musicals. Meanwhile, a flexible 500-seat studio theatre, to be named the Sondheim Theatre, will be added above the Queen's to house extended runs for plays transferring from equivalent smaller spaces like the Almeida, Donmar Warehouse and Cottesloe. Among the design criteria: to take advantage of roof-level views across London.

History

Designed as a sister theatre to the Hicks (subsequently called the Globe and now the Gielgud) on the adjoining corner of Shaftesbury Avenue, the Queen's opened on 8 October, 1907. In 1940 it received the only kind of hit theatres don't like when a German bomb struck. The front-of-house areas and the rear of the circles were destroyed, and it stayed shut until 1959, when it was reconstructed with a modern exterior, retaining the Edwardian auditorium. Usually used for plays, it has also housed musicals from time to time. Notable attractions over the years have included a 1937 season of classics with John Gielgud and Peggy Ashcroft headlining a company that also included Michael Redgrave, Alec Guinness and Anthony Quayle. More recently, the theatre was the original 1982 home to *Another Country* in 1982 that provided West End debuts for Rupert Everett, Kenneth Branagh, Daniel Day-Lewis, Colin Firth and others, and to Maggie Smith's 1999 appearance in Alan Bennett's *The Lady in the Van* and a season by the Royal Shakespeare Company.

Best seat in the house

The Dress Circle overhangs the Stalls quite dramatically so the raked rear seats (from row M back) offer an envelope-like view of the stage. The front Stalls, however, are not well raked, so if you have a tall person in front of you, you can be scuppered. The front of the Dress Circle therefore offers the best views.

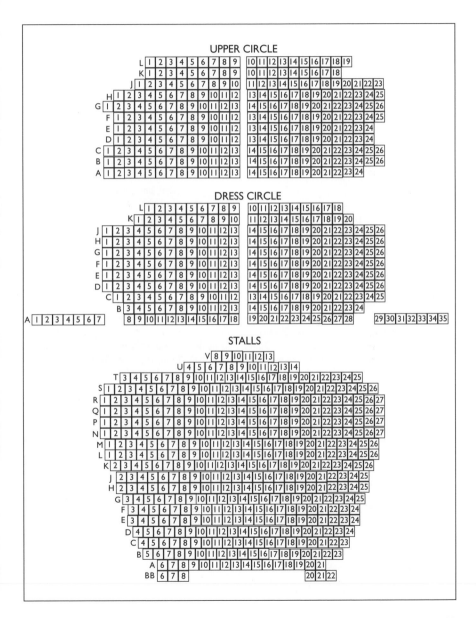

Royal Court Theatre

✉ Sloane Square, SW1W 8AS

🖰 www.royalcourttheatre.com

☎ (Box office) 020-7565 5000, (Stage door) 020-7565 5050

🖶 020-7565 5145

📧 info@royalcourttheatre.com

↑ Located by Sloane Square underground station

🚇 Victoria

⊖ Sloane Square is literally next door to the theatre

P Free on-street parking after 6.30pm

♿ The building is now fully accessible. There's level entrance from the street, down the right-hand side of the theatre, through easy-open doors, to a lift on the inside right that goes to all levels of the theatre from the stalls foyer to the Theatre Upstairs. For the basement bar, restaurant and bookshop, there is a separate platform lift from the stalls foyer area

🎧 Induction loops are fitted in The Jerwood Theatre Downstairs and at the box office's ticket counter. There is an infrared system in both theatres, for which receiving equipment should be collected from the box office. Playscripts are available from the Royal Court Bookshop from the first night of the produc-

tion, usually at £2, but available free to deaf and hard-of-hearing patrons attending the regular sign-interpreted performances

👁 Guide dogs are welcome; an aisle seat should be booked. Alternatively, the theatre staff will dog sit

🎫 The Royal Court's expanded basement area, carved out beneath Sloane Square during the theatre's extensive late '90s refurbishment, includes a large, if smoky, bar that is open all day (11am-11pm) for drinks and coffee. The balcony bar, one level up from the entrance and with an outdoors balcony accessed through French windows overlooking Sloane Square, is better if you want to avoid the smoke! There is also a smart, stylish restaurant, open for lunch from 12noon to 3pm and for dinner from 5pm-11pm, serving an international menu. For further information, contact: 020-7565 5061

ⓘ King's Road – sometime spiritual home of British fashion – continues to be a fashionable shopping street

The basement also contains a small bookshop area, with over 1000 titles on sale. Many Royal Court playtexts (that traditionally double up as the programme) are available for just £2 – a real bargain. For information on titles available or other enquiries, phone 020-7565 5024

Though the theatre's onstage work thrived in the '90s, offstage and behind-the-scenes the building was literally crumbling, and in 1995 the theatre was told that it would be forced to close within 18 months unless it addressed its myriad structural problems. Thanks to the advent of the National Lottery, the Royal Court had an opportunity to reverse the years of rot and after it made a feasibility study of the entire building, put in a bid for a capital development grant, and was awarded £16.2million. During the four-year redevelopment that began in 1996, the Royal Court continued its work by hiring the Duke of York's and Ambassadors (now the New Ambassadors) in the West End, before returning to Sloane Square in February 2000. While major features of the façade and the unique intimacy of the auditorium have been gloriously preserved, in every other way this refurbishment has transformed the theatre inside and out into one of London's best appointed and now most comfortable theatres. In the 400-seater traditional proscenium arch main theatre (known as the Jerwood Theatre Downstairs), plush rows of leather seats offer armrests that can be folded away should the intimacy of the moment warrant it, plus pockets in the seat in front of you (illuminated by individual lights when the houselights are on) to put your programme into. The upstairs studio (known as the Jerwood Theatre Upstairs, originally added in 1969) can now be accessed by a lift if you want to avoid the long climb!

History

Originally designed by Walter Emden and opened in 1888, this intimate Chelsea playhouse became a cinema in 1932. After being bombed in the Blitz, it reopened in 1952. The English Stage Company was established here in 1956 as a subsidised theatre whose first Artistic Director George Devine stated the intention as being to create a writers' theatre: "a place where he play is more important that the actors, the director, the designer". With a whole generation of new writers were nurtured here, from the premiere of John Osborne's ground-breaking *Look Back in Anger* in 1956 to playwrights like Arnold Wesker, John Arden and Edward Bond, it quickly fulfilled that promise, and continues to be at the forefront of new writing to this day, with premieres of plays by Caryl Churchill, Martin McDonagh and Conor McPherson, amongst others, originating here before transferring to the West End and on to America. Other influential young playwrights in recent years include Joe Penhall, Jez Butterworth, the late Sarah Kane, Mark Ravenhill, Roy Williams and American writers Rebecca Gilman and Christopher Shinn.

Best seat in the house

Views from the sides of the shallow horseshoe circles can be a little restricted, but otherwise there's a terrific intimacy from every seat. Best seats are in the centre Stalls or front of the Dress Circle.

BALCONY

CIRCLE

STALLS

Royal National Theatre

✉ South Bank, SE1 9PX

🖰 www.nationaltheatre.org.uk

☎ (Box office) 020-7452 3000 (Mon-Sat 10am-8pm), (Stage door) 020-7452 3333, (Information desk) 020-7453 3400

🖶 020-7452 3030

🕐 foyers open Mon-Sat 10am-11pm.

↑ Located on the South Bank of the River Thames, beside Waterloo Bridge

🚇 Waterloo; also Charing Cross

🚌 Waterloo, or cross the river from Charing Cross via Hungerford Foot Bridge; or from Temple via Waterloo Bridge

P Free onstreet parking available near-by after 6.30pm, but arrive in good time to find a space; otherwise, the National has its own paid car park

beneath the theatre, and there are also other paid public car parking lots in the area

🚲 Racks available outside the Espresso Bar near river level entrance

♿ All three theatres have dedicated wheelchair spaces. Free parking is available for orange badge holders in car park beneath the theatre, from where there is lift access to the Olivier and Lyttelton. Adapted toilets available in all three theatres

🎧 Infrared Audio System is available in all three theatres; headsets are available from the Information Desks

🖐 The theatre regularly holds performances with live sign language interpretation. Minicom for deaf people: 020-7452 3009, Mon-Sat 10am-5pm

👁 Braille/large print cast lists available from Information Desk. There are

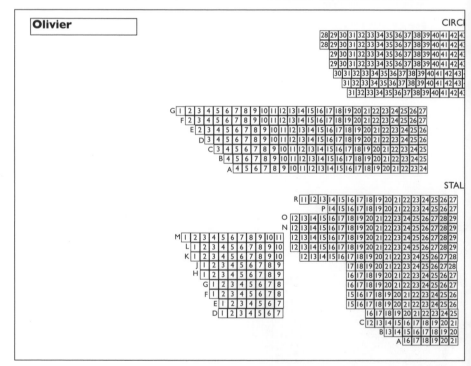

96

also regularly holds audio-described performances. Guide dogs not allowed in theatres; staff will dog sit

★ There are plenty of dining opportunities. The Mezzanine Restaurant offers a full meal service (reservations, 020-7453 3600, open 5.30pm-6.45pm and 8.30pm-11pm, plus before Olivier and Lyttelton matinees from 12noon-2pm). More modest fare is available at the Lyttelton Theatre's Terrace Cafe (020-7452 3555); the Circle Café in the Olivier offers pizza and salad for £5 before all performances in the Olivier; and there are sandwiches, cakes and snacks from the Lyttelton Stalls Foyer counter and Cottesloe bar. Bars available in Lyttelton and Cottesloe Stalls and Circle; two each on either side of Olivier Stalls and Circle foyers

ⓘ Hayward Gallery; National Film Theatre and IMAX Cinema; Royal Festival Hall complex; London Eye.

Foyer music: Free live music, performed every evening in the main (river level) foyer pre-performance and also before Saturday matinees; in the summer, Theatre Square (the area in front of the main, riverside entrance) erupts in a carnival of outdoor music and theatre presented under the title "Watch this Space"

Exhibitions: Free exhibitions in foyers of Olivier and Lyttelton circles

Bookshop: main bookshop (on river level entrance, open daily Mon-Sat 10am-10.45pm, phone 020-7452 3456), stocking extensive range of theatre books, scripts, videos, CDs and magazines; plus bookstalls in Olivier stalls foyer and Cottesloe foyer open from one hour before performance

Backstage Tours: Offered three times daily, Mon-Sat. Book on 020-7452 43400

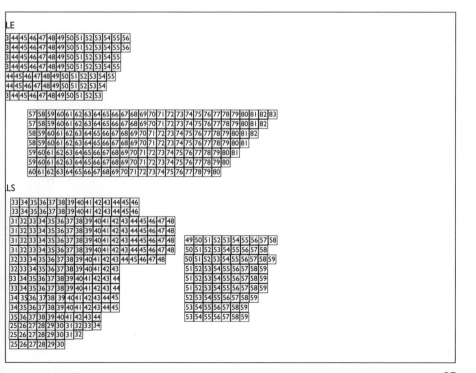

One of the rare London theatre buildings that is open throughout the day and evening and welcoming to everyone regardless of whether they are actually attending a performance, the National Theatre is a wonderfully democratic space. Production standards are consistently high, and this is always a warmly pleasurable place to visit. The most heavily subsidized theatre in Britain (receiving a grant of nearly £13million per annum from the Arts Council), it is very much the flagship venue for theatre in the country. Under new artistic director Nicholas Hytner, who took over in April 2003, it looks set to continue not only to set standards but also to break rules, as with the scabrous *Jerry Springer – The Opera*. It is now also, thanks to a three-year sponsorship deal with Travelex, able to offer a regular six-month season of plays in the main Olivier auditorium with two-thirds of the seats available for just £10, making it a theatre available to nearly everyone.

History

The National Theatre, originally based at the Old Vic with Laurence Olivier appointed as its first artistic director in 1962, moved to its Denys Lasdun designed, purpose-built, three auditoria complex on the South Bank of the River Thames in 1976. The Olivier is the largest auditorium, seating 1150 on two levels in a fan-shaped amphitheatre-like arrangement in front of an open stage. The more conventional, proscenium arch Lyttelton Theatre, seats 890 on two levels, while the flexible Cottesloe studio offers seating for up to 300 on three levels. Under the successive artistic directorships of Peter Hall, Richard Eyre, Trevor Nunn and now Nicholas Hytner, the venue has hosted

Lyttelton

CIRCLE

J	1	2	3	4	5	6	7	8	9	10	11	12	13	14	15	16	17	18
H	1	2	3	4	5	6	7	8	9	10	11	12	13	14	15	16	17	18
G	1	2	3	4	5	6	7	8	9	10	11	12	13	14	15	16	17	18
F	1	2	3	4	5	6	7	8	9	10	11	12	13	14	15	16	17	18
E	1	2	3	4	5	6	7	8	9	10	11	12	13	14	15	16	17	18
D	1	2	3	4	5	6	7	8	9	10	11	12	13	14	15	16	17	18
C	1	2	3	4	5	6	7	8	9	10	11	12	13	14	15	16	17	18
B	1	2	3	4	5	6	7	8	9	10	11	12	13	14	15	16	17	18
A	1	2	3	4	5	6	7	8	9	10	11	12	13	14	15	16	17	18

STALLS

V	8	9	10	11	12	13	14	15	16	17	18					
U	4	5	6	7	8	9	10	11	12	13	14	15	16	17	18	
T	4	5	6	7	8	9	10	11	12	13	14	15	16	17	18	
S	4	5	6	7	8	9	10	11	12	13	14	15	16	17	18	
R	4	5	6	7	8	9	10	11	12	13	14	15	16	17	18	
P	4	5	6	7	8	9	10	11	12	13	14	15	16	17	18	
O	4	5	6	7	8	9	10	11	12	13	14	15	16	17	18	
N	4	5	6	7	8	9	10	11	12	13	14	15	16	17	18	
M	4	5	6	7	8	9	10	11	12	13	14	15	16	17	18	
L	4	5	6	7	8	9	10	11	12	13	14	15	16	17	18	
K	4	5	6	7	8	9	10	11	12	13	14	15	16	17	18	
J	4	5	6	7	8	9	10	11	12	13	14	15	16	17	18	
H	4	5	6	7	8	9	10	11	12	13	14	15	16	17	18	
G	4	5	6	7	8	9	10	11	12	13	14	15	16	17	18	
F	4	5	6	7	8	9	10	11	12	13	14	15	16	17	18	
E	5	6	7	8	9	10	11	12	13	14	15	16	17	18		
D	4	5	6	7	8	9	10	11	12	13	14	15	16	17	18	19
C	4	5	6	7	8	9	10	11	12	13	14	15	16	17	18	
B	5	6	7	8	9	10	11	12	13	14	15	16	17			
A	6	7	8	9	10	11	12	13	14	15	16	17				

premieres and classics, from new plays to old musicals, and in addition also has extensive touring and education departments. There's also a work-in-development department, to nurture new work away from the public gaze in the Studio, located in an
annexe near the Old Vic.

Best seat in the house

The best seats in the house usually go to those on the theatre's mailing list, who in
return for a small annual subscription are able to book ahead of the general public.
Pick up a leaflet at the theatre or phone: 020-7452 3500.

For sell-out shows, a number of day seats are sold from 10am on the day of the performance at the box office only; these may be limited to two per person and queues
may form early.

For shows that are not sold out, bargain standby tickets are available, with all remaining seats sold at lower prices two hours before the performance, and at an even
cheaper prices to students/unemployed/theatre union members from 45 minutes
before the performance.

In the Olivier and Lyttelton, the front Stalls are, when still available, a real bargain,
since they are sold at the cheapest price in the house and invariably offer a fine view
(though they're more cramped than elsewhere, without arm rests). The Cottesloe
is a completely flexible space, with the seating layout changed from production to
production.

CLE

19	20	21	22	23	24	25	26	27	28	29	30	31	32	33	34	35	36
19	20	21	22	23	24	25	26	27	28	29	30	31	32	33	34	35	36
19	20	21	22	23	24	25	26	27	28	29	30	31	32	33	34	35	36
19	20	21	22	23	24	25	26	27	28	29	30	31	32	33	34	35	36
19	20	21	22	23	24	25	26	27	28	29	30	31	32	33	34	35	36
19	20	21	22	23	24	25	26	27	28	29	30	31	32	33	34	35	36
19	20	21	22	23	24	25	26	27	28	29	30	31	32	33	34	35	36
19	20	21	22	23	24	25	26	27	28	29	30	31	32	33	34	35	36
19	20	21	22	23	24	25	26	27	28	29	30	31	32	33	34	35	36

LS

19	20	21	22	23	24	25	26	27	28	29				
19	20	21	22	23	24	25	26	27	28	29	30	31	32	33
19	20	21	22	23	24	25	26	27	28	29	30	31	32	33
19	20	21	22	23	24	25	26	27	28	29	30	31	32	33
19	20	21	22	23	24	25	26	27	28	29	30	31	32	33
19	20	21	22	23	24	25	26	27	28	29	30	31	32	33
19	20	21	22	23	24	25	26	27	28	29	30	31	32	33
19	20	21	22	23	24	25	26	27	28	29	30	31	32	33
19	20	21	22	23	24	25	26	27	28	29	30	31	32	33
19	20	21	22	23	24	25	26	27	28	29	30	31	32	33
19	20	21	22	23	24	25	26	27	28	29	30	31	32	33
19	20	21	22	23	24	25	26	27	28	29	30	31	32	33
19	20	21	22	23	24	25	26	27	28	29	30	31	32	33
19	20	21	22	23	24	25	26	27	28	29	30	31	32	
9	20	21	22	23	24	25	26	27	28	29	30	31	32	33	34
3	19	20	21	22	23	24	25	26	27	28	29	30	31	32
8	19	20	21	22	23	24	25	26	27	28	29	30	31	
8	19	20	21	22	23	24	25	26	27	28	29	30		

Savoy Theatre

✉ Savoy Court, WC2R OET

🖋 www.savoytheatre.co.uk

☎ (Box office) 0870 164 8787 (in person, open Mon-Sat 10am-8.30pm), (Stage door) 020-7828 0600

↑ Located adjoining the front entrance of the Savoy Hotel, just off the Strand – if dropping someone off at the theatre, note that the private street in front of the hotel is the only one in England where traffic drives on the right!

🚇 Charing Cross

🚆 Charing Cross

P Private paid parking in the Savoy Adelphi Garage nearby (020-7836 4838, access from the Embankment), or MasterPark car park in Spring Gardens (off Trafalgar Square)

♿ Access to the Dress Circle can be made through a side entrance from the Embankment side of the fairly steep Carting Lane, approximately 100metres from the main entrance. From here, access is level to the front of the Dress Circle, where there are two spaces for wheelchair users on the right-hand side. Each wheelchair user must bring a non-disabled companion. There is an adapted toilet to the right of the Dress Circle

🎧 An Infrared system is available, for which headsets must be collected from the box office

👁 Guide dogs allowed in auditorium, or staff can dog sit

🍸 Usual bar service

ⓘ The neighbouring Savoy hotel next door provides a plush, if formal, venue for tea or drinks before or after the show

This mostly subterranean theatre (the Upper Circle is at street level), with its Art-Deco-influenced interior, is handsomely appointed, even if the silver panels give it a harsher edge than the previous wooden ones they replaced. Intimate enough for plays yet large enough (with nearly 1200 seats) for musicals, it is regularly used for both.

History

Built at the instigation of Richard D'Oyly Carte (producer to the 19th-century composing team of Gilbert and Sullivan) and opened in 1881, this was where many G&S works, which became known as the Savoy Operas, were premiered. In 1929, the Victorian auditorium was demolished and replaced with a more modern, wood-panelled interior. In 1990, the theatre's interior was completely burnt out in a fire, but three years later re-opened, restored to the 1929 designs but now with glistening silver painted panels replacing the wooden ones. While the modern D'Oyly Carte Company have regularly played seasons of operettas from the Gilbert and Sullivan repertoire here, a bold new plan to establish London's third year-round opera house has run aground after its first season. The good intention was to perform popular operas in English, without subsidy but at affordable prices, but now the Savoy is back on the market as a theatre available to hire, as before, to producers of plays and mid-scale musicals.

Best seat in the house

Rows stretch the width of the Stalls, but there's refreshingly ample legroom and enough space for people to get through. The Stalls are also nicely raked, but do go back a long way, so sit towards the front if you want to feel involved. The Dress Circle, too, divided into two by a central corridor, is better in the front half.

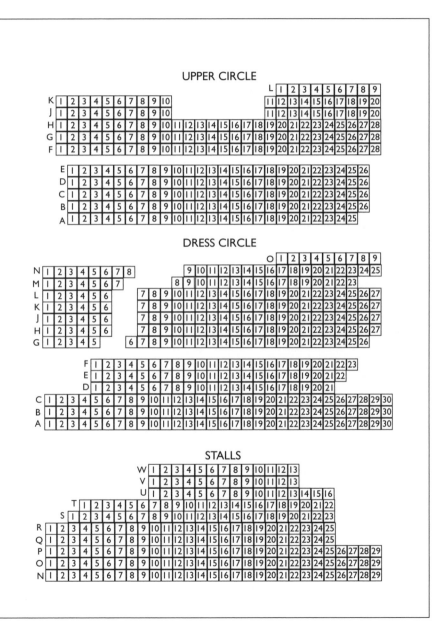

Shaftesbury Theatre

✉ 210 Shaftesbury Avenue, WC2H 8DP

☎ (Box office) 0870 906 3798, (Stage door) 020-7379 3345

↑ Located at the top end of Shaftesbury Avenue, beyond Cambridge Circus and on the edge of Bloomsbury, this theatre occupies an imposing corner site at the junction of Shaftesbury Avenue and High Holborn

⊖ Tottenham Court Road, Holborn or Covent Garden

P NCP in Drury Lane, Museum Street, Parker Mews (below New London Theatre) or short walk to Newport Place Masterpark

♿ There is space for four wheelchairs in the stage side boxes, down 3 steps off a corridor near the box office for which help will be required to negotiate them. Transfer seating is available to seats in the front row of the Dress Circle (here called the Royal Circle), the entrance to which is level from the foyer. An adapted toilet is available

🎧 Infrared system: collect headsets from the box office

👁 Guide dogs allowed in auditorium, or staff can dog sit

🍸 Usual bar service with two bars each in the Stalls and Royal Circle (on the left hand side of the auditorium); one bar in the Grand Circle; and a further bar in the main ground floor foyer

ⓘ Bloomsbury and the British Museum (open to 8.30pm on Thursdays and Fridays; with the Great Court open to 11pm from Thursday to Saturday); Covent Garden

This slightly musty but homely theatre is full of potential: it only needs a hit to bring it back to life again. Unfortunately, the misses have come more frequently than the hits of late.

History

Originally called the Princes Theatre when it opened in 1911, this was the last new theatre to be built on Shaftesbury Avenue. Designed by Victorian architect Bertie Crew, it is an ornate spectacle of plasterwork, some of which still survives in the beautiful boxes on either side of the stage and on top of them, the statues representing the muses of comedy, tragedy, music and poetry. The theatre, with its large capacity of some 1,400 seats, has come to largely be used for music and musicals, and in the last 20 years has been home to such shows as *Follies*, *Kiss of the Spiderwoman*, *Carousel*, *Tommy* and *Rent*. It also housed the Royal Opera for a season while the Royal Opera House was being refurbished.

Best seat in the house

Row M in the Stalls has plenty of legroom thanks to a corridor in front of it separating the front Stalls from the rear Stalls; but otherwise, the front row of the Dress (or Royal, as it is known here) Circle is best for uninterrupted, well-raked views. The Upper Circle (or Grand Circle) is very high up, particularly towards the rear of a steep and deep seating area.

GRAND CIRCLE

J	3 4 5 6 7 8 9 10 11 12 13		25 26 27 28 29 30 31 32 33 34
H	3 4 5 6 7 8 9 10 11 12 13		25 26 27 28 29 30 31 32 33 34
G	3 4 5 6 7 8 9 10 11 12 13	14 15 16 17 18 19 20 21 22 23 24	25 26 27 28 29 30 31 32 33 34
F	3 4 5 6 7 8 9 10 11 12 13	14 15 16 17 18 19 20 21 22 23 24	25 26 27 28 29 30 31 32 33 34
E	3 4 5 6 7 8 9 10 11 12 13	14 15 16 17 18 19 20 21 22 23 24	25 26 27 28 29 30 31 32 33 34 35
D	3 4 5 6 7 8 9 10 11 12 13	14 15 16 17 18 19 20 21 22 23 24	25 26 27 28 29 30 31 32 33 34 35
C	4 5 6 7 8 9 10 11 12 13	14 15 16 17 18 19 20 21 22 23 24	25 26 27 28 29 30 31 32 33 34 35
B	4 5 6 7 8 9 10 11 12 13	14 15 16 17 18 19 20 21 22 23 24	25 26 27 28 29 30 31 32 33 34
A	5 6 7 8 9 10 11 12 13	14 15 16 17 18 19 20 21 22 23 24	25 26 27 28 29 30 31 32 33

ROYAL CIRCLE

N 6 7 8 9 10 11 12   24 25 26 27

M	2 3 4 5 6 7 8 9 10 11 12 13 14 15 16 17 18	19 20 21 22 23 24 25 26 27 28 29 30 31 32 33 34
L	1 2 3 4 5 6 7 8 9 10 11 12 13 14 15 16 17 18	19 20 21 22 23 24 25 26 27 28 29 30 31 32 33 34 35
K	1 2 3 4 5 6 7 8 9 10 11 12 13 14 15 16 17 18	19 20 21 22 23 24 25 26 27 28 29 30 31 32 33 34 35
J	1 2 3 4 5 6 7 8 9 10 11 12 13 14 15 16 17 18	19 20 21 22 23 24 25 26 27 28 29 30 31 32 33 34 35
H	3 4 5 6 7 8 9 10 11 12 13 14 15 16 17 18	19 20 21 22 23 24 25 26 27 28 29 30 31 32 33 34
G	4 5 6 7 8 9 10 11 12 13 14 15 16 17 18	19 20 21 22 23 24 25 26 27 28 29 30 31 32 33
F	4 5 6 7 8 9 10 11 12 13 14 15 16 17 18	19 20 21 22 23 24 25 26 27 28 29 30 31 32 33
E	4 5 6 7 8 9 10 11 12 13 14 15 16 17 18	19 20 21 22 23 24 25 26 27 28 29 30 31 32 33
D	4 5 6 7 8 9 10 11 12 13 14 15 16 17 18	19 20 21 22 23 24 25 26 27 28 29 30 31 32 33
C	4 5 6 7 8 9 10 11 12 13 14 15 16 17 18	19 20 21 22 23 24 25 26 27 28 29 30 31 32 33
B	4 5 6 7 8 9 10 11 12 13 14 15 16 17 18	19 20 21 22 23 24 25 26 27 28 29 30 31 32 33
A	4 5 6 7 8 9 10 11 12 13 14 15 16 17 18	19 20 21 22 23 24 25 26 27 28 29 30 31 32 33

STALLS

X	3 4 5 6 7 8 9 10 11 12		19 20 21 22 23 24 25 26 27 28 29 30 31 32 33
W	3 4 5 6 7 8 9 10 11 12		19 20 21 22 23 24 25 26 27 28 29 30 31 32 33
V	3 4 5 6 7 8 9 10 11 12		19 20 21 22 23 24 25 26 27 28 29 30 31 32 33
U	3 4 5 6 7 8 9 10 11 12	13 14 15 16 17 18	19 20 21 22 23 24 25 26 27 28 29 30 31 32 33
T	3 4 5 6 7 8 9 10 11 12	13 14 15 16 17 18	19 20 21 22 23 24 25 26 27 28 29 30 31 32 33 34
S	3 4 5 6 7 8 9 10 11 12	13 14 15 16 17 18	19 20 21 22 23 24 25 26 27 28 29 30 31 32
R	3 4 5 6 7 8 9 10 11 12	13 14 15 16 17 18	19 20 21 22 23 24 25 26 27 28 29 30 31 32 33 34
P	3 4 5 6 7 8 9 10 11 12	13 14 15 16 17 18	19 20 21 22 23 24 25 26 27 28 29 30 31 32 33 34
O	3 4 5 6 7 8 9 10 11 12	13 14 15 16 17 18	19 20 21 22 23 24 25 26 27 28 29 30 31 32 33 34
N	3 4 5 6 7 8 9 10 11 12	13 14 15 16 17 18	19 20 21 22 23 24 25 26 27 28 29 30 31 32 33 34
M	3 4 5 6 7 8 9 10 11 12	13 14 15 16 17 18	19 20 21 22 23 24 25 26 27 28 29 30 31 32 33 34

L	1 2 3 4 5 6 7 8 9 10 11 12 13 14 15 16 17 18	19 20 21 22 23 24 25 26 27 28 29 30 31 32 33 34 35
K	3 4 5 6 7 8 9 10 11 12 13 14 15 16 17 18	19 20 21 22 23 24 25 26 27 28 29 30 31 32 33
J	4 5 6 7 8 9 10 11 12 13 14 15 16 17 18	19 20 21 22 23 24 25 26 27 28 29 30 31 32
H	5 6 7 8 9 10 11 12 13 14 15 16 17 18	19 20 21 22 23 24 25 26 27 28 29 30 31
G	6 7 8 9 10 11 12 13 14 15 16 17 18	19 20 21 22 23 24 25 26 27 28 29 30
F	6 7 8 9 10 11 12 13 14 15 16 17 18	19 20 21 22 23 24 25 26 27 28 29 30
E	6 7 8 9 10 11 12 13 14 15 16 17 18	19 20 21 22 23 24 25 26 27 28 29 30
D	7 8 9 10 11 12 13 14 15 16 17 18	19 20 21 22 23 24 25 26 27 28 29
C	7 8 9 10 11 12 13 14 15 16 17 18	19 20 21 22 23 24 25 26 27 28 29
B	7 8 9 10 11 12 13 14 15 16 17 18	19 20 21 22 23 24 25 26 27 28
A	8 9 10 11 12 13 14 15 16 17 18	19 20 21 22 23 24 25 26 27 28
CC	8 9 10 11 12 13 14 15 16 17 18	19 20 21 22 23 24 25 26 27 28
BB	8 9 10 11 12 13 14 15 16 17 18	19 20 21 22 23 24 25 26 27 28

Shakespeare's Globe Theatre

✉ 21 New Globe Walk, SE1 9DT

⌖ www.shakespeares-globe.org

☎ (Box office) 020-7401 9919 (Mon-Sat 10am-6pm), (Stage door) 020-7902 1400

🖷 020-7902 1401

↑ Located on the South Bank of the River Thames, between Blackfriars and Southwark Bridges, adjoining the new Tate Modern Gallery

🚇 Nearest rail stations are London Bridge, Cannon Street, Blackfriars and Waterloo

⊖ Mansion House, Blackfriars, Cannon Street; London Bridge; Southwark; St Paul's (then by foot over the Millennium Bridge)

P Limited street parking; there is an NCP car park on Upper Thames Street across the river

♿ There is provision for wheelchair users in the Theatre's Yard (that also accommodates up to 600 standing 'groundlings') and Gentlemen's Rooms; there is also full disabled access throughout the rest of the centre. A dedicated phone line is available for advice on how disabled people are accommodated on 020-7902 1409, from 11am-5pm Monday to Friday

🎧 A hearing aid induction loop is available for all performances, but since the Globe is an open-air theatre it should be noted that the loop will amplify all sounds, not just those coming from the stage. Sign language-interpreted performances are also offered – check with box office for details. The best view of the interpreter is from the Yard

👁 Guide dogs are allowed inside the auditorium.

🍴 You don't have to be a theatregoer to visit the Globe's restaurants, which include a grill restaurant (open for lunch from noon to 2.30pm and for supper from 5.30pm to 11pm; reservations on 020-7928 9444) and café (open from 10am daily to last orders 15 minutes after the end of the performance; reservations 020-7902 1576). Offering panoramic views over the River Thames, St Paul's Cathedral, and the Globe itself, these are open year-round. There are also snacks and drinks available from refreshment stands around the outdoor piazza in front of the entrance doors to the theatre before performances and during the interval

ⓘ The Tate Modern Gallery, in the converted Bankside Power Station, is next door to the theatre; the South Bank cultural complex of the National Theatre and Royal Festival Hall etc is a short walk away

Under artistic director of leading British Shakespearean actor Mark Rylance, the Globe has established itself as far more than a heritage attraction – it is a living, vital theatre that investigates not just the Shakespearean repertoire but also that of his contemporaries. New plays specially created for the theatre are also performed here.

History

The dream to recreate Shakespeare's Globe on Bankside, one of the original sites where the Bard premiered his plays in the early 17th-century, was that of the late American actor, director and producer Sam Wanamaker. After founding the Shakespeare Globe Trust in 1970 dedicated to the reconstruction of the site, he tirelessly campaigned to raise the necessary funds to build it until his death in 1993, by which time building work had already begun on finally making his dream a reality. The thatching of the roof in 1994 was of some note as the first thatched building to have been built in central London since the Great Fire of 1666. In 1995, the first workshop season was held in the substantially completed theatre and a prologue season followed in 1996, before the opening season was held in 1997. Dedicated to the experience and international understanding of Shakespeare in performance, its timber-framed structure is in the form of a wooden 'O' that brings the audience into close proximity to the stage. With standing 'groundlings' in the yard at the front of the stage (for which tickets are just £5), there are three galleries of seating: a lower gallery behind the yard, a middle gallery and an upper gallery, each of which wraps around the theatre below the thatched roof.

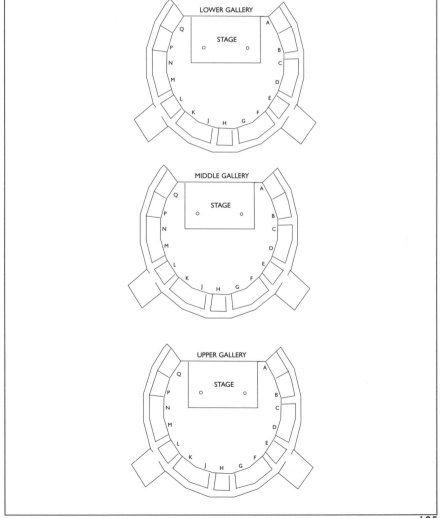

Best seat in the house

Best views and the most dynamic, interactive experience is definitely to be had from being a "groundling" in the yard, though it's tough on the feet and there's no protection against the elements should it rain: umbrellas are not allowed (but the theatre stewards sell inexpensive plastic rain macs). Seats in the galleries are priced according to the views they offer – the roof and all gallery seats are held up by pillars, so there is no seat from which they do not obscure the action at some point. The seats are wooden benches without back rests, so can be numbing, despite cushions that can be hired for a small charge; a new innovation in 2003 saw canvas contraptions being hired out that also offer some support to the lower back.

St Martin's Theatre

✉ West Street, WC2H 9NZ

☎ (Box office) 020-7836 1443, (Stage door) 020-7836 1086

↑ Tucked away off Charing Cross Road. Walking north from Leicester Square turn right onto Lichfield Street (or walking south from Tottenham Court Road, turn left onto Lichfield Street) and the theatre is straight ahead of you.

🚇 Charing Cross

⊖ Leicester Square, Tottenham Court Road, Piccadilly Circus, Covent Garden

P MasterPark at Cambridge Circus, NCP at Upper St Martin's Lane and Bedfordbury

♿ There is a wheelchair entrance through an exit door on Tower Court, with space for one wheelchair

user in a Dress Circle box, access to which is via a ramp that will be put over five steps by staff. Transfer to seats in the rear of the Dress Circle are also possible. Wheelchair users must be accompanied by a non-disabled companion. There is an adapted toilet by the Tower Court entrance.

🎧 Induction loop and single track infrared systems with headsets that should be booked in advance and will require a deposit

👁 Guide dogs not allowed inside auditorium, but staff can dog sit

🍸 Usual bar service

ⓘ The Ivy (probably the most fashionable theatrical restaurant) is across the street, as will be witnessed by the inevitable posse of paparazzi outside

The St Martin's is an intimate, wood-panelled gem – the only pity is that so few people will actually get to see it more than once in their lives, as *The Mousetrap* looks set to hold onto the lease here for many years to come. But it's a real beauty, with an impressive columned façade that leads into a delightful, intimate auditorium seating 550 people.

History

Home to *The Mousetrap* (which is booking "to doomsday" according to *Time Out*), the St Martin's Theatre has, contrary to what one might think, also hosted other plays. In fact, *The Mousetrap* didn't even begin here, but rather transferred from the Ambassadors Theatre next door – a theatre for which the St Martin's was coincidentally built as a companion. But the Ambassadors opened first, in 1913, with the out-break of the First World War interrupting building on the St Martin's, that finally opened in 1916. Between then and the arrival of *The Mousetrap* in 1974, it housed many hits – including another (rather superior) thriller, *Sleuth*. But no play can beat *The Mousetrap*, which has played half a century now, and more than half of that time here.

Best seat in the house

The Mousetrap proudly proclaims that it never discounts seats through any source – but then seats are reasonably priced to begin with. Like The Tower of London or Buckingham Palace, this show is on the tourist itinerary – and though far from the best that London has to offer, the production is kept in shape by replacing the cast annually. There are good views from most seats in the intimate Stalls and Dress Circle; only the rear rows of the Upper Circle feel a little remote.

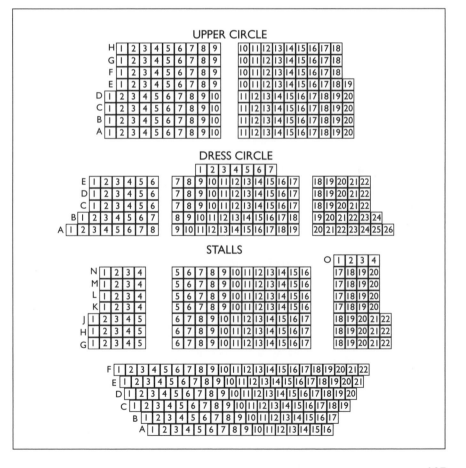

Strand Theatre

✉ Aldwych, WC2B 4LD

⌂ www.delfont-mackintosh.com

☎ (Box office) 0870 060 2335 (Mon-Sat 10am-7.45pm), (Stage door) 020-7836 4144

↑ Located in the Aldwych just off the Strand, this Covent Garden theatre has a grand frontage on its corner site with Catherine Street

🚇 Charing Cross

⊖ Covent Garden; Charing Cross; Holborn

P NCP in Drury Lane

♿ There is separate access for wheelchair users through an exit door off Catherine Street, from which there are four steps down. There are two spaces for wheelchair users in a box, with transfer seats available in the front row of the Dress Circle. Each wheelchair user must be accompanied by a non-disabled companion. There is no adapted toilet

🎧 No facilities at present

👁 Guide dogs allowed in auditorium, or staff can dog sit

🍸 Usual bar service, with dress circle bar open from 45 minutes before the performance and other parts of the theatre 30 minutes beforehand

ⓘ One Aldwych (a modern boutique hotel, with an excellent Cinnamon coffee bar facing the Strand Theatre's entrance), Covent Garden, the Theatre Museum, Somerset House (including the Courtauld Institute Gallery, and riverside promenade), the Royal Courts of Justice

Now under the ownership of Cameron Mackintosh, the Strand (seating just over 1000 people) is in the midst of a £1.7million refurbishment whose priority is to recreate the glamour of the original interior as well as to upgrade and expand the public areas and facilities. Part of the Waldorf Chambers next door, facing the Aldwych and the fifth floor of which were once the London apartment of the composer/performer Ivor Novello, are being absorbed into the new front-of-house areas.

History

Opened in 1905 as the Waldorf Theatre, in its early years it was leased to legendary American theatre owners the Shubert brothers. In 1909 the theatre changed hands – and its name to the Strand – before another American manager FC Whitney took over and changed its name again to the Whitney Theatre. He, too, had little success, and in 1913 the theatre reverted again to being called the Strand. Many owners came and went over successive generations. During the Blitz, actor-manager Donald Wolfit kept the theatre open with lunchtime performances of Shakespeare, with the actors having to negotiate piles of rubble to get to the stage since a bomb had damaged the dressing rooms. Then came the first of the theatres record-breaking runs, when in 1942 the Broadway comedy *Arsenic and Old Lace* (recently revived at the same theatre, with less success) began a 1337-performance run. In August 1974, that record was broken when the sex comedy *No Sex Please – We're British!* overtook it. More recently, the theatre housed seven of the 13-year run of *Buddy!*, transferred here from the Victoria Palace.

Best seat in the house

The Stalls are gently raked and afford good views from around the fifth or six row back. Legroom, however, is currently very poor all around. The central section of the

Dress Circle is recommended – avoid the seats that wrap around the sides of the front row, as views are restricted. The Upper Circle is called the Grand Circle – and what's called the Upper Circle is in fact the Balcony (i.e. 4th level), so very high up indeed!

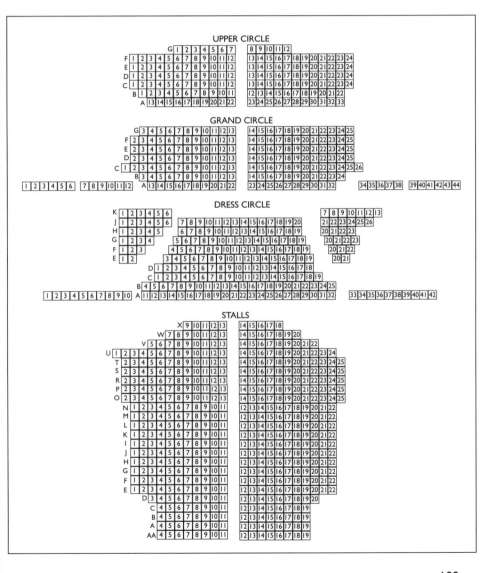

Vaudeville Theatre

✉ 404 Strand, WC2R ONH

☎ (Box office) 0870 890 0511, (Stage door) 020-7836 3191

↑ Located on the north side of the Strand, a few minutes walk from Trafalgar Square and Charing Cross Station

🚇 Charing Cross

⊖ Charing Cross, Embankment

P There is a MasterPark in Spring Gardens, off Trafalgar Square, and a NCP car park in Drury Lane

♿ There are no spaces for wheelchair users in the auditorium, but transfer seating is available to any aisle seat on the left-hand side of the Stalls –

five steps down from the foyer. The Dress Circle can be accessed via a side exit door on Lumley Court, with a shallow step immediately inside the door and a further two steps down to the front row of the Dress Circle. There is no adapted toilet. Each wheelchair user must bring a non-disabled companion

🎧 No facilities at present

👁 Guide dogs allowed in auditorium, or staff can dog sit

🍸 Usual bar service – tiny Stalls bar in entrance foyer, a more spacious bar upstairs adjoining the Dress Circle, and another bar in the Upper Circle

ⓘ Trafalgar Square

This is an appealing little theatre, though be careful where you sit – see below!

History

The third building on this site, having originally opened in 1870, been substantially re-designed in 1891 and again improved in 1926, this still – despite its name – isn't a vaudeville theatre at all! Instead, it's a small playhouse that specialises in plays and occasionally small-scale musicals or revues.

Best seat in the house

This intimate West End playhouse, with seating for nearly 700, has a surprisingly deep Stalls area that goes a very long way back in rows that go the width of the auditorium, so it's best to sit as centrally as possible towards the front. The Dress Circle seating is notable for a lack of legroom, and the Upper Circle seems very far away from the stage.

UPPER CIRCLE

```
J       15 14 13 12 11 10  9  8  7  6  5  4  3  2  1
H    17 16 15 14 13 12 11 10  9  8  7  6  5  4  3  2  1
G 18 17 16 15 14 13 12 11 10  9  8  7  6  5  4  3  2  1
F 18 17 16 15 14 13 12 11 10  9  8  7  6  5  4  3  2  1
E 18 17 16 15 14 13 12 11 10  9  8  7  6  5  4  3  2  1
D 18 17 16 15 14 13 12 11 10  9  8  7  6  5  4  3  2  1
C 18 17 16 15 14 13 12 11 10  9  8  7  6  5  4  3  2  1
B 18 17 16 15 14 13 12 11 10  9  8  7  6  5  4  3  2  1
A    16 15 14 13 12 11 10  9  8  7  6  5  4  3  2  1
```

DRESS CIRCLE

```
K 19 18 17 16 15 14 13 12 11 10  9  8  7  6  5  4  3  2  1
J 19 18 17 16 15 14 13 12 11 10  9  8  7  6  5  4  3  2  1
H 19 18 17 16 15 14 13 12 11 10  9  8  7  6  5  4  3  2  1
G    18 17 16 15 14 13 12 11 10  9  8  7  6  5  4  3  2  1
F       17 16 15 14 13 12 11 10  9  8  7  6  5  4  3  2  1
E 19 18 17 16 15 14 13 12 11 10  9  8  7  6  5  4  3  2  1
D 19 18 17 16 15 14 13 12 11 10  9  8  7  6  5  4  3  2  1
C 19 18 17 16 15 14 13 12 11 10  9  8  7  6  5  4  3  2  1
B 19 18 17 16 15 14 13 12 11 10  9  8  7  6  5  4  3  2  1
A 19 18 17 16 15 14 13 12 11 10  9  8  7  6  5  4  3  2  1
```

STALLS

```
S 18 17 16 15 14 13 12 11 10  9  8  7  6  5  4  3  2  1
R 18 17 16 15 14 13 12 11 10  9  8  7  6  5  4  3  2  1
Q 18 17 16 15 14 13 12 11 10  9  8  7  6  5  4  3  2  1
P    17 16 15 14 13 12 11 10  9  8  7  6  5  4  3  2  1
O       15 14 13 12 11 10  9  8  7  6  5  4  3  2  1
N    16 15 14 13 12 11 10  9  8  7  6  5  4  3  2  1
M 18 17 16 15 14 13 12 11 10  9  8  7  6  5  4  3  2  1
L 18 17 16 15 14 13 12 11 10  9  8  7  6  5  4  3  2  1
K 18 17 16 15 14 13 12 11 10  9  8  7  6  5  4  3  2  1
J 18 17 16 15 14 13 12 11 10  9  8  7  6  5  4  3  2  1
H 18 17 16 15 14 13 12 11 10  9  8  7  6  5  4  3  2  1
G 18 17 16 15 14 13 12 11 10  9  8  7  6  5  4  3  2  1
F 18 17 16 15 14 13 12 11 10  9  8  7  6  5  4  3  2  1
E 18 17 16 15 14 13 12 11 10  9  8  7  6  5  4  3  2  1
D 18 17 16 15 14 13 12 11 10  9  8  7  6  5  4  3  2  1
C 18 17 16 15 14 13 12 11 10  9  8  7  6  5  4  3  2  1
B 18 17 16 15 14 13 12 11 10  9  8  7  6  5  4  3  2  1
A    16 15 14 13 12 11 10  9  8  7  6  5  4  3  2  1
AZ                  10  9  8  7  6  5  4  3  2  1
AY                      8  7  6  5  4  3  2  1
```

The Venue

✉ 5 Leicester Place, off Leicester Square, WC2

☎ (Box office) 020-7434 9629

↑ Tucked in a side street just behind the Empire cinema on the North Side of Leicester Square, this venue – called simply, The Venue – is easy to miss. Since it's entirely subterranean, the only marking is a small doorway at street level – next door to the Prince Charles Cinema

🚇 Charing Cross

⊖ Leicester Square, Piccadilly Circus

P MasterPark at Trafalgar Square, NCP at Upper St Martin's Lane and Cambridge Circus

♿ Subterranean location means disabled access is very difficult, unless able to negotiate a steep flight of stairs

🌟 Cramped basic bar

ⓘ Leicester Square cinemas

They said this was the first "completely new" commercial theatre to open in the West End for nearly three quarters of a century when it opened in 2002, but "new" and "theatre" are stretching it a bit. Not only is it an old room, but also its conversion into a theatre has simply entailed installing banks of temporary, stadium-like plastic tip-up seating for 329 people that are also deeply uncomfortable. There's no legroom and even less butt-room. It looks and feels like one of those hasty conversions that take root in church halls, very like this one, for the Edinburgh Fringe every summer. Being asked to pay West End prices might strike one as a bit rich, given the rudimentary circumstances; but as an alternative, intimate venue, it's also just the kind of space that London's commercial theatre has hitherto lacked. It has a raffish, fringe quality that makes it less intimidating, perhaps, to audiences unaccustomed to the West End's faded glamour; but a few more comfort factors, particularly on the seating, wouldn't have gone amiss. The tiny bar also makes for a tight squeeze, particularly as it's the main throughway to the auditorium. Good sightlines, however, bring most of the audience close to the action. And manager Perry makes sure that his staff are unusually friendly, too.

History

This basement venue used to be the Notre Dame Hall for the church of that name above it, and was formerly a music venue where, amongst other things, it hosted the first-ever gig by The Sex Pistols, and appearances by The Damned, Blondie and The Clash. Subsequently it has seen use as a dance hall, but in 2002, it acquired a new life as a West End Theatre when a musical called *Taboo*, written by Boy George, opened here, followed by a throwback to radio days, *Round the Horne Revisited*.

Best seat in the house

The front few rows have old-fashioned, traditional theatre seating, obviously salvaged from a "real" theatre, so are more comfortable but are unraked; the rest of the audience sits on stadium-like tip-up plastic seats installed on scaffolding rostra.

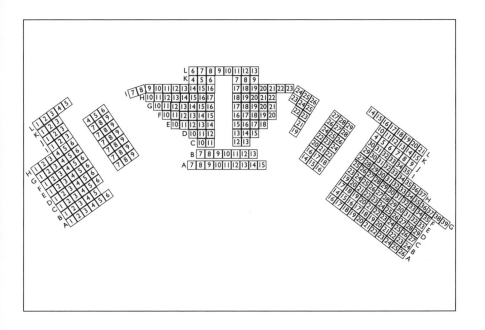

Victoria Palace Theatre

✉ Victoria Street, SW1E 5EA

☎ (Box office) 020-7834 1317 (24 hours by phone; in person, open Mon-Sat 10am-8pm), (Stage door) 020-7834 2781

🖨 020-7931 7163

↑ Located on a prominent corner site directly opposite Victoria Station as you exit the main concourse, a little way away from the traditional heart of the West End but on a busy commuter route

🚇 Victoria Station is across the street

⊖ Victoria

P MasterPark at Rochester Row (behind Army and Navy department store); some free on-street parking behind the theatre and environs after 6.30pm

♿ Entry via exit door on Allington Street brings level access to the rear Stalls, with spaces for wheelchairs and companion seating available in rows M and P. Transfer seating is also available to any aisle seat. Wheelchair users must be accompanied by a non-disabled patron. There is an adapted toilet available beside the side entrance

⌒ Induction loop and single track infrared system with headsets, which must be booked in advance and for a deposit is required

👁 Guide dogs allowed in auditorium, or can be looked after in the manager's office

🍸 Usual bar service

ⓘ Victoria Station; Buckingham Palace; St James Park

Though away from the main West End loop, this is a popular musicals destination since transport connections are so good and there is a built-in local commuter audience. Though this is not one of architect Frank Matcham's most classically beautiful theatres, it has an air and functional grace that still sets it apart from most other theatres of this size.

History

The present theatre dates from 1910, but there has been a theatre on this site since 1832 – well before the arrival of the railways put Victoria on the map as a major station in the 1870s. Originally the Royal Standard Music Hall, what was London's oldest licensed music hall was demolished so that new technology and electricity could be introduced, and – with the great Victorian architect Frank Matcham at the helm – this grand and spacious theatre replaced it. A small grey marble foyer area beside the box office, with gold mosaic and pillars of white Sicilian marble, leads up to the Dress Circle, with a larger entrance bar area to the right. The theatre features a sliding roof – a precursor to air-conditioning (which the theatre now blissfully has, a rare feature in London). The theatre has often boasted long runs, such as: the original production of *Me and My Girl* (originally in 1937 until the Second World War broke out, and revived in 1954), the Crazy Gang who ran riot here for 15 years; the *Black and White Minstrel Show*, which reigned supreme for 10 years; the original London run of *Annie*; a revival of *Barnum*, starring Michael Crawford in the late '70s and '80s; *Buddy* which ran here for six years from 1989 before transferring to the Strand; and the Rod Stewart musical, *Tonight's The Night*.

Best seat in the house

The Stalls, with seats ranged in two blocks on either side of a centre aisle, are surprisingly intimate in a theatre so large (it seats 1517)and afford a good view from most seats. The Dress Circle is similarly arranged, and has similarly good views, as does the Upper Circle, though a steep rake up there can make the rear rows seem remote (but at the same time affords an uninterrupted view of the stage).

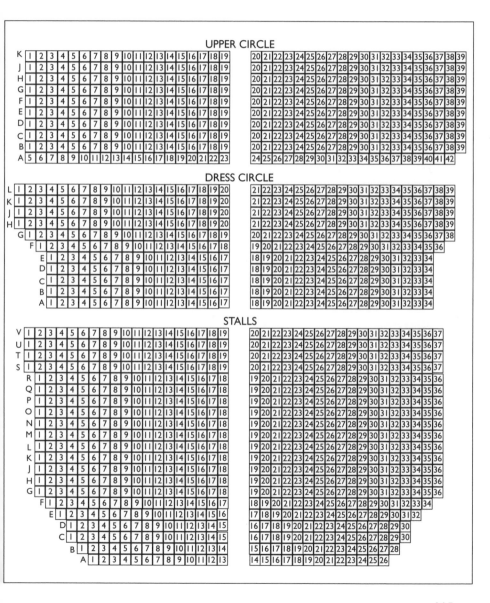

Whitehall Theatre: Trafalgar Studios

✉ 14 Whitehall, SW1A 2DY

🖰 www.theambassadors.com/ trafalgarstudios

☎ (Box office) 0870 060 6632 (24 hours), (Stage door) 020-7321 5400

↑ Located at the top of Whitehall near where it meets Trafalgar Square, this theatre is in the governmental and ceremonial heart of London

🚇 Charing Cross

🔵 Charing Cross, Embankment

P MasterPark in Spring Gardens, Trafalgar Square; NCP at Befordbury

♿ As layout of the venue will be changed, please check for specific details

🎧 Check for details

👁 Check for details

🌟 Check for details

ⓘ Trafalgar Square; Horse Guard's Parade; Downing Street; Houses of Parliament

Despite an excellent location just off the recently revamped Trafalgar Square at the top of Whitehall, and a smart mid-80s refurbishment that restored many of the theatre's lovely art deco features, this theatre has long had difficulties attracting long-running tenants. But now a bold new plan has just been implemented that preserves the fabric and integrity of the building, and also gives it (and the West End) a much needed new lease of life with its adventurous £750,000 conversion into two smaller theatre studios, as briefly happened to the New Ambassadors when the Royal Court took it over while their home theatre was being refurbished in the mid-90s. Though Cameron Mackintosh's extensive plans for the refurbishment of the Queen's and Gielgud Theatres include installing a brand-new 500-seat studio theatre above the Queen's, this plan pre-empts that with considerably less fanfare.

The larger of the newly-named Trafalgar Studios rises from the existing stage, itself raised and extended to create a larger, more flexible footprint over part of the front stalls, with seating for 380 rising in steeply raked rows that meet and continue at the former Dress Circle level. It will offer the chance to commercially extend the life of productions from other smaller studio theatres in London, like the Donmar, Almeida and Young Vic, as well as transfers from the likes of Stratford-upon-Avon's Swan Theatre. The smaller studio, built within the former stalls area, has seating for 80, and is intended to offer the opportunity to develop new work in the heart of the West End.

Best seat in the house

These two intimate spaces should allow great views from any seat in the house, though they are yet to be tested.

```
  L  1  2  3  4  5  6  7  8  9 10 11 12 13 14 15 16 17
  K  1  2  3  4  5  6  7  8  9 10 11 12 13 14 15 16 17 18 19 20
  J  1  2  3  4  5  6  7  8  9 10 11 12 13 14 15 16 17 18 19 20
  H  1  2  3  4  5  6  7  8  9 10 11 12 13 14 15 16 17 18 19 20
  G  1  2  3  4  5  6  7  8  9 10 11 12 13 14 15 16 17 18 19 20 21
  F  1  2  3  4  5  6  7  8  9 10 11 12 13 14 15 16 17 18 19 20 21 22 23 24 25 26 27 28 29 30
  E  1  2  3  4  5  6  7  8  9 10 11 12 13 14 15 16 17 18 19 20 21 22 23 24 25 26 27 28 29 30
  D  1  2  3  4  5  6  7  8  9 10 11 12 13 14 15 16 17 18 19 20 21 22 23 24 25 26 27 28 29 30
  C  1  2  3  4  5  6  7  8  9 10 11 12 13 14 15 16 17 18 19 20 21 22 23 24 25 26 27 28 29 30
  B  1  2  3  4  5  6  7  8  9 10 11 12 13 14 15 16 17 18 19 20 21 22 23 24 25 26 27 28 29 30
  A  1  2  3  4  5  6  7  8  9 10 11 12 13 14 15 16 17 18 19 20 21 22 23 24 25 26 27 28 29 30 31
 AA  1  2  3  4  5  6  7  8  9 10 11 12 13 14 15 16 17 18 19 20 21 22 23 24 25 26 27
 BB  1  2  3  4  5  6  7  8  9 10 11 12 13 14 15 16 17 18
 CC  1  2  3  4  5  6  7  8  9 10 11 12 13 14 15 16 17 18 19 20
 DD  1  2  3  4  5  6  7  8  9 10 11 12 13 14 15 16 17 18 19 20 21 22 23 24 25 26
```

Wyndham's Theatre

✉ Charing Cross Road, WC2H 0DA

⌨ www.theambassadors.com/wynd-hams/

☎ (Box office) 020-7369 1736, (Stage door) 020-7438 9700

↑ Directly above Leicester Square station, diagonally opposite the Hippodrome nightclub on the edge of Leicester Square

🚇 Charing Cross

⊖ Leicester Square is directly next door; Covent Garden

P MasterPark at Trafalgar Square, NCP at Upper St Martin's Lane and Cambridge Circus. Limited on-street parking on yellow lines and metres is free after 6.30pm in St Martin's Lane and Long Acre

🚲 Racks in Upper St Martin's Lane

♿ Entrance is through a side entrance to the right of the main entrance on Charing Cross Road, with three steps down into a box where there is space for two wheelchair users, or eight steps down to the Stalls where transfer seating is available to aisle seats. Each wheelchair user must bring a non-disabled companion. There is a toilet in the box, but it is not adapted for wheelchair use

🎧 Free infrared system, though deposit required for headsets available from the manager

👁 Guide dogs are allowed in auditorium, or staff can dog sit

🍸 Usual bar service, in basement bar before you enter the Stalls, or rear of the Royal Circle and Balcony

ⓘ Leicester Square; Covent Garden

This jewel-box of a theatre with seating for nearly 800 offers a sense of occasion from the moment you enter its tiny, circular entrance foyer with its domed ceiling and wood box office window, from where steps lead up to the circles and down to the Stalls. The theatre itself is another miniature gem, with its ornate classical curtain and petite boxes on either side of the proscenium.

History

Actor-manager Charles Wyndham had a 20-year stint running the Criterion Theatre at Piccadilly Circus, but always hankered to build his own theatre, an ambition he finally realised when Wyndham's Theatre opened in 1899, with Wyndham himself starring in the title role of a play about another great actor-manager, David Garrick. The theatre has long been a keenly sought playhouse since, for everyone from great Dames of the stage like Maggie Smith, Judi Dench and Diana Rigg, to dames like Madonna (who made her West End theatrical debut here in *Up for Grabs*). Considering its ideal proportions for plays, it has also occasionally staged small-scale musicals to great success, from the transfer of *The Boy Friend* in 1954 (where it ran 2078 performances) to *Godspell* in 1972 and *Side by Side* by Sondheim later in the 70s. More recent hits include several years of housing the play *Art*, two seasons of *The Play What I Wrote*, *Democracy* from Michael Barrymore's disastrous stage comeback and the transfer of *Dinner* for the National Theatre

Best seat in the house

The front four rows of the Stalls are arranged in continuous rows; from the fifth row back, they are broken into two sections by a central aisle. These centre aisle seats are best. The small Royal (Dress) Circle, with seats in continuous rows, also affords great views from the centre of the front few rows. A four-level house with a Balcony extending behind the Grand (Upper) Circle, the upper levels are quite high and remote.

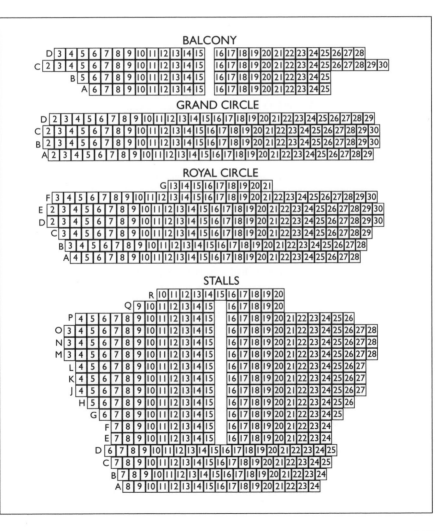

Classical Venues

Conway Hall

✉ 25 Red Lion Square, WC1R 4RL

⌂ www.conwayhall.org.uk

☎ (Box office) 020-7272 9619

🖃 conwayhall@ethicalsoc.org.uk

↑ Red Lion Square is a three-minute walk from Holborn station

⊖ Holborn

P Metered parking in Red Lion Square and adjacent streets, unrestricted after 6.30pm, Saturdays after 1.30pm and Sundays all day

Established in 1929 by the South Place Ethical Society, the Conway Hall is one of the last bastions of free thinking. The series of Sunday evening chamber music concerts, stretching back a hundred years to before the construction of the main hall must surely make this multi-purpose educational venue unique among concert halls, which is so acoustically clear that it's often used as a recording studio.

London Coliseum

✉ St Martin's Lane, WC2N 4ES

⌂ www.eno.org

☎ (Box office) 020-7632 8300, (Stage door) 020-7836 0111

🗏 020-7379 1264

🖃 info@eno.org

↑ At the bottom end of St Martin's Lane, near to Trafalgar Square, the London Coliseum cuts an imposing figure, and is visible from further afield thanks to the twinkling globe on top of it

🚇 Charing Cross

⊖ Charing Cross, Leicester Square, Embankment, Covent Garden

P Discounts available to ENO patrons at Masterpark carparks – nearest ones are in Spring Gardens and Whitcomb Street. Ask the Box Office or information desk to validate your parking ticket.

♿ ENO runs an Access Programme, offering a range of services and support materials for patrons with disabilities. Contact the box office on 020-7845 9258 for details.

𝔇 Regular sign-language interpreted performances.

👁 Regular audio-introduced performances, with synopsis and vivid descriptions of sets, costumes and characterisations.

🍴 Bar service and snacks on all levels.

ⓘ Trafalgar Square

London's largest lyric theatre, the London Coliseum has been home to the English National Opera (or Sadler's Wells Opera, as it was originally known) since 1968, and the company acquired the freehold to the building in 1992.

Designed on epic Romanesque lines, as its name suggests, by the renowned theatrical architect Frank Matcham, this spectacular theatre with seating for nearly 2400 people on four levels has gone through many uses, housing variety and music hall, musicals and dance, but it is as a classical opera house – epic yet surprisingly intimate – that it has found its true calling.

The London Coliseum was recently restored to its former 1904 glory in a spectacular £41million restoration, re-opening its doors in February 2004 almost exactly a century after the theatre was originally created.

Some 40 per cent additional public space has been carved out, with new and expanded bar facilities throughout; all areas of the theatre are reachable from staircases off the main foyer, with the Balcony entrance no longer to be found in a separate side alley; there's been a the welcome doubling of the ladies loos; and Matcham's original curved glass roof, long ago dismantled, has been reinstated over the Balcony Bar to afford a dramatic view of the Coliseum's landmark tower. On top of that tower, the Coliseum's famous globe, spelling out the theatre's name, has been recreated and actually revolves for the first time in a century – owing to safety rules, the original basket work revolve made of iron had been removed and replaced, until now, with a green fibreglass model that contained a flickering light to recreate the moving effect.

The Balcony foyer has also been extended into the tower to create a new public foyer in a space that used to be a kitchen that, as well as creating the cosy Clore Education Room with a fluorescent-lit ceiling, opens out onto an outdoor balcony that affords spectacular views towards Trafalgar Square – you can even see the London Eye from here!

But it is the auditorium itself that is even more stunning, with Matcham's original 1904 colour scheme of rich imperial purple, Italian reds and shades of gold and cream gorgeously reinstated, replacing the dull veneer of grey paint that used to hide so much of this theatre's extraordinary detail. Conceived with imposing friezes and figures to

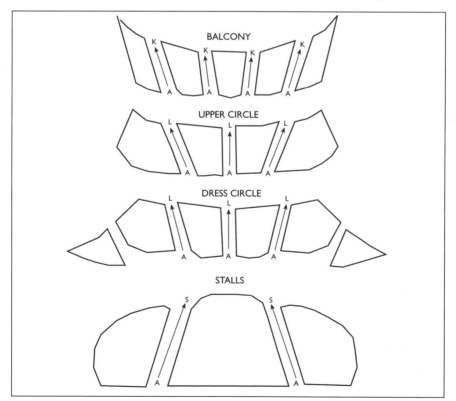

explicitly evoke the Colosseum in Rome, the theatre gleams with marble and mosaics, while the splendid terracotta façade comes complete with ornamental lions and slaves.

Best seat in the house:

The Stalls are surprisingly intimate for so vast a house and bring you closest to the action, but the front of the Dress and Upper Circles are also great for uninterrupted views of the stage. Further back in both circles you suffer from the overhang effect of the circles above them, which makes it feel like you're looking at the stage through a letterbox opening, and the sound can be muffled, too. Those in the know say that the sound is best in the stratospheric Balcony – but it's so high that nosebleeds might well result!

Royal Albert Hall

✉ Kensington Gore, SW7 2AP

⌁ www.royalalberthall.com

☎ (Box office) 020-7589 8212, or in person beside Door 12

↑ Located near South Kensington tube station and the myriad of museums there, the Royal Albert Hall is situated on the south side of Hyde Park directly opposite the Albert Memorial

⊖ South Kensington and High Street Kensington are a ten-minute walk away

P There is limited street parking on surrounding streets and even immediately outside the hall after 7pm, but beware residents' restrictions that are often in force beyond 6.30pm. The RAH offers limited parking from 6pm for patrons attending concerts. Spaces are £7.50 and must be booked in advance

♿ The Hall has many entrances at ground level – there are ramped entrances at 2, 4, 8, 9 and 12. There are lifts at doors 2, 8 and 11 serving all areas of the hall. There is a plat-

form lift from basement level at Door 2 into the Arena. There are wheelchair spaces with adjacent companion spaces in the stalls and circle

🎧 Infrared system, plus personal receivers for use with or without hearing aids, with the use of a free receiver that can be collected from the information desk at Door 6 on the ground floor

👁 Welcome in the hall, but advise when booking for the most appropriate seats

🍴 Three restaurants: the Elgar Room Restaurant (Circle level, book in advance on 020-7589 8212), the Victoria Room Brasserie (also on the Circle level, a self-service restaurant offering light meals) and the Prince Consort Wine Bar and Café Consort (entrance via door 12 to South Porch, offering light meals). Six Bars

ⓘ Hyde Park is opposite; the great South Kensington Museums – the Victoria and Albert Museum, the Natural History Museum and the Science Museum – close by

One of the world's most monumental concert halls, the Royal Albert Hall (named for Queen Victoria's late husband and built in his honour) opened in 1871, a decade after his death at the age of 42. Classical music has predominated over the years (most notably, perhaps, in its annual summer hosting of the BBC Proms season), but the hall has seen various uses as cinema (as early as 1905), tennis court (1970), ice-skating arena (1984), sumo wrestling arena (1991), and circus stadium (for Cirque du Soleil's now annual post-Christmas appearances). Over the years the Royal Albert Hall became a little shabby, but a major refurbishment has been completed, including re-seating of the Stalls and Circle, air cooling in the auditorium, new and dramatic public foyers underneath the Stalls seating and restoration and redecoration of all the public areas – and at long last the shop and restaurant are open to daytime visitors. With hundreds of concerts held over the course of a year, there's always a sense of occasion about arriving in the inviting womb of this auditorium that wraps the audience around a massive atrium in ever-ascending levels.

Best seat in the house:

Many of the private boxes on each of the three tiers below the high top Balcony are "lost" (and often shamefully unoccupied) thanks to the private subscriptions that are held to them by companies and individuals, but the best seating is in the Stalls level anyway, on comfortable swivel chairs. The Arena immediately in front of the stage (with seating removed for the Proms season so that that promenaders can stand and congregate) is unraked, so if you are sitting there views can be problematic should a tall person be immediately in front of you!

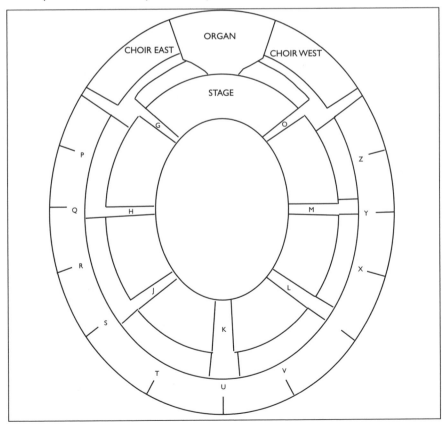

Royal Festival Hall, Queen Elizabeth Hall and Purcell Room

✉ South Bank Centre, SE1 8XX

🖰 www.rfh.org.uk

☎ (Box office) 020-7960 4201

🖨 020-7921 0821

↑ Located on the south bank of the River Thames, half way between Westminster and Waterloo Bridges, the South Bank Centre (as these three concert halls are collectively known, together with a major contemporary art gallery, the Hayward Gallery, next door) is now easily reached from the West End by the new Golden Jubilee Bridges (formerly the Hungerford Footbridge) that lead straight to its terraces, or from Waterloo Station

🚇 Waterloo, Charing Cross

⊖ Waterloo, Charing Cross, Embankment, Westminster

P There are car parks below the Hayward Gallery and National

Royal Festival Hall

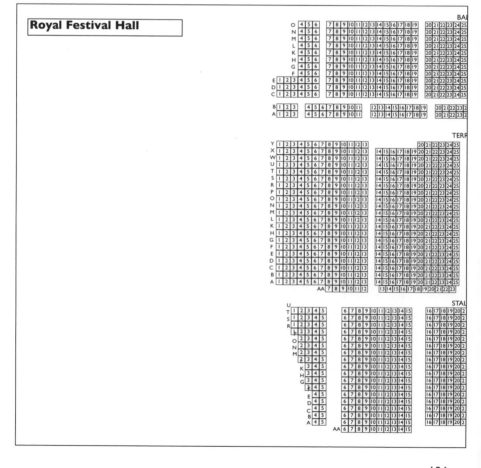

Theatre, as well as limited free street parking after 6.30pm.

♿ There are places for eight wheelchair users, plus opportunities to transfer to seating, in various parts of the Royal Festival Hall auditorium, with lifts to most areas and accessible toilets on levels 1, 3 and 5. For the Queen Elizabeth Hall, level access is available form the Artists' Entrance, with an adjacent accessible toilet, and five wheelchair spaces available in the auditorium. For the Purcell Room, wheelchair access is by a platform lift from the Queen Elizabeth Hall foyer, with space available for two wheel-chair users

⍓ Sennheiser infrared system in all auditoria – receivers available from the cloakroom on Level 2 for the Royal Festival Hall, or in the main foyer of the Queen Elizabeth Hall and Purcell Room

◉ Spaces for patrons with guide dogs available in all three auditoria

▣ Foyer bars and EAT coffee bars in both the Royal Festival Hall and QEH/Purcell Room foyers; the Royal Festival Hall also has a Festival Buffet in the main foyer, a café and coffee bar beside the box office entrance,

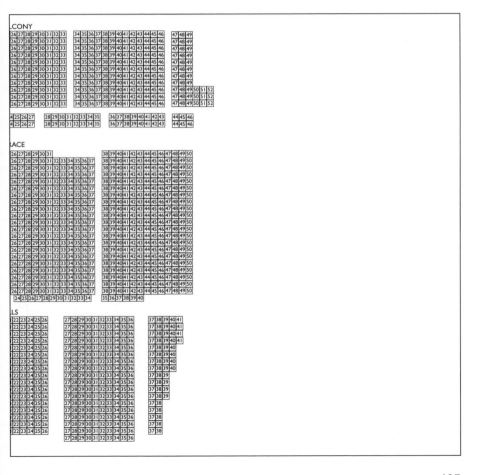

and a new café around the back of the building in Belvedere Road, plus the People's Palace waiter-service restaurant on Level 3 with fine river front views (Reservations: 020-7928 9999)

ⓘ The London Eye Millennium Wheel; the National Film Theatre; the National Theatre

The Royal Festival Hall is the only permanent legacy of the Festival of Britain that was held in 1951 to mark the country's emergence from the austerity that resulted from the Second World War, but is now part of a much bigger scheme that makes it one of the most distinctive cultural areas in London. The Festival Hall, designed in a 'modernist' style with glazed screens and a green roof of weather-exposed copper, was the first post-war building to receive a Grade listed status. With seating for up to 2900 people on two levels — a deep Stalls area that continues after a break into a similarly deep terrace, with a grand tier over it — it undoubtedly has scale if not intimacy. The banks of side boxes look like car ashtrays that are sticking out of their holders. During the interval, be sure to go out onto the upper outside terraces in fine weather for views onto the river. The Queen Elizabeth and Purcell Room concert halls, housed in a brown concrete bunker structure next door, are much less loved from the outside, though inside both rooms are sparsely decorated but comfortably appointed modern auditoria. The South Bank Centre is currently in the midst of a £60million redevelopment programme, so much will be changing there over the next few years.

Queen Elizabeth Hall

Seating plan for the Queen Elizabeth Hall showing the REAR STALLS (rows PP, OO, NN, MM, LL, KK, HH, GG, FF, EE, DD, CC, BB, AA) and STALLS (rows M, L, K, H, G, F, E, D, C, B, A), with seats numbered from 1 to 39 across each row.

Best seat in the house:

For the Royal Festival Hall, central Stalls are always best; the rear terrace can be claustrophobic with the Grand Tier hanging over it. The front row of the side annexes often represent good value; though you're viewing side on, you are close to the stage, particularly for concerts. In the 1,100-seat Queen Elizabeth Hall, the front half of the Stalls is preferred; the rear Stalls can feel pretty remote. The 372-seat Purcell Room is so tiny that every seat is good.

Purcell Room

R	1	2	3	4	5	6	7	8	9	10	11	12	13	14	15	16	17	18	19	20	21	22	23	24	25
P	1	2	3	4	5	6	7	8	9	10	11	12	13	14	15	16	17	18	19	20	21	22	23	24	25
O	1	2	3	4	5	6	7	8	9	10	11	12	13	14	15	16	17	18	19	20	21	22	23	24	25
N	1	2	3	4	5	6	7	8	9	10	11	12	13	14	15	16	17	18	19	20	21	22	23	24	25
M	1	2	3	4	5	6	7	8	9	10	11	12	13	14	15	16	17	18	19	20	21	22	23	24	25
L	1	2	3	4	5	6	7	8	9	10	11	12	13	14	15	16	17	18	19	20	21	22	23	24	25
K	1	2	3	4	5	6	7	8	9	10	11	12	13	14	15	16	17	18	19	20	21	22	23	24	25
H	1	2	3	4	5	6	7	8	9	10	11	12	13	14	15	16	17	18	19	20	21	22	23	24	25
G	1	2	3	4	5	6	7	8	9	10	11	12	13	14	15	16	17	18	19	20	21	22	23	24	25
F	1	2	3	4	5	6	7	8	9	10	11	12	13	14	15	16	17	18	19	20	21	22	23	24	25
E	1	2	3	4	5	6	7	8	9	10	11	12	13	14	15	16	17	18	19	20	21	22	23	24	25
D	1	2	3	4	5	6	7	8	9	10	11	12	13	14	15	16	17	18	19	20	21	22	23	24	25

C	1	2	3	4	5	6	7	8	9	10	11	12	13	14	15	16	17	18	19	20	21	22	23	24
B	1	2	3	4	5	6	7	8	9	10	11	12	13	14	15	16	17	18	19	20	21	22	23	24
A	1	2	3	4	5	6	7	8	9	10	11	12	13	14	15	16	17	18	19	20	21	22	23	24

Royal Opera House and Linbury Studio

✉ Covent Garden, WC2E 9DD

🏛 www.royaloperahouse.org

☎ (Box office) 020-7304 4000

🖨 020-7212 9460

↑ Located in the heart of Covent Garden, there are entrances into the Opera House from the Covent Garden Piazza and on Bow Street

🚇 Charing Cross

🚉 Charing Cross, Covent Garden

P There is no designated parking at the Royal Opera House – the nearest NCP car parks are a five-minute walk away at Drury Lane and Shelton Street, or there is limited onstreet parking after 6.30pm

♿ There is wheelchair access to the Stalls Circle, Grand Tier, Balcony and Upper Amphitheatre, as well as the Linbury Studio Theatre. Phone 020-7212 9123 for details

🎧 Assisted-hearing facility in both theatres

★ All areas of the house are open one-and-a-half hours before curtain-up, for ticket-holders only: for enquiries and reservations for the restaurants, phone 020-7212 9254. Restaurants include the Amphitheatre restaurant, with views across Covent Garden Piazza from the Terrace; the Vilar Floral Hall Balconies Restaurant in the spectacularly restored Floral Hall; and the Crush Room (cold food only). Bars include a long bar in the Floral Hall, with drinks, hot beverages and light snacks; the Champagne Bar in the Floral Hall; and the Amphitheatre bar, reached by the long bank of escalators from the Floral Hall

ⓘ Covent Garden Piazza; London Transport Museum; Theatre Museum

The third theatre on this site after its Theatre Royal predecessors burnt down in 1808 and 1856, the building that is now the Royal Opera House first opened for business in 1858 though it didn't take its current name until 1892. Now known as one of the finest lyric theatres in the world, it wasn't always thus: Covent Garden was, in its original incarnation, one of only two theatres, together with the Theatre Royal in Drury Lane, to be granted a royal patent to perform spoken drama in the capital, since theatre was considered a potentially subversive art.

As successive theatres opened on this site, opera and ballet became part of the fare that also included plays, cabarets and dancing. During the First World War, the theatre was requisitioned by the Ministry of Works for use as a furniture repository, and during the Second World War it became a Mecca Dance Hall.

After the war, Sadler's Wells Ballet became resident ballet company here, and a resident opera company was established thereafter. These for the forerunners to The Royal Ballet and The Royal Opera that were granted their Royal Charters in 1956 and 1968 respectively, and became the house companies.

While plans for refurbishment and expansion were mooted as early as 1975, with land being bequeathed to the Opera House by the then Labour Government for it, it wasn't until the establishment of the National Lottery in 1995 and a successful application for some of its proceeds that the long-heralded refurbishment finally took place. This included the addition of the excellent, versatile new Linbury Studio, a three-level theatre in the basement of the Royal Opera House for more small-scale work.

It is now as spectacular a theatre as it is possible to visit in London, though it comes at quite a price: severely restricted upper slips seats might let you hear for as little as £4 but to actually see can cost you as much as £130 or more. Ballet performances are substantially cheaper. But those are the extremes: there are definite attempts by the current management to shake off the venue's elitist image and make its work more accessible to all – whose tax pounds after all are its main form of funding. These plans include simultaneous live broadcasts on video screens to the Piazza outside.

Best seat in the house:

Seating is on five levels, rising in horseshoe configurations from the Stalls. The Orchestra Stalls, though closest to the action, isn't raked much so views can be obstructed; the shallow Stalls Circle, Grand Tier and Balcony levels are far better bets, though side seats can also lose views of parts of the stage. Views from the massive Amphitheatre are mostly uninterrupted, but very far and high from the stage, especially the further back you go.

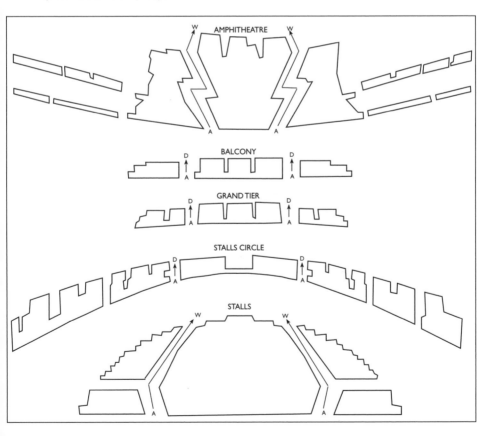

Sadler's Wells Theatre and Lilian Baylis Theatre

✉ Rosebery Avenue, EC1R 4TN

🖱 www.sadlerswells.com

☎ (Box office) 020-7863 8000

↑ Angel tube station in Islington is a short walk from the theatre. Turn left on exiting the station into Upper Street, and at the traffic lights continue straight into St John Street, and then second right into Rosebery Avenue

🚇 King's Cross then bus or 15-minute walk up Pentonville Road to Angel

⊖ Angel. If arriving by bus routes 19, 38, 73 or 341 and you present your single fare ticket at the Ticket Office before the start of the performance with your ticket for that performance, you will be refunded its cost and given the same cash amount for your return journey. A special Sadler's Express Bus service (SWX) leaves eight minutes after each evening performance to take patrons directly to Waterloo, Waterloo East and Victoria station, for which a fare

is payable

P Free street parking in surrounding streets after 6.30pm on weekdays and 1.30pm on Saturdays.

♿ Sadler's Wells maintains a free-to-join Access Address Book that offers appropriate seat locations and significantly reduced ticket prices, where possible, to patrons with particular needs. Contact 020-7863 8128 for details

🎧 BSL interpreted performances are offered, as well as captioned performances

👁 Audio introduction and audio described performances are offered, usually preceded by a touch tour of the stage

★ The Stage Door Café Bar, accessed via the glass doors from Rosebery Avenue, serves hot food, drinks and wine before matinee and evening performances. There are also bars in the Foyer and both circles

One of London's newest theatres, Sadler's Wells is the latest in a line of venues that have occupied this site for over 300 years. Originally a "musick house" that one Dick Sadler opened here in the 1680s, it has gone through several incarnations to arrive at its current opulent state as a state-of-the-art theatre that specialises in modern and classical dance. At various times housing a music hall and cinema, it was the legendary Lilian Baylis who put it on the map in the 1920s as an extension of her populist drive to bring drama to the South Bank at the Old Vic by adding dance and opera. It was here that the seeds were sown for both what became the Royal Ballet and English National Opera, but when those companies found their own feet elsewhere, Sadler's Wells became a receiving house for other companies from around the world.

While the theatre struggled with finding an identity at times, Lilian Baylis's remarkable legacy was honoured by the opening of a new studio theatre named in her honour in 1988, but a bigger step was taken when the old theatre was entirely demolished in 1996 and a new one built in its place. This gleaming, glass-fronted theatre – with the wells that partly give the theatre its name still visible under a panel at the rear of the Stalls – is now one of the most impressive dance houses in the capital.

Best seat in the house:

This large, modern theatre affords excellent views throughout, though rows in the Stalls and both circles are very wide and accessible by side aisles only, so arrive early if you are seated centrally!

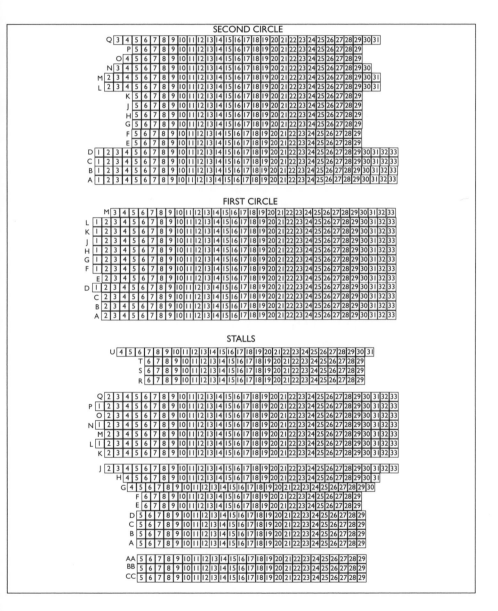

Sadlers Wells at The Peacock Theatre

✉ Portugal Theatre, WC2A 2HT

🖰 www.sadlerswells.com

☎ (Box office) 020-7863 8222

↑ Located off Kingsway, turn left on exiting Holborn station and walk down Kingsway towards the Aldwych. Bush House, the headquarters of the BBC's World Service, is at the bottom of Kingsway. Portugal Street is a turning on the left

⊖ Holborn

P Car park in Parker Street, or free onstreet parking behind the Peacock Theatre around Lincoln's Inn Field after 6.30pm

♿ Access and wheelchair spaces for disabled people are very limited – phone for details

🌠 Spacious Stalls and circle bars

Formerly the site of a spectacular theatre originally called the London Opera House and later the Stoll Theatre that was demolished and replaced by an office block in the '60s with a bleakly functional theatre in its basement, the Peacock Theatre is an attempt to re-brand the previously unloved Royalty Theatre that was for a long time the West End's biggest white elephant that no show wanted to appear in. While legend has it that the star of one of those shows — a dolphin called Flipper who died during its run — now haunts the theatre, it subsequently passed into use as a TV studio for *This is Your Life*.

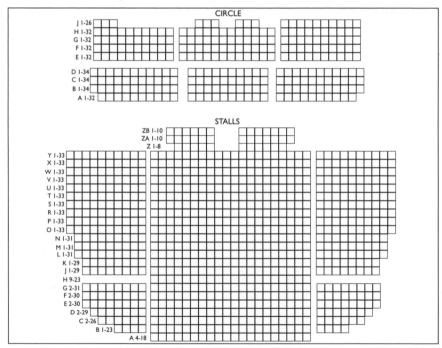

When Sadler's Wells had to relocate from Islington, however, during the rebuilding of their Islington base, they hired this theatre – now owned by the nearby London School of Economics and used by them as a sometime lecture theatre – to be their base, but since re-opening their Islington home has continued to operate this as a sister theatre in the West End, presenting a mixed bag of visiting dance, music and lyric theatre productions. Though the theatre itself is still a somewhat bleak subterranean experience, the foyers and spacious bars are now spruced up and inviting.

Best seat in the house:

Seating is on two levels – the Stalls goes back a long way so avoid the rear.

St John's, Smith Square

✉ Smith Square, SW1P 3HA

⌨ www.sjss.org.uk

☎ (Box office) 020-7222 1061

🖳 020-7233 1618

↑ From Westminster station go past Big Ben and the Houses of Parliament on your left, continue along Millbank then just before Lambeth Bridge turn into Dean Stanley Street. St John's in the middle of Smith Square

🚌 Victoria

⊖ Westminster, St James's Park

P Metered parking during the day, Monday-Friday

♿ Access for wheelchair users is difficult. Call the box office for details

◠ The hall is equipped with an induction loop system

⊠ The Footstall restaurant in the Crypt offers pre and post-concert buffet meals. Licensed bar

This grandiose Baroque church-turned-concert hall presents a wide rage of music, from solo performances to symphony orchestras. The acoustics are superb but some seats at the side, sold at a reduced price, are either restricted view or no view at all. Down in the vaulted crypt the restaurant is called 'The Footstool'. St John's became known as "Queen Anne's Footstool" after architect Thomas Archer apparently consulted Queen Anne on the design of his new church. The haughty monarch simply kicked over her footstool and said 'like that!' – thus the church's four towers are said to give the building the semblance of an upturned footstool. Charles Dickens, however, wrote in *Our Mutual Friend* that it was "a very hideous church with four towers at the corners resembling some petrified monster". Either way, the music inside always comes across with crystal clarity.

St Martin-In-The-Fields

✉ Trafalgar Square, WC2N 4JJ

🕆 www.stmartin-in-the-fields.org

☎ (Box office) 020-7839 8362

↑ The Church is located at the north-eastern corner of Trafalgar Square.

🚇 Charing Cross

⊖ Charing Cross, Embankment

P MasterPark in Spring Gardens, Trafalgar Square; NCP at Befordbury

🍴 The Café in the Crypt

Musical history was made at St Martin's. Handel played here on the first organ and Mozart is also reputed to have given a concert. Since then chamber groups, instrumental soloists and choirs from all around the world have taken advantage of the fine acoustics, and it's also home to the Academy of St Martin in the Fields, founded here by Sir Neville Marriner in 1959. So whether it's classical music, evening concerts by candlelight, or free lunchtime concerts, there's nothing like wandering in to this central London church and hearing the choir in full voice backed by the magnificent organ, followed by a Gothic slap-up meal in the Café in the Crypt downstairs.

The Place

✉ 17 Dukes Road, WC1H 9AB

🕆 www.theplace.org.uk

☎ (Box office) 020-7387 0031

🖨 020-7387 3504

↑ Dukes Road is on the south side of Euston Road, next to Upper Woburn Place

🚇 Euston

⊖ Euston Square

P Limited on-street parking

♿ Four wheelchair spaces available in the Robin Howard Dance Theatre (by prior arrangement)

🍴 Licensed café, open Monday to Saturday 9am -8pm (6.30pm on non-performance days). The Place Bar opens one hour before the start of performances.

ⓘ British Library

For a venue all about movement, The Place has certainly moved on after a major refurbishment in 1991. Housed in an impressive Victorian drill hall originally built for the Middlesex Artists' Rifle Volunteers, it's now home to the 300-seat Robin Howard Dance Theatre, the London Contemporary Dance School and Richard Alston Dance Company, and also provides a range of services for dance professionals, from dance classes to education projects. Seats for the Robin Howard Dance Theatre are unreserved and sold at a range of prices – the earlier you book, the cheaper the ticket. The contemporary-look downstairs café is not just a hang-out for dancers either: it's a handy local meeting point where they serve low-cost meals of high quality all day.

Wigmore Hall

✉ 36 Wigmore Street, W1U 2BP

🖰 www.wigmore-hall.org.uk

☎ (Box office) 020-7935 2141

🖨 020-7935 3344

📠 info@ wigmore-hall.org.uk

↑ Wigmore Hall is near the intersection of Wimpole Street and Wigmore Street

⊖ Bond Street

P Metered parking free after 6.30pm

Monday to Saturday and all day Sunday. NCP car park in Welbeck Street. MasterPark in Cavendish Square

♿ Three wheelchair spaces in the auditorium

🎧 Induction loop available

👁 Guide dogs welcome

🌟 Licensed bar, Wings café 020-7487 4874

Over 400 concerts a year are presented in this famous concert venue with pin-drop acoustics and comfortable seating, best enjoyed downstairs. Built in 1901, by the German piano firm Bechstein next to its showrooms on Wigmore Street, the Hall was intended to provide a venue both grandly impressive and yet intimate enough for recitals. It's so grandly appointed that you can spend half your time at a concert gazing at the wondrous Arts and Crafts cupola above the platform depicting the 'Soul of Music' gazing in rapture at the "Genius of Harmony" with the figures of Love and Psyche hovering somewhere in the background making music. If music still be the food of love, then it's worth a visit to Wings at Wigmore Hall (open evenings and all day Sundays), the Wigmore's excellent café serving freshly prepared food.

BALCONY

D 20 19 18 17 16 15 14 13 12 11	10 9 8 7 6 5 4 3 2 1
C 18 17 16 15 14 13 12 11 10	9 8 7 6 5 4 3 2 1
B 18 17 16 15 14 13 12 11 10	9 8 7 6 5 4 3 2 1
A 22 21 20 19 18 17 16 15 14 13 12	11 10 9 8 7 6 5 4 3 2 1

STALLS

4 3 2 1

X	19 18 17 16	15 14 13 12 11 10 9 8 7 6 5	4 3 2 1
W	19 18 17 16	15 14 13 12 11 10 9 8 7 6 5	4 3 2 1
V	19 18 17 16	15 14 13 12 11 10 9 8 7 6 5	4 3 2 1
U	19 18 17 16	15 14 13 12 11 10 9 8 7 6 5	4 3 2 1
T	19 18 17 16	15 14 13 12 11 10 9 8 7 6 5	4 3 2 1
S	19 18 17 16	15 14 13 12 11 10 9 8 7 6 5	4 3 2 1
R	19 18 17 16	15 14 13 12 11 10 9 8 7 6 5	4 3 2 1
Q	19 18 17 16	15 14 13 12 11 10 9 8 7 6 5	4 3 2 1
P	19 18 17 16	15 14 13 12 11 10 9 8 7 6 5	4 3 2 1
O	19 18 17 16	15 14 13 12 11 10 9 8 7 6 5	4 3 2 1
N	19 18 17 16	15 14 13 12 11 10 9 8 7 6 5	4 3 2 1
M	19 18 17 16	15 14 13 12 11 10 9 8 7 6 5	4 3 2 1
L	19 18 17 16	15 14 13 12 11 10 9 8 7 6 5	4 3 2 1
K	19 18 17 16	15 14 13 12 11 10 9 8 7 6 5	4 3 2 1
J	19 18 17 16	15 14 13 12 11 10 9 8 7 6 5	4 3 2 1
I	19 18 17 16	15 14 13 12 11 10 9 8 7 6 5	4 3 2 1
H	19 18 17 16	15 14 13 12 11 10 9 8 7 6 5	4 3 2 1
G	19 18 17 16	15 14 13 12 11 10 9 8 7 6 5	4 3 2 1
F	19 18 17 16	15 14 13 12 11 10 9 8 7 6 5	4 3 2 1
E	19 18 17 16	15 14 13 12 11 10 9 8 7 6 5	4 3 2 1
D	19 18 17 16	15 14 13 12 11 10 9 8 7 6 5	4 3 2 1
C	19 18 17 16	15 14 13 12 11 10 9 8 7 6 5	4 3 2 1
B	19 18 17 16	15 14 13 12 11 10 9 8 7 6 5	4 3 2 1
A	19 18 17 16	15 14 13 12 11 10 9 8 7 6 5	4 3 2 1
BB	19 18 17		3 2 1
AA	19 18		2 1

Children's Theatres

Chicken Shed Theatre Company

✉ Chase Side, Southgate, N14 4PE

🖱 www.chickenshed.org.uk

☎ (Box office) 020-8292 9222

↑ Ten minute walk from Cockfosters tube

⊖ Cockfosters

P On-street parking nearby

♿ Wheelchair-friendly venue

🎧 Infrared hearing loop system for all performance spaces

𝔇 Signed performances and stagetext for main house shows

👁 Touch tours and audio described performances. Braille printing, speech recognition software and other access aids available

🃏 Café

Was this the original Fame Academy? Established as a charity almost 30 years ago with the aim of aim of introducing theatre to children and young people from all backgrounds, Chicken Shed's bustling purpose-built red brick and glass premises has become a pioneering youth performance powerhouse with a community reach generating theatre activity and workshops right across London. The theatre itself has four performance spaces, a main 300-seat auditorium, a recording studio and a dance studio. Everyone loves Chicken Shed. The kids have performed with the Spice Girls, Meatloaf, Barnet-born Elaine Paige, Ricky Martin and Gabrielle. Chicken Shedders have appeared on numerous television specials and recorded "I Am In Love With The World" on the tribute album to Diana, Princess of Wales, who became a Chicken Shed patron. It's also supported by the likes of Dame Judi Dench, Trevor Nunn, Kenneth Branagh, and Emma Bunton, ensuring that this North London institution continues to live up to its Mission Statement to: "produce excellent, original and creative theatre which demonstrates that the performing arts belong to everyone."

Polka Theatre For Children

✉ 240 The Broadway, Wimbledon, SW19 1SB

🖱 www.polkatheatre.com

☎ (Box office) 020-8543 4888

📧 boxoffice@polkatheatre.com

↑ From Wimbledon and South Wimbledon stations several bus routes stop outside the theatre

🚉 Wimbledon/Wimbledon South

⊖ Wimbledon

P Pay and Display bays near the theatre. Car parks in Wimbledon town centre.

♿ Wheelchair spaces available

🎧 Sound amplification induction loop system

🃏 Café

Resembling a bright little Swiss chalet on a dull stretch of Wimbledon Road, the Polka Theatre is just what it says it is: a theatre exclusively for children – from toddlers and tiny tots to young teenagers, from school coach parties to family outings – serving a local community and the entire Greater London area. The staff are all child-experienced and the facilities are as child-friendly as you can get – a main 300-

seat auditorium with small seats, a 90-seat Adventure Theatre, a large foyer and box office space, a souvenir shop and café and even a playground. The Polka is famous way beyond the confines of Wimbledon, yet it still has to struggle for funding. Productions are invariably of a high standard. There are even 'Watch with Baby' performances for the under fours and their carers.

The Little Angel Theatre

✉ 14 Dagmar Passage, Cross Street, N1 2DN

⌂ www.littleangeltheatre.co.uk

☎ (Box office) 020-7226 1787

✉ info@littleangeltheatre.com

↑ Cross Street is mid-way between Highbury Corner and Angel, near to

St Mary's Church

⊖ Angel, Highbury & Islington

P Limited on-street metered parking

♿ Four wheelchair spaces

ᑎ Sound amplification induction loop system

A former bombed-out temperance hall hidden in the back passages of Islington has been home to the only permanent puppet theatre in London for more than 40 years. A recent funding crisis almost meant an end for the marionettes, rod and glove puppets and shadow-play figures, many of them carved in the 100-seat theatre's workshop, that have entertained generations of children. Fortunately an appeal in 2002 put this very special theatre back on a less precarious financial basis and it's really only thanks to the £180,000 raised by a "Save The Little Angel" campaign and the establishment of a Guardian Angel supporters scheme that strings are still being pulled at this internationally renowned institution.

The Puppet Theatre Barge

✉ Moored at Blomfield Road, Little Venice, W9

⌂ www.puppetbarge.com

☎ (Box office) 020-7249 6876 or via email

✉ puppet@movingstage.co.uk

↑ Moored along the Regent's Canal, close

to the Edgware Road and the Marylebone flyover

🅿 Paddington

⊖ Warwick Avenue, Paddington

P Very restricted on-street parking

🅇 Café

L ook out for the red and white candy striped awning of this former working canal barge converted by the Hackney-based Movingstage company into a curious little 50-seat space for puppet shows. Performances take place at Little Venice until mid-summer when the Puppet Theatre Barge wends its way along London's waterways for a summer tour.

Unicorn Theatre

✉ Unicorn Administration Offices, St
Mark's Studios, Chillingworth Road,
N7 8QJ

🖰 www.unicorntheatre.com

☎ (Box office) 020-7700 0702

In 1947 Caryl Jenner had a dream. She had formed the touring Unicorn Theatre but her vision was always to create a purpose-built theatre for children. For more than 20 years, the Unicorn lived at the Arts Theatre in the West End. More recently productions in London have been staged at venues as varied as the Open Air Theatre Regent's Park and the Cochrane Theatre. But soon Jenner's dream will finally come true when Unicorn's new £11.5 million home opens in Tooley Street, Southwark. Opening in 2005, and funded by the Arts Council of England (with Lottery funds), the Pool of London Partnership and private and public sources, the Unicorn will be London's first ever purpose-designed children's theatre venue. Plans for the project, part of the More London development near Tower Bridge, include a 350-seat main auditorium; a 120-seat studio, the Foyle Education Studio (funded by The Foyle Foundation) for projects, workshops and drama groups with children, families and teachers; a rehearsal studio and welcoming child-friendly public areas, with a café. In the meantime, Unicorn is touring its productions to various venues in London and the UK.

Major Fringe Theatres

BAC

✉ Lavender Hill, SW11 5TN

🖰 www.bac.org.uk

☎ (Box office) 020-7223 2223. (Stage door) 020-7223 6557, (Administration) 020-7602 3703

🖷 020-7978 5207

📠 boxoffice@bac.org.uk

↑ BAC is the Old Town Hall building half way up Lavender Hill, near the junction with Elspeth Road and Latchmere Road

🚇 Clapham Junction

⊖ Clapham Common or Stockwell. Both stations are a 15-minute bus journey away by the 345 bus.

P Single yellow line parking outside after 7pm

♿ The building has ramps and rails to the front door, and adapted toilets. To arrange seats in advance wheelchair users should call 020-7344 0055. Discounts available for wheelchair users and their companions

⌒ Induction loops in the theatres

🖑 Some signed performances

👁 Guide dogs welcome

🌟 A licensed bar and a café selling snacks, meals, confectionery and coffee

ⓘ Clapham shops and restaurants, Battersea Park

As one of the largest multimedia arts centres in the UK, the BAC is more than just a theatre. In fact there are three theatres: a multipurpose performance space seating around 150 people, Studio One and Studio Two, each with a seating capacity of 45. There are also rehearsal and meeting rooms, darkrooms, and the Lower and Grand Hall bringing BAC's total audience capacity to 1360. After an eight-year tenure as Artistic Director, Tom Morris left BAC early in 2004 to join the National Theatre as an Associate Director. Much of the BAC's experimental artistic energy has derived from the annual 'scratch programme' of innovative works in progress performed in front of a live audience, including most famously, *Jerry Springer – The Opera* that was fully developed at the National Theatre before transferring to the West End.

History:

Such was the civic pride of the citizens of 19th-century Battersea that they hired the architect for the Old Bailey to build them a magnificent Town Hall on Lavender Hill and even placed a plaque in the Grand Hall vestibule proclaiming their mission statement: 'Not for me, Not for you, But for us'. This superb Renaissance-style building was therefore always a community centre where entertainment, education and politics easily mixed. It was used for wedding receptions, theatre, concerts, a polling station and community events until demolition loomed in the late 1960, with Poet Laureate John Betjeman leading the fight to save it. By the 1970s it had become a council-run community centre, only to face closure again in 1979. This time local actors, including Timothy West and Prunella Scales, led the protests and eventually an independent trust was formed to re-open it 1981 as Battersea Arts Centre. By 1993 the splendid high Victorian mosaic and marble interior had been restored, and with the name changed to the BAC it has gone on to become one of London's top independent theatre venues, though still very much a community centre 'for us'.

Best seat in the house:

We like the BAC. Apart from the amazing diversity of productions, most performances have "Pay What You Can" nights on Tuesdays if they are running for two weeks or more. So you can see some amazing shows at knock-down prices. But there are no best seats. The unallocated seating is movable, depending on the style of the production, so it's best to arrive early, form a queue and stake your claim as soon as the doors open.

Bridewell Theatre

✉ Bride Lane, off Fleet Street, EC4Y 8EQ

🖥 www.bridewelltheatre.co.uk

☎ (Box office) 020-7936 3456, (Stage door) 020-7353 0259, (Administration) 020-7353 0259

📠 020-7583 5289

↑ Located near Blackfriars station, in a tiny lane located just off Fleet Street in the shadow of the imposing St Bride's Church

🚇 Blackfriars

🚌 Blackfriars, St Paul's

P Free street parking off Fleet Street after 6.30pm

♿ Contact the theatre in advance to make arrangements – there is a stair-lift available to bring patrons from street level to the box office foyer and theatre entrance level

🍸 Excellent spacious bar is an unusual feature of this non-pub based fringe theatre

ⓘ St Paul's Cathedral; Fleet Street; St Bride's Church with its wonderful wedding-cake spire

The Bridewell, like many fringe theatres, has typically existed on a wing-and-a-prayer of hope and charity; but now that the charity has been withdrawn, hope has not entirely been extinguished yet. Recently threatened with closure after its landlords The St Bride's Institute withdrew their rent-free status and grant, a vociferous campaign was launched to save it that resulted in the Corporation of London and Arts Council England providing one-off core funding of £30,000 each, which together with an additional £50,000 raised by an appeal to its audience has meant that it has been happily reprieved for now and been able to sign a new two-year lease at its current location. Since it was founded in 1994, it has become a powerhouse for the production of new and interesting musicals, and after a decade of the kind of adventurous work that isn't being done anywhere else in London in this field, it deserves to live on.

History:

A former indoor Victorian swimming pool – the changing booths still exist and the pool, beneath the floorboards, sometimes doubles as the orchestra pit – this wonderful "found space" was converted into an extremely versatile theatre in 1994.

Best seat in the house:

One of this theatre's most impressive facilities is its endless versatility, where the staging and seating can be adapted from show to show (or even removed entirely, so that the audience promenade). We've seen the theatre used with the stage end-on (in both directions), side-on with the seating arranged in three sides around it, and down-the-middle, with the seating arranged on either side of a traverse stage; but in every variation, it works. Seating is mostly unreserved, though a new strategy sells select allocated seating at a small additional price to save you having to scramble for the best seats when you arrive.

Bush Theatre

✉ Shepherd's Bush Green, W12 8QD

⌂ www.bushtheatre.co.uk

☎ (Box office) 020-7610 4224, (Stage door) 020-7602 3703, (Administration) 020-7602 3703

↑ Located on the south-west corner of Shepherd's Bush Green, next door to the Shepherd's Bush Empire pop concert venue and above the O'Neill's Irish-theme pub on the corner of Goldhawk Road

⊖ Shepherd's Bush, Goldhawk Road

P Free parking on local streets after 6.30pm, though it can be a mission to find a space!

& The theatre is located above a steep flight of stairs, but the theatre will do its best to accommodate

⊞ Rowdy pub downstairs; drinks bought there can be taken into the auditorium in plastic beakers

ⓘ Shepherd's Bush Green is across the street

New writing is the lifeblood of the theatre, and the Bush – which promises to read every script it receives – is at the forefront of this important genre, second only perhaps to the Royal Court in the London theatres whose raison d'etre it is. In its amazingly combustible auditorium, some wonderful theatre regularly takes place in the kind of highly intimate conditions for both actors and audience that has made it unique.

History:

One of London's longest-established, and most important, new writing venues, the Bush opened in April 1972 in what used to be the upstairs dining room of the Bush Hotel and had previously found service as Lionel Blair's dance studio. Since then, it has gone on to premiere new work by an international range of playwrights, many of them discovered here, including Stephen Poliakoff, Snoo Wilson, Ron Hutchinson, Terry Johnson, Kevin Elyot, Billy Roche, Tony Kushner, Catherine Johnson, Jonathan Harvey, Conor McPherson, Joe Penhall and Charlotte Jones, to name a few. Amongst the actors who have appeared here over the years, Victoria Wood and Julie Walters first worked together here, with Victoria writing her first sketch on an old typewriter backstage; and other actors who have appeared on its stage include Antony Sher, Bob Hoskins, Alan Rickman, Simon Callow, Jim Broadbent, Tim Roth and Jane Horrocks.

Best seat in the house:

Seating is unreserved in this L-shaped auditorium, and though recently refurbished, the new seating (now complete with backrests instead of the previous arrangement where you sat against the legs of the person behind you) is just as reassuringly uncomfortable as ever!

Gate Theatre

✉ 11 Pembridge Road, above Prince Albert Pub, Notting Hill Gate, W11 3HQ

☎ (Box office) 020-7229 0706

🖷 020-7221 6055

📠 gate@gatetheatre.freeserve.co.uk

↑ Take the Portobello Road exit at Notting Hill Gate tube station. With Notting Hill Gate behind you, the Gate Theatre is on your left, above the Prince Albert pub

🚄 Paddington

⊖ Notting Hill Gate

P Limited single yellow line parking outside

♿ Wheelchair users must transfer to a seat and be accompanied. Theatre is reached up a flight of stairs

🎧 Occasional sign interpreted performances. To book, call 020-7229 5387

👁 Guide dogs welcome

❌ No bar. Prince Albert pub is downstairs

ⓘ Portobello Road market

Strictly speaking, the Gate isn't really pub fringe. The pub in question, the Prince Albert, is separate, so you've no need to have anything to do with the chummy Toby Young types quaffing downstairs if you don't want to. You reach the theatre foyer by climbing a flight of stairs next to the pub entrance, usually with a sense of expectation that is invariably met by the production itself. If you do go downstairs during the interval, it's wise to keep one eye on your watch, as theatregoers have been known to forget to go back.

History:

The Gate was established in 1979, when the rush to open black box theatre venues in redundant function rooms above pubs was beginning to peak. Between 1979 and 1985 the founding Artistic Director was Lou Stein, who also opened the Gate at the Latchmere, Battersea, later known as the Grace and now simply known as the Latchmere. At the Gate, Stein laid down a marker for high-quality productions of new and classic work, often experimental or European and always essential viewing. Subsequent artistic directors have included Stephen Daldry (before he became an international film director), Mick Gordon and Erica Whyman who have picked up the challenge and developed major international and often 'themed' programming. Key London Arts Board and Cameron Mackintosh Foundation funding ensured that this important little theatre continued to present new writers and revivals of classics. As the LAB has said, it is creative spaces like this that "demonstrate innovation, high-quality work and who are supporting emerging talent and building new audiences."

Best seat in the house:

Monday evenings at the Gate are always worth considering. A "happy Mondays" policy means that the first 30 tickets on the door are sold for as much (or little!) as you can afford. Given that this is a tiny 100-seat black box space where the playing area varies dramatically from production to production, it's also worth arriving early as well in order to choose a good vantage point, as the seating is unreserved.

Hackney Empire

✉ 291 Mare Street, Hackney, E8 1EJ

🖑 www.hackneyempire.com

☎ (Box office) 020-8985 2424, (Stage door) 020-8510 4515

🖨 020-8510 4530

🕓 Box office open from 12noon-6pm.

↑ The Hackney Empire is in Mare Street, adjacent to Hackney Town Hall. The Bullion Room Theatre is at the rear of the Hackney Empire, in Wilton Way

🚇 Hackney Central

⊖ Bethnal Green

P Some on-street parking off Mare Street. Beware! Restrictions apply until 11 pm

♿ Phone for access details

⭐ Bars at all levels.

ⓘ The Ocean music venue, Geffrye Museum

A glorious show biz history hangs over the Hackney Empire, but for donkey's years the glum fabric of the building has been more reminiscent of a dodgy flea-pit. The £15 million rejuvenation programme to restore it to its former gleaming glory has been led by Griff Rhys Jones, backed by the likes of David Baddiel, Ben Elton, Josie Lawrence and Harold Pinter. It reopened in 2004, with a brand new orchestra pit, high-tech backstage facilities, restored features and new seating, and the Hackney Empire is sure to bring theatrical riches to one of London's poorest boroughs.

History:

Hackney Empire is a true Palace of Varieties. Built by Frank Matcham for the famous Stoll circuit in 1901 it was an East End rival to the London Palladium and Victoria Palace, designed on a lavish scale to resemble an Italian opera house, with an elaborate Moorish, Gothic and Rococo interior unrivalled in London's theatreland. Marie Lloyd, Charlie Chaplin and Stan Laurel are among the artistes appearing on the then state-of-the-art all-electric stage. Variety continued until well after the Second World War. Like the Palladium, all the great names played the Empire. But by the 1960s, variety was in its death throes, and the Empire had become the home of the new weekend commercial television channel, ATV. Ironically, when Mecca Bingo moved in, much of the theatre's threadbare Edwardian splendour was covered in Formica, thus preserving it for the future. In 1986 a touring theatre group, CAST, established New Variety at the Empire, developing, under the direction of Roland Muldoon, new generations of performers and presenting an eclectic mix of stand-up, plays, opera, musicals and pantomime – all geared to attract diverse local multi-ethnic audiences. An exciting new phase began in 2004 when the Empire reopened after a major £15 million refurbishment.

Best seat in the house:

You can see from almost anywhere in this fabulous auditorium, which is so spectacular it becomes part of the show.

Hampstead Theatre

✉ Eton Avenue, NW3 3EU

🖊 www.hampsteadtheatre.com

☎ (Box office) 020-7722 9301, (Stage door) 020-7449 4200

🖨 020-7449 4201, (Administration) 020-7449 4200

↑ Located just off the massive Swiss Cottage gyratory traffic system in a quiet, mainly residential side street, a minute from Swiss Cottage tube station

🚇 Silverlink to Finchley Road and Frognal (on the Richmond-North Woolwich line), or Silverlink to South Hampstead (on the Watford Junction-London Euston line)

⊖ Right next to Swiss Cottage, or a five-minute walk to Finchley Road

P Limited street parking after 6.30pm

♿ The theatre is fully wheelchair accessible. The main entrance is at ground floor level, with accessible toilets on all three levels of the theatre, and wheelchair spaces both in the main auditorium and studio space

🎧 Induction loops and infrared audio reinforcement in both auditoria

👁 Orientation tapes and scripts can be provided in advance on free loan. Guide dogs can be taken into both auditoria, or the theatre can look after them

🎫 Café bar is open throughout the day from 9am till after the performance, serving hot food, snacks and drinks. Pre-show supper or interval snacks can be ordered in advance. Call 020-7449 4205 for details

ⓘ Though called Hampstead Theatre, it's actually at Swiss Cottage – Hampstead Village is a short drive (or long walk) up Fitzjohns Avenue

Hampstead Theatre has long nurtured new writing at the top of its artistic agenda, and is continuing to do so in its splendid new home that replaces the ragged charm of its intimate old auditorium with a splendidly curved new main theatre with seating on two levels that can be flexibly arranged to accommodate audiences from 140 to 325 people. A zinc drum that rises from the lower foyer to jut up through the roof encloses the elliptical-shaped Stalls and Balconies that run behind and over the Stalls. In the basement, a large education studio, The Space, is a workshop area that is dedicated to the theatre's work with young people and the community. The whole building, filled with natural light during the daytime, is intended to be a great new public space for the area, with a café that is open all day and evening.

History:

Founded in a Scout Hall in the heart of Hampstead Village with an opening season that included two new plays by Harold Pinter (*The Room* and *The Dumb Waiter*), the theatre moved to a temporary prefab in Swiss Cottage in 1962 – and continued to occupy it for the next 40 years! In 2002, however, that site – next to Swiss Cottage Library, just around the corner from its current location – finally closed, to be replaced by the spanking new wood-and-glass rectangular building just 50 metres away, as London's first purpose-built, stand-alone, producing indoor theatre to be built since the National opened in 1976. At a cost of £15.7million, it opened its doors on 13 February 2003.

Best seat in the house:

The seating is flexible so may change from production to production, but the Stalls area includes long rows of comfortable seating (the legroom is dreadful). Sit to the sides if you don't want to feel trapped!

King's Head Theatre

✉ 115 Upper Street, Islington, N1 1QN

⌂ www.kingsheadtheatre.org

☎ (Box office) 020-7226 1916

🖷 020-7226 8507

↑ Opposite St Mary's Church and next to the Post Office in Upper Street

🚉 Highbury & Islington, King's Cross

⊖ Angel, Highbury & Islington

P Upper Street is a Red Route. Some parking bays outside theatre. NCP at the Business Design Centre, off

Upper Street

♿ Racks at front of theatre

♿ Level but limited access across an invariably crowded pub. One adapted toilet

🌟 Pub open during licensing hours. Pre-show dinner menu served in the theatre. Food and snacks also available in the pub

ⓘ Upper Street shopping, Chapel Market, Screen on the Green cinema, Islington Business and Design Centre

The longest-running joke about the King's Head is that when the plays are good the food is bad and when the food improves the plays get worse. But however serious its financial, artistic or culinary ups and downs may be, the King's Head remains an obstinate maverick among fringe theatres and too unkempt for the arts funding industry. It's always a fun place to visit at any time of the day, although the grim downstairs loos are like slop tanks. But it's at its roar-of-the-greasepaint-smell-of-the-crowd best during the noisy pre- and apré-show meleé in the pub, where theatregoers, bar flys, old peculiars and young trendolas rub shoulders and shout at each other. Nowadays, the contrast between this human vagabondage and the bland restaurants and bars in the rest of Upper Street is startling.

History:

Ever since the early 1970s Dan Crawford and the King's Head Pub and Theatre have gone together like Highbury & Islington. By a fluke of chance, Crawford, who is still the Artistic Director, obtained a lease on the shabby old pub that dated back to the 1850s, and in the spirit of true fringe set about putting on a show with no money. The back room of the pub, a ramshackle den which had been variously employed as a boxing booth and a pool room, became recycled as the auditorium. Crawford begged and borrowed red velvet drapes, elderly lamps and moth-eaten old seats from the Theatre Royal, Haymarket and the soon-to-be-demolished Scala Theatre in Goodge Street, and was soon in business, putting on an eclectic and sometimes eccentric programme of old and new plays, musicals, revue, Sunday night shows and lunchtime productions which has continued until today. Always teetering on the edge of financial catastrophe, the theatre has nevertheless got by, thanks to the pub takings and its supporters known as 'Plums' (Baby, Sugar, Golden and Life), and has always attracted big star names (a very young Victoria Wood cut her comedy teeth here and still does fund-raising performances for the venue at the Albert Hall), waning old stars (Anthony Newley bombed here at the end of his career) and eager new writers. Recent renovations have included new seating and air cooling, and an upgraded pre-show menu. More than 35 plays and musicals have transferred from this tiny stage in a 120-seat back room to the West End and Broadway, winning no less than four Tony Awards.

Best seat in the house:

The King's Head has never quite managed to solve the problem of serving food before the show and having to keep the tables and chairs screwed to the floor for fire safety reasons. For years you used to come out with lumber pain because of the awful viewing angle. But new bench tables have been installed parallel with the stage, which means that after your meal you just turn round to watch the show. Seats are unreserved, so if you don't eat it's best to stick like superglue to the front of the queue and make for the row of front row seats to the left of the stage. If that's too close, stake you claim to the benches at the back, or wait for the serving hatch to close and perch on the fold-down form.

Lyric Hammersmith Theatre and Lyric Studio

✉ King Street, Hammersmith, W6 0QL

⌨ www.lyric.co.uk

☎ (Box office) 020-8741 2311/ 08700 500 511

🖳 020-8741 7694

📠 tickets@lyric.co.uk

↑ At the eastern end of King Street, next to the King's Mall shopping centre

⊖ Hammersmith

P Limited on-street parking nearby. NCP at King's Mall shopping centre.

♿ All levels accessible by lift. Main theatre: space for three wheelchairs in row R at the back of the Stalls. The theatre also has accessible transfer seats at the end of rows on the left hand side of the auditorium.

Wheelchair users must transfer to a seat and be accompanied. The Studio: two wheelchairs positioned at the front of the seating area

🎧 Regular sign interpreted performances

𝄢 Regular open-captioned performances

👁 Guide dogs are welcome in the auditorium or dog-sitting can be arranged. Touch tours of the set can be arranged. Audio described performances for certain performances

🌟 Two bars. Cafe Brera counter-service restaurant open from 9:30am for breakfast, lunch, dinner and snacks, Monday to Saturday

ⓘ Hammersmith Palais, London Apollo Hammersmith, Riverside Studios

However varied the quality of the productions, red plush past and plain present always collide when you visit the Lyric. But it's a theatre approaching the future with confidence. Adjacent Lyric Square has been transformed with an outdoor performance space, a grove of trees, new seating and lighting, a water feature and a market area. With it have come ambitious plans that have created a dramatic new glass-fronted entrance for the theatre, plus a new box office and café and new backstage spaces.

History:

Designed by theatre architecture maestro Frank Matcham and opened by Lillie Langtry in 1895, the Lyric is one of London's great theatrical survivors. From its glamorous Victorian heyday to Edwardian era "Blood and flea pit", from West End appendage to outright closure, from burning to the ground and wholesale demolition to becoming the centrepiece of a 1970s development, the Lyric has entered the 21st century looking as if its here to stay. Behind the unimpressive office block exterior and bland but ample public spaces, is a truly magnificent three-tiered interior, carefully recreated in 1978 from original Matcham plasterwork. It's just like walking into a Tardis. Under Neil Bartlett's artistic direction the Lyric has become a community hub, offering free first nights and cheap tickets for local residents and an eclectic programme of in-house and visiting productions. The 540-seat gilt-edged auditorium contrasts with the stark 110-seat black box Lyric Studio which is now targeting young adults with cutting-edge companies like Frantic Assembly and Peepolykus.

Best seat in the house:

Much of the seating at the Lyric looks and feels as if it was installed in the 1970s and has stayed put ever since. Many springs have lost their bounce, so if you are unlucky you could be forced to slouch when you should be sitting up and paying attention. That said, sightlines are good throughout the main auditorium, even if legroom is cramped. Best Stalls seats for protecting your knees are at the ends of rows D, F and R. The configuration of the Studio changes depending on the production. You watch from no-frills, tip-up, bum-aching chairs that bring new meaning to the term "cutting-edge theatre".

Orange Tree Theatre

✉ 1 Clarence Street, Richmond, Surrey, TW9 2SA

⊕ www.orangetreetheatre.co.uk

☎ (Box office) 020-8940 3633

↑ The Orange Tree Theatre is about 50 yards from Richmond Station. After leaving the station, turn right into Kew Road until you reach Clarence Street. The daytime box office is at 53 Kew Road, Richmond

🚇 Richmond

⊖ Richmond

P   Old Deer Park. Limited on-street parking

♿ Wheelchair spaces by arrangement. Ramps fitted to staircases. Disley seat available – a high, firm orthopaedic seat with arms

🎧 Sennheiser infrared hearing system

♪ Regular signed performances

👁 Guide dogs are welcome. Regular audio-described performances. Talking brochure available at the Box Office. A touch tour of set and props can be arranged prior to any performance

🍸 One licensed bar

ⓘ Richmond Green, Richmond Park

For Richmondites, the Orange Tree is now an indispensable local resource, reaching out to local schools and even to old folk's homes. Perhaps unfairly, for outsiders, the words "middle" and "class" sometimes come to mind when you turn up and find yourself surrounded by an audience of pashmina-wearing ladies and their husbands. But once you leave your prejudices in the cloakroom, it really does feel like a family night out where everyone knows everybody else – a far cry from impersonal West End venues. Oh, and the plays are generally well worth seeing too.

History:

Once affectionately described as a "theatrical totter", the Orange Tree's artistic director Sam Walters founded the theatre in 1971 in a room above the Orange Tree pub where a group of enthusiastic actors and directors presented drama, musicals, classics and revivals, bringing locals an new alternative to nearby Richmond Theatre's touring fare. Fame spread far and wide and by the 1980s the pub ambience was restricting the growth of this expanding community theatre. After a long fund-raising campaign a brand new 170-seat theatre was opened in 1991 in a former a Victorian school just opposite the pub, and the Orange Tree made history – as the first purpose-built theatre-in-the-round in London, leading to a long-standing natural synergy with Alan Ayckbourn's Stephen Joseph theatre in Scarborough. Walters, now an MBE, is still the Orange Tree's theatrical totter, presenting and often directing high-standard revivals, new plays and neglected classics. He's also overseen a £500,000 fund-raising campaign, launched by Lord Attenborough and Victoria Hamilton, to build new rehearsal rooms and much needed wardrobe space in the Bank building next door.

Best seat in the house:

Not so much in-the-round as in-the-square, seats are unreserved in this compact auditorium, but they are all good for sightlines and you can choose downstairs or upstairs. Downstairs there are three long rows of well-padded benches surrounding a boxing ring-size stage. Upstairs there's only one row edging the performance space and you do have to look down, but you feel so close-up to the actors that you can almost reach out and touch their wigs.

Riverside Studios

✉ Crisp Road, Hammersmith, W6 9PL

🖰 www.riversidestudios.co.uk

☎ (Box office) 020-8237 1111

↑ Walking from the bus station or District/Piccadilly tube, walk through Hammersmith Broadway shopping centre, take the south exit by Tesco Metro, continue in front of the London Apollo Theatre, turn left into Queen Caroline Street and left into Crisp Road. Riverside Studios is on your right

⊖ Hammersmith

P Limited on-street parking in Crisp

Road and Queen Caroline Street.

🖲 Hammersmith

♿ Wheelchair spaces by prior arrangement. Adapted toilet in the main corridor.

𝄞 Hearing loop

🖐 Some signed performances.

👁 Guide dogs are welcome, by prior arrangement

🍴 Large licensed bar and café with a menu including pasta meals

ⓘ London Apollo Theatre, Hammersmith Bridge, Lyric Theatre, Hammersmith Palais

Once you've found it, the Riverside's contemporary-look glass frontage welcomes you to a kind of arty feeding frenzy, with theatregoers mingling with cinema fans and workshop people tangling with those here to see the art hanging on the walls. At most times of the day the echoing café-bar located at one end of the building seems to be the throbbing heart of the place, jam-packed with a friendly young going-out crowd creating a happy alcoholic melee that can sometimes be heard in the main theatre studio. If you are having a pre-show meal, and the food is actually very good and affordable here, make sure you grab a table quick.

History:

Now a bustling arts and media centre on the north bank of the Thames, this venue goes back to the 1930s when it opened as Riverside Film Studios. Later it was used as a scoring stage to record music in stereo for early CinemaScope films. In 1955 the BBC bought it and classic TV comedies like *Hancock's Half Hour* were recorded here. It was also the first studio in the UK to broadcast colour television. Today the building houses a contemporary art gallery, a cinema and two studio theatre spaces as well as a popular bar and a café. The theatre productions from visiting companies can range from the magnificent Complicité to the downright awful.

Best seat in the house:

The main studio is huge, accommodating around 400 people on steeply raked rows of reserved grandstand seating. Depending on the production, you can usually see from most corners of the auditorium, except that you can feel too far away the further back you get. Ask for the front row and you won't go too far wrong. The seats are of the tip-up plastic variety so don't expect any concessions to audience comfort. The same applies in the smaller studio.

Soho Theatre and Writers' Centre

✉ 21 Dean Street, WID 3NE

🖳 www.sohotheatre.com

☎ (Box office) 020-7478 0100,
(Stage door) 020-7287 5060,
(Administration) 020-7287 5060

↑ Located in the heart of Soho, north of Old Compton Street and south of Oxford Street

🚇 Charing Cross

⊖ Short walk from Piccadilly Circus, Oxford Circus and Tottenham Court Road; the latter is closest

P Not advisable! On-street parking in Soho is mostly resident-bay only, and is strictly enforced by Westminster City Council!

♿ Fully accessible, by lift to the theatre

🎧 Infrared hearing system

🖐 Sign-language interpreted performances are given for every in-house production; check with box office for schedule

👁 audio-described performances are given for every in-house production; check with box office for schedule

🍴 Small terrace bar on the 2nd floor, next to entrance to the theatre; main theatre bar is in the downstairs restaurant, the Cafe Lazeez brasserie, an attractive, fashionable space serving attractive, fashionable food

ⓘ Soho Square and Oxford Street heading north; Piccadilly heading south

Though the Royal Court, Bush and Hampstead theatres still lead the way in new writing, Soho Theatre is rapidly gaining ground, trailblazing in discovering new writers and not merely premiering new plays. This emphasis on nurturing writers is reflected in the very name of the splendid building the company has acquired for itself.

History:

Originally founded in 1969 and occupying basement premises called the Soho Poly, located in Riding House Street near Oxford Circus until 1990, the company had a peripatetic physical existence for most of the '90s except for a three year residency at Lisson Grove's Cockpit Theatre from 1992-5, though it produced work elsewhere and continued its extensive education and community programmes. It also secured and found new premises at 21 Dean Street, which it purchased (largely with Lottery funding) and converted into a smart new purpose built theatre. The rental of the smart, street-level restaurant below it goes to pay all the building's overheads and frees the theatre's funding to be spent purely on artistic activities.

Best seat in the house:

This intimate house, with seating on comfortably cushioned benches arranged in a generous rake, has excellent sightlines everywhere, but to feel close to the action without being squashed up, arrive early to get a seat towards the front – seats are unreserved.

Southwark Playhouse

✉ 62 Southwark Bridge Road,, SE1 OAS

🌐 www.southwarkplayhouse.co.uk

☎ (Box office) 020-7620 3494 (Stage door) 020-7652 2224, (Administration) 020-7652 2224

📧 boxoffice@southwarkplayhouse.co.uk

↑ A block from Southwark Bridge, just south of the river and near to Shakespeare's Globe and the Tate Modern, this tiny theatre is located

off a lovely little courtyard

🚇 London Bridge

🚇 Borough, Southwark, London Bridge

P Free street parking after 6.30pm

♿ The theatre is accessible – ring for details

🍸 Tiny bar just next to theatre entrance

ⓘ Tate Modern; Shakespeare's Globe

This versatile little theatre now attracts national media attention and in 2003 even had a West End transfer when its production of *Through the Leaves*, starring Simon Callow, moved to the Duchess Theatre. Great things have come from this theatre already – it's one of the ones to watch for the future.

History:

A former Victorian tea and coffee warehouse, Southwark Playhouse took on a theatrical life in 1993 and in just a decade has established itself as a leading London studio theatre that also serves the local community. Its stated mission is to present "innovative, high quality drama in an historic building accompanied by a professional and comprehensive education programme for local children and adults" and that just about sums it up.

Best seat in the house:
A flexible space means seating changes from production to production.

Theatre Royal Stratford

✉ Gerry Raffles Square, Stratford, E15 1BN

🖰 www.stratfordeast.com

☎ (Box office) 020-8534 0310

🖳 020-8534 8381

📠 theatreroyal@stratfordeast.com

↑ From either Stratford Broadway or Stratford station head for Stratford Shopping Centre and follow the signs

🚇 Stratford

🚌 Stratford

P Very little on-street parking. Use the Shopping Centre car park.

🖈 Racks outside the theatre

♿ Wheelchair spaces in theatre, with lifts to the upper level. Phone the Community Liaison Officer 020-8279 1121, who helps with booking seats and any other access queries

🎧 Sennheiser Infrared system

🤟 Occasional signed performances

👁 Guide dogs allowed

🔲 Theatre Workshop Bar open from 11am Mon-Sat, whether you are seeing a show or not. The Ken Hill Bar is the Dress Circle bar

ⓘ Stratford Shopping Centre

The Theatre Royal is unique among London's theatres. You don't just go to see a show: it's an entire way of life. Nowhere else attracts such intense loyalty among both those who work there and the audience. It was like that in Joan's Littlewood's time and it's still like that today, when anyone who is old enough to have actually seen one of her Theatre Workshop productions simply wouldn't recognise Stratford, which is now a kind of regeneration boomtown. Newham Council recently refurbished the theatre, adding a new booking office space, a new bar and terraces and new dressing rooms. It must be the only theatre in town where you'll see cockney teenagers selling programmes one minute and appearing on stage in the latest urban musical theatre project the next. Production quality control varies, but the community feeling is a constant and the audience is usually part of the show.

History:
Built in 1884 when the East End was all gaslight and pea-soupers, the Theatre Royal never enjoyed an impressive frontage. But the interior was, and still is, charming without too much Victorian ornamentation. It's a miracle that any of this has survived. Two world wars, various closures and the indignity of taking in touring nude shows with titles like *Strip, Strip Hooray* brought this shabby, neglected pile close to collapse. Until in 1953, at a time when redundant theatres were being demolished all over London, an unknown company called Theatre Workshop turned up to perform *Twelfth Night*. The rest is history. Joan Littlewood's ensemble changed the face British theatre forever, let alone the fate of the dingy old Theatre Royal. Eventually they became the darling of the West End with groundbreaking productions like *A Taste of Honey* and *Oh, What A Lovely War*. After Littlewood left in 1974, the theatre retained its community pulling power, which is currently enjoying a new renaissance within Newham's multi-culturally

diverse population, producing community-oriented drama, musicals and revues.

Best seat in the house:

The 460-seat, three-tiered auditorium was restored in 1992. Apart from the front few rows most seats in the Stalls, the cosy Dress Circle, and even the Upper Circle have a good view of the stage. If they don't, you'll get hefty discount off your ticket price to make up for any restrictions.

Tricycle Theatre

✉ 269 Kilburn High Road, NW6 7JR

🖰 www.tricycle.co.uk

☎ (Box office) 020-7328 1000

↑ Located in the heart of the Kilburn High Road, just beyond a railway bridge next to Brondesbury Railway station.

🚉 Brondesbury (Silverlink) station is nearby

⊖ Kilburn

P Free on-street parking after 6.30pm, but can be difficult to find!

ᕕ Level access through both entrances

to the foyer, bar, café and box office areas; access to the Stalls of the theatre is by steps or to the wheelchair seats by lift. Space for two wheelchairs – staff are happy to assist, but each wheelchair user must be accompanied. Accessible toilet to the left of the theatre box office, and a second in the basement, accessible by lift from the main foyer

∩ Induction loop; sign-interpreted performances in British sign language is offered for some shows

✖ Small food counter offering hot and cold specials of the day

One of London's most community-minded local theatres, the Tricycle (or Trike, as it universally known) presents work that reflects the cultural diversity of its neighbourhood, with plays by Irish, African-Caribbean, Jewish and Asian writers in particular. It has regularly presented UK premieres for plays by American black writer August Wilson, and its productions of the musicals *Ain't Misbehavin'* and *Kat and the Kings* have all transferred to the West End. It was also at the Tricycle that the Irish hit comedy *Stones in His Pockets* began its London life, as did the theatrical reconstruction of the Stephen Lawrence Inquiry, *The Colour of Justice*, that subsequently played at the National Theatre and was televised.

History:

Founded in 1980 by Shirley Barrie and Ken Chubb, this theatre in the converted Foresters' Hall was almost totally destroyed by a fire that started in a neighbouring timber-yard in 1987, but it was totally rebuilt with expanded front-of-house facilities. In 1998, a new 300-seater cinema building was completed alongside the theatre.

Best seat in the house:

Seating is mostly on unreserved benches, though some allocated seating can now be bought at an additional charge. The best row of these is the front row of the first Gallery, though the cramped Stalls benches have the advantage of bringing you really close to the action.

Young Vic Theatre

✉ 66 The Cut, SE1 8LZ

⌂ www.youngvic.org

☎ (Box office) 020-7928 6363 (Stage door) 020-7922 8400, (Administration) 020-7922 8400

🗄 020-7922 8401

📧 boxoffice@youngvic.org

↑ Located in the Cut, diagonally opposite and further along the street from the Old Vic, near Waterloo Station and the new Southwark tube stop

🚇 Waterloo and Waterloo East

⊖ Waterloo, Southwark

P Free onstreet parking after 6.30pm

♿ Level access to foyer and (usually, depending on configuration) into auditorium, with adapted toilets available

🎧 Sennheiser Infrared system.

🍴 Pre-performance restaurant and full bar service operated by Konditor and Cook, a local bakery.

ⓘ Old Vic; South Bank

This "temporary" building – built of breezeblock and steel – hides behind an entrance foyer that used to be a butcher's shop (the tiling is still apparent). It's one of London's best flexible studio spaces, with seating on two levels, plus a tiny Studio theatre next to the bar restaurant. The theatre pursues a vigorous artistic agenda of classical and new plays targeted at a youthfully democratic audience.

History:

Built in 1969 as a studio space for the National Theatre when it as based at the Old Vic and intended to last just five years, this temporary building has lasted over thirty – but is now in serious need of redevelopment. An extensive rebuild will finally commence in the summer of 2004 that will see the theatre closed for two years, though the company will continue to produce during this time elsewhere, as the Royal Court did during its lengthy re-fit. After the National left it in 1973, the theatre has had its own artistic identity – one embodied by its mission statement that it's "a theatre for everybody but, above all, for younger artists and a younger audience". The largest flexible space in London, productions can take place in the round, thrust, traverse or even proscenium, for an audience of up to 450 people.

Best seat in the house:

Arrive early to secure the best seats, since the theatre is unreserved; though often what are the best seats won't be apparent until after the show has actually started, since every show here is arranged to a different seating configuration.

Minor Fringe Theatres

Arcola Theatre

✉ 27 Arcola Street, E8 2DJ

⌂ www.arcolatheatre.com

☎ (Box office) 020-7503 1646 (Stage door) 020-7503 1645, (Administration) 020-7503 1645

📠 info@arcolatheatre.com

↑ Located on the Dalston and Stoke Newington border, Arcola Street runs off Stoke Newington Road, a few minutes from Dalston Kingsland BR

🚊 Dalston Kingsland

🚇 Highbury & Islington, then bus 30 or Liverpool Street, then bus 149

P Street parking after 6.30pm

♿ phone theatre for access details

🍴 Café bar is open daily 10am-10pm

Opened in 2001 in a former clothing factory, the Arcola has quickly established itself as a vibrant local community theatre, attracting interest from far afield. It has already been recognised with the Time Out Award in 2003 for Outstanding Achievement and the Peter Brook Empty Space Award in 2002. Though it is publicly unfunded, it is run on the immense enthusiasm and commitment of founding artistic director Mehmet Ergen, who lives, breaths and sleeps the place. Its diet of new and old plays is never obvious, but consistently challenging.

Barons Court Theatre

✉ The Curtain's Up pub, 28A Comeragh Road, W14 9RH

☎ (Box office) 020-8932 4747

↑ From Barons Court tube exit into Gliddon Road then turn right, walk down Palliser Road and take the third left. The Curtain's Up pub is on the corner of Vereker Road. From West Kensington tube, turn left into North End Road, then right into Barons Court Road until you reach Vereker Road on your left

🚇 Barons Court or West Kensington

P Resident's parking bays. Limited on-street parking

🚊 Barons Court or West Kensington

♿ The basement theatre is not fully wheelchair accessible

🍴 The Curtain's Up serves pub grub meals

ⓘ The Queen's Club, Earl's Court Exhibition Centre, Olympia

A theatre in a basement? Barons Court Theatre is a good example of what you can get away with on the shoestring fringe. Unless you are barking mad, you'd never think of staging plays deep down in the cellar of an old Victorian pub where the original vaulting obstructs the view of the performance space. But that's just what they've been doing at Barons Court Theatre, where for a dozen years or more directors, actors and audiences have nosed their way in and around the downstairs dankness for the sake of the drama. The seats, wedged on three sides of a stage between the archways, feel as if they've been plundered from a bug-hutch biograph cinema. Maybe this what's meant by in-yer-face theatre – the actors are so close you can smell their breath. The mini box office is also down here, looking like an entrance to a bargain basement grotto. Upstairs the Curtain's Up pub, previously known as Barons Ale House and the Barons Court Tavern, is decorated with theatrical memorabilia, but the clientele is mostly an un-luvvie West London crew of noisy Antipodeans and overseas students. The pub grub's good, there are tables outside, and they even ring a bell to let you know when to descend to the dramatic cavern beneath this theatrical tavern.

Blue Elephant Theatre

✉ 59A Bethwin Road, SE5 OXT
🖱 www.blueelephanttheatre.co.uk
☎ (Box office) 020-7701 0100
🖷 020-7701 7870
↑ Located off Camberwell Road that leads from the Walworth Road from Elephant and Castle, this theatre is tucked away but worth discovering. Even when you find Bethwin Road that gives the theatre its address, its actual entrance is in Thompson's

Avenue
⊖ Elephant and Castle then a bus; or Oval then a bus
P Limited street parking after 6.30pm
🚌 Elephant and Castle then a bus; or Oval then a bus
♿ Level access to the ground level studio theatre, with adapted toilet available
🎧 Induction loop available
🎫 Small upstairs bar

Established in 1999, this excellent studio theatre on the ground floor and welcoming bar upstairs is in a hard-to-find location, but worth the effort. With just 66 seats, it is extremely intimate, and the versatile stage is relatively large.

Brick Lane Music Hall

✉ 443 North Woolwich Road, E16 2DA
🖱 www.bricklanemusichall.co.uk
☎ (Box office) 020-7511 6655
📧 fun@bricklanemusichall.co.uk
↑ North Woolwich Road is reached via the A13 and Silvertown Way
🚌 Silvertown (Silverlink from Stratford East or Richmond)
⊖ Canning Town, then 69 or 474 bus to Thames Barrier Park stop. Prince

Regent DLR, then 473 bus to Silvertown station
P Ample car and coach parking on-site
♿ Access at ground level, with no steps. Wheelchair access into auditorium and bar. Guide dogs welcome. Advise box office when booking
🎫 A three-course meal is included in the ticket price. Fully licensed bar
ⓘ London City Airport, Thames Barrier

After the success of the original Brick Lane Music Hall in Brick Lane (in a former brewery canteen), which then moved to nearby Curtain Road (to a former button factory), this unique supper and show venue has upped sticks and moved further east to Silvertown. This time, East End impresario and comedian Vincent Hayes has completely refurbished a beautiful deconsecrated Victorian church and created an oasis of sparkling nostalgia. A three-course candle-lit meal is followed by a music hall-style entertainment with a modern twist. The theatre also reaches out into the community, providing special pensioners' matinees, with cream tea served in the interval. Seating around 200 people, its essential to book a table in advance for this truly unique cockney fun palace.

Camden People's Theatre

✉ 58-60 Hampstead Road, NW1 2PY

🕙 www.cpt.dircon.co.uk

☎ (Box office) 020-7916 5878

📧 cpt@dircon.co.uk

↑ Turn left out of Warren Street station, cross Euston Road and make for Hampstead Road. The theatre is on your right.

🚇 Euston

⊖ Warren Street

P On-street parking after 6.30pm

♿ Access at ground level, with no steps. Wheelchair access into auditorium and bar. Advise box office when booking

🍸 Small licensed bar

ⓘ Tottenham Court Road shopping

Surrounded by gleaming corporate office towers, swanky modern furniture stores and a local low-rise community north of Euston Road, the Camden People's Theatre was formed in 1994 in what always feels like a concrete bunker when you venture inside. With a resident ensemble company, the aim here has always been to develop community links and create accessible theatre without necessarily relying on text-based performance. An annual Sprint festival provides a platform for emerging companies, showcasing performers who have taken part in the theatre's TONIC training sessions. As its name suggests, it's very much a community arts resource with a programme of work that reaches out to non-theatre folk. But with the noise from the traffic zooming past the Hampstead Road frontage spilling into the no-frills, no thrills bare box performance space it can be an uphill battle to concentrate on the innovations on stage.

Canal Café Theatre

✉ Above The Bridge House Pub, Delamere Terrace, W2 6ND

🕙 www.canalcafe.fsnet.co.uk

☎ (Box office) 020-7289 6054

↑ Located in the heart of London's picturesque Little Venice, right beside the canal, it can be found by leaving Warwick Avenue tube station by the right exit, carrying on up Warwick Avenue to the traffic lights, then turning right along the canal. Cross the first bridge on the left, and the Bridge House pub is on the corne.

🚇 Paddington

⊖ Warwick Avenue

P Limited canal-side parking after 6.30pm

♿ The theatre is located up a flight of steps so access is difficult

🍸 Pub downstairs, from where drinks can be taken into the auditorium; the pub also does good food

ⓘ Little Venice is outside the door

This charmingly located pub theatre is laid out in cosy cabaret style, with seating around small tables. Strangely, and annoyingly, smoking is allowed even during the performances. The long-time home of the constantly updated topical comedy show *NewsRevue* (founded in 1979, and here since 1984), presented every Thursday to Saturday evenings, the theatre also hosts other productions, often with a comedic slant, on other nights.

Chelsea Theatre

✉ World's End Place, King's Road, SW10 0DR

⌖ www.chelseatheatre.com

☎ (Box office) 0870 990 8454

✉ admin@chelseatheatre.org.uk

↑ From Sloane Square station catch a bus to World's End.

⊖ Sloane Square, then bus

P Car Park in Edith Grove.

♿ Wheelchair space available.

🎭 Licensed bar and café open before and after theatre performances

ⓘ King's Road

If the Royal Court is at the Sloane Ranger end of King's Road, the Chelsea Theatre is very much not, where you'll find the drab-looking Chelsea Theatre lurking in the shadow of a cluster of high-rise flats. Opened in 1978 as a community education centre, its bland civic architectural style makes it look more like a cross between a small lending library and a council home for the bewildered. Inside, a refurbishment has provided a café and spruced up a predictable black-box 110-seat theatre as a centre for developing new theatre writers through commissions, courses and workshops and a range of arts, education and community group activities, including a new young people's project for local kids, aiming to produce four shows a year. It's just a pity that all this activity takes place in one of the dreariest buildings in the Royal Borough of Kensington & Chelsea.

Cochrane Theatre

☎ (Box office) 020-7242 7040

✉ Southampton Row, WC1B 4AP

✉ cochranetheatre@linst.ac.uk

↑ On the corner of Southampton Row and Theobalds Road.

⊖ Holborn

P On-street parking after 6.30pm

🚲 Racks outside theatre

♿ A lift provides access to all levels. Four wheelchair spaces in auditorium

♫ Infra-red system

🎭 Licensed bar and café upstairs

The driving force behind the building of a theatre at the junction of Southampton Row and Theobalds Road in 1963 was Jeanetta Cochrane, Head of Costume Design at Central Saint Martins College of Art and Design next door, who got the London County Council to build the venue, mainly for use by theatre design students. Forty years on, this 314-seat proscenium arch theatre is part of the London Institute of Higher Education Corporation, and intermittently presents professional dance, comedy, drama and music productions as well as work by London Institute students and staff. Ballet Rambert once made its home here, as did the National Youth Theatre and Talawa, the celebrated black theatre company. It's just a pity that this attractive sixties building, with a friendly café overlooking the Southampton Row traffic, isn't used much. The seats are comfortable and the raked auditorium ensures uninterrupted views.

The Courtyard Theatre

✉ 10 York Way, Kings Cross, N1 9AA
🕮 www.thecourtyard.org.uk
☎ (Box office) 020-7833 0876
📧 tickets@thecourtyard.org.uk
↑ Within yards of the junction of York Way and Euston Road, next to King's Cross station

🚇 King's Cross, King's Cross Thameslink, St Pancras
🚌 King's Cross
P Some single yellow lines nearby.
♿ Disabled accessible auditorium
🌟 Small licensed bar
ⓘ British Library

A long entrance leading to an original open air Victorian cobbled courtyard makes this a unique fringe theatre which still retains a Dickensian atmosphere, much sought after by film companies. Founded by the Court Theatre Company in 1989, the same team behind the opening of the Finborough in 1980, the tiny premises began life in the 1890s as Malvisi's Stables, owned by the Great Northern Stable Company. Old plans show seven stables in the present theatre space, foyer and rehearsal studios. It was owned by the eponymous family until the end of World War Two and the theatre is in contact with the remaining family members (whose father was actually born in what are now theatre administration offices). Under the guiding hand of director June Abbott, this 70-seat theatre has grown into an independent professional theatre with a separate training school and a programme of work ranging from classics to the experimental. It's slap bang in the middle of seedy but furiously regenerating King's Cross. In collaboration with the King's Cross Partnership, the former air of draughty make-do-and-mend has been replaced by a complete makeover, which has transformed the front of house. New, padded bench seating has been installed in the auditorium, but the configuration changes for each production.

Drill Hall

✉ 16 Chenies Street, WC1E 7EX
🕮 www.drillhall.co.uk
☎ (Box office) 020-7307 5060
🖨 020-7307 5062
↑ Chenies Street is off Tottenham Court Road, at the Goodge Street end
🚇 Euston

🚌 Goodge Street
P Metered parking in Chenies Street before 6.30pm Monday to Saturday, free thereafter
♿ Twelve wheelchairs can be accommodated in the theatre.
🎧 Induction loop in theatre
🌟 Licensed bar

Theatrically speaking the Drill Hall was once a home to a 1970s political theatre outfit called Action Space and has since gathered a reputation as a right-on lesbian and gay venue, although it is actually a multiple-purpose off-West End arts venue that can swing lots of ways: it offers a 200-seat theatre, a new 50-seat cabaret-style "Drill Hall 2", rehearsal studios, meeting rooms, a photography darkroom and an extensive programme of courses and classes. The main theatre is wide enough to accommodate the gathered ranks of the Bloomsbury Rifles who used to drill here in Victorian days, sometimes giving productions a CinemaScope effect when viewed from the tiered banks of reserved seating. Views are uninterrupted, but these unforgiving tip-up seats are not kind to the nether regions. Downstairs, Drill Hall 2 is small and gets hot.

Etcetera Theatre

✉ Oxford Arms, 265 Camden High Street, NW1 7BU
🖰 www.etcetera-theatre.co.uk
☎ (Box office) 020-7482 4857
(Information desk) 020-7482 0378
📠 etceteratheatre@hotmail.com
↑ From Camden Town tube station turn right into Camden High Street. The Oxford Arms is on your left on the corner of Jamestown Road

🚇 Camden Road
⊖ Camden Town
P Some single yellow lines in nearby streets
♿ 20 steep stairs lead up to the theatre which is not accessible for wheelchair users. Front row seats have most legroom
🍴 Food served in pub downstairs
ⓘ Camden Lock and markets

Twice-nightly was once the rule in variety theatres, and that tradition is continued here. A two-different-plays-a-night policy, combined with occasional two-for-the-price-of-one ticketing, makes this 50-seat pub theatre unusual on the London fringe. It must be a programmer's nightmare finding enough decent product from small theatre companies with limited resources, but Artistic Director David Bidmead has kept the black-painted former function room fully booked. Apart from the playbills outside the Oxford Arms, drinkers are probably unaware of the theatrical goings on upstairs. You have to find you way through the hubbub of the bar to get to the theatre entrance at the back of the pub, where you collect tickets from a small box office before climbing a couple of flights of stairs to reach the auditorium. The bench seating is steeply raked in rows with a gangway at one end. Try and grab the end spaces for optimum comfort, especially on busy nights. At the back, you might find yourself coming face-to-face with the lighting person ensconced in a glass-fronted control room. On your way down, you're quite likely to bump into the actors, emerging from the dressing room.

Finborough Theatre

✉ 118 Finborough Road, SW10 9ED
⌖ www.finboroughtheatre.co.uk
☎ (Box office) 020-7373 3842
(Stage door) 020 7244 7439
↑ Leave Earl's Court tube by the Warwick Road (Exhibition Centre) exit, turn left, cross the lights at Old Brompton Road, and continue straight ahead. Warwick Road becomes Finborough Road, and the theatre is located on your right, above the grey-coloured 'Finborough' on the corner of Ifield Road.

⊖ Earl's Court, West Brompton
P Limited on-street parking after 6.30pm
Ġ There is no disabled access at present to the theatre, which is located up a steep and curving staircase of 23 steps. Unusually there is full disabled access to the main bar and an accessible toilet
☒ Smart café-bar downstairs – good food and designer drinks
ⓘ Earl's Court Exhibition Centre

The Finborough Arms (built in 1868) changed its name to the Finborough in 2002, when the pub underwent an expensive refurbishment in 2002 that has made it into a smart café-restaurant. The cramped little black-box that serves as the theatre upstairs, however, which was founded in 1980 is mainly untouched, and remains at the uncomfortable end of fringe theatregoing. But even if the creature comforts are few (and hot weather making it unbearable, with no air at all), the artistic standards are frequently high, makes this one of London's most consistently interesting pub venues. And with seating capacity of just 50, it's also one of the more exclusive! Since 1999, Neil McPherson has been Artistic Director.

Greenwich Playhouse Theatre

✉ St Christopher's Inn, Greenwich Station Forecourt, 189 Greenwich High Road, SE10 8JA
⌖ www.galleontheatre.co.uk
☎ (Box office) 020-8858 9256
✉ BoxOffice@Galleontheatre.co.uk
↑ The theatre is upstairs in the St Christopher's Inn adjacent to Greenwich rail station.
🚇 Greenwich

⊖ Greenwich/Cutty Sark (DLR)
P Limited on-street parking.
Ġ Wheelchair spaces by prior arrangement. Theatre is reached via a steep flight of stairs
☒ Food served in pub downstairs
ⓘ Maritime Museum, Naval College, Royal Observatory, the Cutty Sark, the Gypsy Moth tea clipper, Greenwich Park

A pub theatre with a difference, part of the backpacker's chain, St Christopher's Inn. The theatre upstairs has a track record of producing entire seasons of plays in-house, a rarity on the pub fringe where artistic directors are often just "rent collectors". Since 1995, Greenwich Playhouse has been run by the energetic Galleon Theatre Company, former residents at what used to be called the Prince Theatre. The renamed Playhouse was re-opened by the company in 2000 with new facilities and air conditioning. An entrance at one end of the pub leads to a smart box office and some steep stairs. The cool auditorium is a black box with rows of raked seating along two sides.

Hen and Chickens Theatre

✉ 109 St Paul's Road, Islington, N1 2NA
🖰 www.henandchickens.com
☎ (Box office) 020-7704 2001
↑ Located above a pub called the Hen and Chickens on Highbury and Islington corner
⊖ Highbury and Islington

P Free onstreet parking after 6.30pm
🚇 Highbury and Islington
♿ Difficult – the theatre is located at the top of a steep flight of stairs
🍴 Downstairs pub
ⓘ Upper Street, Islington, with plentiful restaurants and shopping

Tiny hothouse of a fringe theatre above a lively Islington pub, with cushioned but still uncomfortable bench seating and run by the Unrestricted View resident company. The occasional gem sometimes makes it worth the effort. Also holds comedy nights on the first and third Sundays of the month and poetry events.

Jackson's Lane Theatre

✉ 269a Archway Road, N6 5AA
🖰 www.jacksonslane.org.uk
☎ (Box office) 020-8341 4421 (Stage door) 020-8340 5226
🖨 020-8348 2424
↑ Located in a converted red brick church at the corner of Archway Road and Jackson's Lane, this arts centre is directly opposite Highgate tube station.
⊖ Highgate
P Limited street parking in nearby residential streets – the main Archway

Road is a red route. A new car share scheme aims to help by linking drivers and passengers together online. See website
♿ The box office, café, bar and theatre are fully accessible to wheelchair users. Phone theatre to discuss your requirements.
🎧 Induction loop.
🍴 'Big Daddy Kwaks' runs the vegetarian café and there's a bar, offering hot food, snacks and drinks

A thriving and diverse local arts centre that once won a Times/RIBA award for its enterprising community spirit, Jackson's Lane opened in 1975 and has since been offering a year-round programme of drama, dance, comedy and music performances from visiting companies in its comfortable village hall-like raked auditorium, with a seating capacity that can vary between125 and 163. The Lavender Room, Primrose Room, Youth Space and a Multipurpose Space are also available for meetings, training sessions, conferences, rehearsals and performances, while the vast range of classes and courses on offer makes this small but big-hearted venue a valued community treasure chest for this part of North London.

Jermyn Street Theatre

✉ 16b Jermyn Street, SW1Y 6ST
🖰 www.jermynstreettheatre.co.uk
☎ (Box office) 020-7287 2875,
(Administration) 020-7434 1443 (Stage
door) 020-7434 1443
↑ Located just off Piccadilly Circus in
Jermyn Street, take the exit for the
south side of Piccadilly from the station, and walk south on Lower Regent
Street. Jermyn Street is the first turning
on the right

⊖ Piccadilly Circus
P Very limited street parking in the area,
but after 6.30pm there is free parking
in St James Square

♿ Very difficult – there's a steep staircase
down to the box office, then further
steps down into the theatre itself

🖼 Tiny bar hatch as you enter the theatre
is open before performances and during the interval

ⓘ Piccadilly Circus

Once the changing rooms for the staff of the restaurant upstairs, Jermyn Street
Theatre is a small but perfectly formed studio theatre in the heart of the West
End that accommodates audiences in comfortable traditional theatre seating on just
six rows, with two more on the side of the stage. Since opening in August 1994, it has
become one of the most important outlets for London cabaret and small-scale musicals, but it also regularly hosts plays. Whether its one-night magic shows, cabaret
evenings or longer runs of small-scale musicals, they are passionate about theatre in
this bijou basement. Run by volunteer trustees, there's a welcome on the mat, once
you wend your way down the stairs. For best seats, we recommend the front row of
the rear block. With an aisle in front, you can stretch out a bit.

Landor Theatre

✉ Above the Landor pub, 70 Landor
Road, Clapham
🖰 www.landortheatre.co.uk
☎ (Box office) 020-7737 7276
📧 bookings@landortheatre.co.uk
↑ In the heart of Clapham, come out of
Clapham North tube station and
turn right into Landor Road. The the-

atre is a three-minute walk on the
right hand side.

⊖ Clapham North
P Limited on-street parking after
6.30pm

♿ Difficult, as theatre is located upstairs
🖼 Pub downstairs

A small pub theatre with cushioned bench seating that specialises in its own productions of small-scale musicals, as well as renting the space to other visiting companies. There's always a hubbub in the smoky downstairs pub, and you have to reach the
theatre itself – a large former function room with rows of seats usually arranged
lengthways along one side – via several flights of musty stairs. The actor's dressing
room seems to be located off here as well, so on the way in you might well bump into
one of them peeping through the curtains.

Latchmere Theatre

✉ 503 Battersea Park Road, SW11 3BW

🏮 www.latchmeretheatre.com

☎ (Box office) 020-7978 7040

↑ This south London pub theatre is above The Latchmere Pub on the corner of Latchmere Road and Battersea Park Road, near Battersea Bridge

🚆 Clapham Junction (from Victoria or Waterloo) then bus 345 or 344

⊖ Sloane Square then bus 319 towards Battersea; or South Kensington then

bus 49 or 345 towards Battersea

P Free onstreet parking on local streets after 5pm

♿ Difficult – the theatre is located up a flight of stairs into its own bar area, from where another smaller flight of stairs goes into the auditorium itself.

🍴 Pub open daily 12noon-11pm, with food served 12noon-9pm weekdays and to 8pm Saturdays and 6pm on Sundays

ⓘ Battersea Park

O riginally set up as an offshoot of the Gate Theatre in Notting Hill in 1982, the theatre was first known as the Gate at the Latchmere, and scored an instant hit when its first production, *Fear and Loathing in Las Vegas*, transferred to the West End. Several incarnations later, which included a spell when it was known as The Grace Theatre, it has recently been relaunched as The Latchmere Theatre, with a focus on new writing, as well as continuing to provide a showcase for comedians in a theatrical setting.

The Menier Chocolate Factory

✉ 51–53 Southward Street, SE1 1TE

🏮 www.menierchocolatefactory.com

☎ (Box office) 020-7378 1712

↑ Located behind the Tate Modern gallery in Southwark, a short walk from London Bridge tube station – leave by the West Side exit for Borough High Street

⊖ London Bridge

🚆 London Bridge

P Free street parking after 6.30pm, NCP car park adjacent

♿ phone box office for details

🍴 Full bar/restaurant is part of the theatre complex

P art of a building that was constructed in 1870 to house a chocolate factory, the Menier Chocolate Factory is London's latest 'found' space to offer a versatile and atmospheric theatrical environment, complete with exposed wooden beams, cast iron columns and an exposed brick interior. Laid out with seating on two sides (that can be changed, as required), seating capacity is surprisingly large; if an adventurous artistic policy complements the uniqueness the space, this theatre could become a major player.

Millfield Theatre

✉ Silver Street, Edmonton, N18 IPJ
🖥 www.millfieldtheatre.co.uk
☎ (Box office) 020-8807 6680
📧 info@millfieldtheatre.co.uk
↑ Silver Street loops off the North Circular Road just east of the Great Cambridge Roundabout junction with A10
🚌 Silver Street
⊖ Turnpike Lane, Arnos Grove, Bounds

Green
P Free car parking facilities
♿ Level access to the auditorium, box office, bar, toilets and car park. Limited number of wheelchair users in the auditorium
🎧 Infrared or loop sound amplification hearing systems in auditorium
★ Licensed bar

W ith up to 362 seats (depending on the stage layout), the Millfield Theatre is a small but important performance venue in the London Borough of Enfield. A non-profit-making company, Millfield Arts Trust, which presents a broad-based programme of drama, dance, musicals, cabaret, music, children's events and an ever-popular Christmas pantomime, jointly manages both the theatre and the Millfield House Arts Centre of which it is a part.

New End Theatre

✉ 27 New End, Hampstead, NW3 IJD
🖥 www.newendtheatre.co.uk
☎ (Box office) 020-7794 0022, (Stage door) 020-7472 5803, (Administration) 020-7472 5803
↑ Located in the heart of Hampstead Village, turn right on leaving Hampstead tube station and walk up the hill till you reach New End. Turn right, and the theatre is halfway down the block on the left, next door to a pub

⊖ Hampstead
P The streets in the immediate vicinity are all residents only up to 8pm, but there are free spaces in the High Street from 6.30pm.
🚌 HampsteadHeath
♿ There are two steps up to the box office and foyer but then level access into the auditorium. There is an adapted toilet.
★ Little upstairs bar
ⓘ Hampstead Heath and Village

I t was here that Karl Marx was laid out in what are now the theatre's administration offices, for this building, constructed in 1890 was originally the mortuary for the former New End Hospital. Since 1974, however, the place has been more alive than dead and has been a thriving local fringe theatre, where local artists like Judi Dench and her late husband Michael Williams have appeared, and the likes of Ken Russell have directed. New seating, in steeply raked rows, is more comfortable than before, but the legroom is dismal – and the air-conditioning non-existent!

Old Red Lion Theatre

✉ 418 St John Street,, EC1V 4NJ
🖰 www.oldredliontheatre.co.uk
☎ (Box office) 020-7837 7816
↑ Located in Islington, turn left on exiting Angel tube station, and walk straight ahead. After crossing the lights, the theatre is above the Old Red Lion pub a minute away.
🚇 King's Cross and then a bus up to Angel, or a 20 minute walk

⊖ Angel
P Limited onstreet parking is available after 6.30pm; from 7pm, the 'red route' immediately outside the theatre is also available to park on
♿ The theatre is located up a flight of steps, so access is difficult, though there is level access to the pub
🍴 Downstairs pub
ⓘ Islington shopping and markets

Founded in 1979, this quintessential (and sometimes, essential) small upstairs pub theatre has bizarre seating in what look like old wooden church pews, arranged in a L-shape around the tiny stage. Despite cushioning, they are a hard sit. Though standards are variable, you might, if you're lucky, catch the occasional gem – interesting names have passed through its doors. And the occasional production has even transferred to the West End.

Oval House Theatre

✉ 52-54 Kennington Oval, SE11 5SW
🖰 www.ovalhouse.com
☎ (Box office) 020-7582 7680
📧 bookings@ovalhouse.com
↑ From Oval station, turn left into Kennington Oval. The theatre is on your left on the corner of Harlyford Street
⊖ Oval
P Unrestricted on-street parking after 6.30pm. Disabled drivers may use staff

car park
♿ Downstairs theatre, cafe, foyer and toilets are wheelchair accessible. Staff help required for Upstairs Theatre. Free entrance for wheelchair user's companion
🎧 Induction loop in both theatres
🍴 Small café serving homely meals
ⓘ The Oval cricket ground, Kennington Park

Lambeth is famous for many things: Charlie Chaplin and its walk for starters. It also has a well-known cricket ground overlooking the Oval House where the two studio theatres – one tiny 50-seater upstairs, the other 100-seater downstairs – are uninspiring open spaces with stackable seats arranged to suit the production. Performance is the focus of the arts activities taking place in this former South London youth centre, where you'll catch up on emerging talent and visiting companies, mostly with a worthy women's, lesbian, black or gay slant. Exhibitions, other events, youth arts classes, workshops and a kids' summer school are regularly held here and the café usually has some tasty home cooking on the go to round off your multicultural experience.

Pleasance Theatre and Pleasance Stage Space

✉ Carpenters Mews, North Road, Islington, N7 9EF

🖰 www.pleasance.co.uk

☎ (Box office) 020-7609 1800

📧 tickets@pleasance.co.uk

↑ From Caledonian Road tube, turn left. North Road is on your left. Keep going until you reach Carpenters Mews on your left

🚊 Caledonian Road & Barnsbury

⊖ Caledonian Road

P Local street parking from 6.30pm.

♿ Theatre is reached via a long cast iron staircase.

🍴 Licensed bar serving snacks. Full menu at Shillibeers restaurant and bar next door

Located at the less salubrious end of Islington in a cobbled courtyard shared with Shillibeers bar and restaurant, the independently run 300-seat Pleasance is tucked away up a cast iron staircase just off the wasteland end of Caledonian Road. Before Pleasance founder Christopher Richardson hit on the idea of turning it into a sister theatre to the Pleasance Edinburgh, the building was the timber store for the London Omnibus Company, and later became a home for the Circus Space. The reinvention of the building was completed in 1996, and a home created for a wide, varied and often risk-taking programme of plays and musicals, many co-produced with other commercial managements. Padded seats are banked in long rows in a well-raked auditorium. All of the seats have good views. The new Pleasance Stage Space is an intimate 54-seater showcasing new writing and the latest up-and-coming comedy talent.

Rosemary Branch Theatre

✉ 2 Shepperton Road,, N1 3DT

🖰 www.rosemarybranch.co.uk

☎ (Box office) 020-7704 6665

↑ The location is between Islington and Hoxton, beside the Grand Union Canal. It's a 15-20 minute walk or short bus ride from three different tube stations. From Old Street, take 76, 141 or 271 buses, or walk north on New North Road, cross the canal, turn right on Baring Street and walk ahead until you meet the junction of Southgate Road. From Angel, take 38, 56, 73 or 171A buses, or turn right into Upper Street, and when you reach Islington Green, take the right fork down Essex Road until you reach New North Road; turn right, then left when you reach Shepperton Road. From Highbury and Islington, take the 271 bus, or walk down New North Road until you reach Shepperton Road on your right

⊖ Old Street, Angel, Highbury & Islington (see directions above)

P Free street parking in the evenings and on weekends.

🚊 Highbury & Islington (see directions above)

♿ Theatre is located up a steep flight of steps, so very difficult.

🍴 Excellent bar and restaurant as part of the pub, but doesn't serve food on weekends except for Sunday roast.

ⓘ Grand Union Canal

This Victorian pub has a long performance history – it is rumoured that Charlie Chaplin appeared here, and music hall stars Marie Lloyd and Little Titch certainly did. Nowadays, a tiny upstairs room offers a variety of entertainments on well-raked wooden chairs, decorated with beautiful hand-crafted cushion covers. The theatre is also mercifully air-conditioned, a rare feature in pub theatreland.

Shaw Theatre

✉ The Shaw Park Plaza Hotel, 100-110 Euston Road, NW1 2AJ

🕾 www.shawtheatre.com

☎ (Box office) 020-7387 6864. Theatre Hotline: 0870 730 1180

↑ The hotel and theatre are adjacent to British Library on Euston Road

🚇 St Pancras, Euston, King's Cross

⊖ Euston Square

P Meter parking on nearby streets. Car parks at Euston and St Pancras stations.

🌠 Licensed bar. Mirrors Restaurant in hotel

It's a crying shame that the Shaw has become a theatre without an audience. It's a small but comfortably designed space with excellent sightlines of a thrust stage, and it's also centrally located near the new British Library in a part of London which is sure to boom once the Eurostar arrives and King's Cross is regenerated. The Shaw got its name when it opened in 1971 as part of a new civic complex including St Pancras Library (George Bernard Shaw having once served as a local councillor). The National Youth Theatre moved in for a while, but eventually municipal pride gave way to commercial considerations and the adjoining building was turned into a four-star hotel – the Shaw Park Plaza – and the theatre refurbished. A bit like the Savoy Theatre and the almost defunct Mayfair Theatre, the Shaw found itself in bed with a luxury hotel. But productions were few and feeble and conferences made more financial sense for the owners, much to the annoyance of Camden Council that wanted it used for the "community". A planning inspector has now over-ruled Camden's ban on conferences and said that the venue should be used mostly for drama productions, but with some measure of conference use to defray the running costs and secure its long-term viability. So let's hope the Shaw will soon come out of the cold.

Tabard Theatre

✉ 2 Bath Road, Turnham Green, Chiswick, W4 1LW

☎ (Box office) 020-8995 6035

↑ One minute from Turnham Green station

🚊 Chiswick Park

⊖ Turnham Green

P Local street parking from 6.30pm.

♿ Wheelchairs users by prior arrangement.

❎ The Tabard Inn serves a menu of affordable pub meals

It's hard to believe it, but Turnham Green was once a hive of arts activity. Built in the 1880s, the utopian Bedford Park development in Turnham Green was Britain's first garden city and its Arts and Crafts movement connections gave its Victorian inhabitants a reputation for being a rather arty lot. They also had the use of a rather fine new 'local', the Tabard Inn designed by Norman Shaw, the architect of the Savoy Theatre and Scotland Yard. The Inn, with its William Morris details and gleaming wall tiles, is still open for business and the locals still have an arty ambassador in the form of the Tabard Theatre, a small 49-seat theatre which opened in 1985 as a writers' venue. and which was saved from closure in 1999 by the ambitious Two Colour Theatre Company. Under the guidance of Hamish Gray it has continued to present a mixed programme of in-house productions and outside visiting companies. Hiding behind shrubs and bushes, this is a sylvan location for a fringe theatre. Better still, enjoy a pre-show meal in one of the most unusual 'locals' anywhere in London.

The Lion and Unicorn Theatre Club

✉ The Lion and Unicorn Pub, 42-44 Gaisford Street, Kentish Town, NW5 2ED

☎ (Box office) 020-7419 1685

📧 boxoffice@lionandunicorn.co.uk

↑ Turn left out of Kentish Town station. Gaisford Street is the third turning on the left

🚊 Kentish Town

⊖ Kentish Town

P On-street parking after 6.30pm

❎ Bar snacks in Lion and Unicorn Pub

Since August 2002 Act Provocateur has been the resident company at this scruffy back-to-basics pub theatre close to Kentish Town Road. Formed in Russia in 1985 and now UK-based, the company's leading light is bearded theatrical experimentalist Victor Sobchak. But this large side street tavern has long maintained a theatrical fringe connection. In 1995 The Red Room producing house for new writing was launched above the pub. Forget the sometimes wonky seats: this is pub fringe as it should be – innovative, alternative and scary.

Theatro Technis

✉ 26 Crowndale Road, NWI ITT
🖰 www.theatrotechnis.com
☎ (Box office) 020-7387 6617
📠 info@theatrotechnis.com
↑ From Mornington Crescent station turn right, cross Camden High Street to Crowndale Road; the theatre is five minutes walk, on your left.
🚇 Euston

⊖ Mornington Crescent
P On-street parking after 6.30pm
♿ Wheelchair spaces by arrangement. Access via side entrance.
🎧 Induction loop in auditorium
🍸 Small bar in foyer
ⓘ Camden markets

Mostly run by volunteers, this unusual fringe theatre has always had a dual function – as a performance space and a community centre. Theatro Technis goes back to 1957 when a group of Camden Town Cypriots with a theatre background set up shop in an old garage. Eventually, in 1978 the company converted its present home – a former church – into a theatre which now also offers studio hire, dance, music, film, a photographic darkroom and a welfare rights, legal and family advisory service for the many and varied ethnic communities in Camden. The plain parquet-floored auditorium has basic green plastic chairs arranged on three sides of the acting space, where classic and contemporary work of varying quality is presented. After a successful season at this 100-seat space, *The Madness of George Dubya* transferred to the West End. But, after the loss of its community funding, an appeal has been launched to improve and develop the theatre side of this North London institution.

UCL Bloomsbury

✉ 15 Gordon Street, WC1H 0AH
🖰 www.ucl.ac.uk/bloomsburytheatre
☎ (Box office) 020-7388 8822
🖨 020-7383 4080
📠 j.maisey@ucl.ac.uk (Box Office Manager)
↑ The theatre is a short walk from Euston Square tube station

🚇 Euston, St Pancras, King's Cross
⊖ Euston Square
P Meter parking on nearby streets. Car parks at Euston and St Pancras stations
♿ Two wheelchair spaces
🎧 Infrared hearing system in auditorium
🍸 Licensed bar. Bloomsbury Theatre Cafe adjacent to box office

They proudly proclaim that you get unrestricted views from all 550 seats at the UCL Bloomsbury Theatre. They are right. The leg room is ample, there are no pillars and they'll even give you a free ticket to another show if you think a production is not up to scratch. Opened in 1968 as the "Collegiate Theatre", it was became the "Bloomsbury" in 1982, (although it still retains its links with the nearby University College London campus). Today you can see professional music, drama and film productions, there's a gallery space squeezed in to the lively bar and foyer areas, and this is one of the best auditoriums for stand-up comedy in town.

Union Theatre

✉ 204 Union Street, SE1

🖰 www.uniontheatre.freeserve.co.uk

☎ (Box office) 020-8261 9876

↑ Union Street is directly opposite Southwark tube station – cross at the lights and walk straight ahead, and the theatre is on the left just after you go under a railway bridge.

🚇 Waterloo (exit on Waterloo Road, turn right, and then left onto The Cut; walk past the Old Vic and the Young Vic until you get to Blackfriars Road, go straight ahead into Union Street)

⊖ Southwark

P ample free street parking after 6.30pm

♿ Level access to the foyer and bar, and into auditorium.

☒ Small pavement café open during the day up to 7.30pm and an indoor bar.

ⓘ A short walk to the South Bank and on to the Tate Modern and Shakespeare's Globe

This very basic fringe theatre, located underneath a railway arch, can be cold and damp, but can also be redeemed by strong productions from the array of small fringe companies that regularly hire it. A pleasant wooden bar is an improbable luxury in the midst of the bleak surroundings.

Upstairs At The Gatehouse Theatre

✉ The Gatehouse Pub, junction of Hampstead Lane and North Road, Highgate, N6 4BD

🖰 www.upstairsatthegatehouse.com

☎ (Box office) 020-8340 3488, (Stage door) 020-7387 2342, (Administration) 020-7387 2342

↑ Located in Highgate Village, a ten-minute walk up Southwood Lane from Highgate tube station

⊖ Highgate, or Archway (then bus 143, 210, or 271 up Highgate Hill)

P Onstreet parking after 6.30pm or all day Sunday

🚇 Highgate, or Archway (then bus 143, 210, or 271 up Highgate Hill)

♿ The theatre is located up a flight of steps, so access is difficult

☒ Pub and pub grub downstairs

ⓘ Hampstead Heath, Highgate Village, Highgate Cemetery

Self-styled as London's "top theatre", as the pub of which it is a part of is 446 ft above sea level! Probably the oldest pub in Highgate – records date from 1670 – it was renovated in 1905 in the mock-Tudor style we see today. The auditorium that now houses the theatre opened in 1895 as "a place suitable for balls, Cinderellas and Concerts" and its various uses have included a music hall, a cinema, a Masonic Lodge and a jazz and folk club. Now run by Ovations Theatre Limited's John and Katie Plews, it is one of London's most welcoming and professionally-run fringe theatres, though the onstage standards don't always match the offstage ones. Seating is on three sides, but the centre block enjoys the best views.

Warehouse Theatre Croydon

✉ Dingwall Road, Croydon, CR0 2NF
🖰 www.warehousetheatre.co.uk
☎ (Box office) 020-8680 4060
📠 warehouse@dircon.co.uk
↑ Exit right from East Croydon station. Dingwall Road is the first turning on your right.
🚇 East Croydon
P Limited local on-street parking in

Dingwall Road.
♿ Unable to offer wheelchair access.
🎧 Induction loop.
🏩 Licensed bar is open all day (11am - 11pm) Monday-Friday, on Saturdays the bar opens at 7pm and on Sundays at 4pm. During some productions there is a special pre-show menu.

Up to six in-house productions a year, an annual International Playwriting Festival Theatre, education and outreach programmes, writers' workshops, a bar popular with Croydon commuters – just how much activity can you squeeze into a miniscule studio theatre? Even more intriguing, how do you achieve all of this and champion new and established writers in a building that worked well as a Victorian cement warehouse, but is now falling apart at the seams? Since 1985, when he took over as artistic director, Ted Craig has achieved the impossible and turned the Warehouse into a South London powerhouse, keeping audience loyalty while launching the career of many successful writers – for much of the time without proper Arts Council funding. The long-running drama over finding new premises seems never ending, although a final scene must be looming as the site is due for redevelopment. In the meantime, despite the uncertainty and its physical ailments, the Warehouse is always a treat to visit. The indomitable staff are always cheery, the 100-plus seat upstairs auditorium is always cozy – except when it rains or if it's just too hot in warm weather – and the always-busy and newly extended bar, on the site of the old stables, is itself a local institution.

White Bear Theatre Club

✉ 138 Kennington Park Road, SE11 4RB
☎ (Box office) 020-7793 9193
↑ Two minutes from Kennington tube station – turn right when you exit, and the theatre is on your right, behind the White Bear pub.
🚇 Kennington

P Beware the red route the theatre is located on, but after 7pm you can park on it free of charge.
♿ A few steps up to the pub, then level access inside the pub to the theatre itself.
🏩 Pub bar

This tiny but appealing fringe theatre, with seating for fewer than 50 on two sides of an L-shaped auditorium, was established in 1988 and has played an important role in nurturing various budding careers of actors, directors and playwrights. A rough and ready Kennington pub is the less-than-welcoming foyer, but the theatre itself is a treat.

Wimbledon Studio Theatre

✉ 103 The Broadway, Wimbledon, SW19
1QG

☎ (Box office) 020-8540 0362

↑ Turn left after exiting from Wimbledon Station. After a five-minute walk you will see Wimbledon Theatre on your right. The Studio entrance is at one side of the theatre in The Broadway

🚇 Wimbledon

⊖ Wimbledon

P Car parking available next to Wimbledon Theatre in Russell Road and Hartfield Road.

♿ Lift access for wheelchairs from The Broadway

🔲 Tiny licensed bar

ⓘ Wimbledon Lawn Tennis Club

For years a dance hall, where legend has it Fred Astaire once appeared, the Wimbledon Studio Theatre has recently come under the management of Wimbledon Theatre. Since 1987, the enterprising Attic Theatre Company has programmed this intimate 80-seat venue with everything from one-night comedy gigs to straight plays, musicals and children's shows. After running into a cash crisis Wimbledon Civic Theatre Trust, which ran the theatres, was forced to close them both but The Ambassador Theatre Group (ATG), the second biggest theatre group in the West End, has taken over the theatre. With backing like this, the Studio could take on a new lease of life.

Outside Central London

Bromley: Churchill Theatre

✉ High Street, Bromley, Kent BR1 1HA

⌂ www.theambassadors.com/churchill

☎ (Box office) 020-8460 6677

↑ From Bromley South station follow the signs to the Glades Shopping Centre

🚊 Bromley South

P Limited on-street parking. Car parks nearby at Beckenham Lane and Civic Centre

♿ Direct access from Foyer to Circle for nine wheelchair users

Very much a community asset for leafy Bromley, this spacious air-conditioned theatre seats 785 in deluxe style, offering uninterrupted views from both the Stalls and the Circle. It was built by Bromley Council after Bromley's New Theatre was destroyed by fire in 1971 and was officially opened in 1977 by HRH The Prince of Wales. Since April 2000 it has been managed by the Ambassador Theatre Group, presenting a mixed bag of popular plays, musicals, comedies and dramas that often begin their touring life here and transforming the Churchill into a major producing venue.

Chichester: Chichester Festival Theatre & Minerva Theatre

✉ Oaklands Park, Chichester, West Sussex, PO19 4AP

⌂ www.cft.org.uk

☎ (Box office) 01243 781312 (Stage door) 01243 784437

↑ Located in the small Roman-founded cathedral city in West Sussex in the Sussex Downs. By Road – M3/A3 and A29, A259 and A24 connect Portsmouth, Southampton, mid-Sussex and London. The roads to London are quite windy – a pleasant country drive by day, but you have to concentrate at night! For printable directions, contact the website.)

🚊 Chichester, 15 minutes walk away, with direct connections to and from London Victoria

P Car parking: 900 space pay-and-display car park adjoins the theatre, free after 5pm weekdays and 4pm on Saturday. Allow plenty of time on Saturday matinee days, as you need

to compete with city shoppers for space

♿ Allocated wheelchair and companion seats available

🎧 Free Sennheiser units from programme/disability access point in the Festival Theatre and front-of-house staff in Minerva. Sign-language interpreted performances are given for all productions

👁 Blind/visually impaired patrons: Audio described performances are given for all productions. Guide dogs are welcome in the Festival Theatre only, not the Minerva

🍴 Food and bars – Full meal service is available at Leith's Restaurant in the Minerva complex; and light menu in the Gallery Café (on the first floor of the Minerva). Advance booking recommended for both, 01243 782219. Or bring your own picnic hamper, or pre-book one from the theatre.

ⓘ Nearest seaside town: Bognor Regis. Goodwood House and Estate, home to the Dukes of Richmond and Gordon for over three centuries, is to the north of Chichester, 01243 755040.

Shop: in Minerva Theatre foyer offers books, gifts, cards and souvenirs.

Backstage Tours: Every Saturday at 11am. Book through the box office.

Laurence Olivier combined his job as first director of the National Theatre with being the first director at Chichester when it opened its doors in 1962, and duly used the latter to provide the nucleus of his company and established the reputation of both. The 1,206-seat Festival Theatre was the first modern theatre to be built in this country with an open thrust stage, around which the audience are seated on three sides. The studio Minerva, which follows a similar layout but in much more intimate terms, seats up to 283 people, and was added in 1989 in a new complex that also contains the theatre's main restaurant, Gallery Café and a theatre shop.

In the summer months, from May to late September, Chichester functions as a leading producing theatre. Previously reputed for starry productions of classics, revisiting recent new plays, and the occasional British premiere (often of an American-originated musical), a new triumvirate of artistic directors took over in 2003 and with their first "themed" season, seem to have succeeded in putting the "festival" back into the theatre's name, giving the place a sense not only of occasion but also of cohesion. In the winter, it is largely a receiving house for touring product.

Best seat in the house:

Chichester's loyal local audience book well ahead, so the best seats might be gone. But if you can plan ahead, it is best to sit centrally in the main house – the side seats offer distorted angles – though the problem isn't as acute in the side seats of the more intimate Minerva.

Croydon: Ashcroft Theatre

✉ Fairfield, Park Lane, Croydon, CR9 9EE

🖰 www.fairfield.co.uk

☎ (Box office) 020-8688 9291

🖳 info@fairfield.co.uk

↑ Turn right when exiting from East Croydon station. Fairfield is on your left a few minutes walk away

🚇 East Croydon

P Car park outside Fairfield Hall

♿ Spaces for four wheelchair users at the rear of the upper stalls. Limited parking for Orange Badge holders immediately outside the building, by arrangement with the box office

🎧 Infrared induction loop

🖐 Selected sign language performances

🍽 Licensed bar. Green Room restaurant.

Croydon – England's tenth largest town – is dominated by an office block skyline, the Whitgift shopping centre, commuters, trams and chic bars. Kate Moss went to school here and Roy Hudd, Martin Clunes and David Bowie were Croydon-born, as was Dame Peggy Ashcroft – hence the name of the Ashcroft Theatre which is part of the multi-purpose Fairfield Hall. When it was opened in 1962 by the Queen Mother this was state-of-the-art leisure – the largest entertainment complex between London and the South Coast. These days the 763-seat Ashcroft, with its excellent sightlines, presents Croydon with a constant cavalcade of touring (and local amateur) productions of drama, musicals, ballet, opera, children's shows, pantomime, concerts, films, conferences and product launches.

Greenwich: Greenwich Theatre

✉ Crooms Hill, SE10 8ES

🖰 www.greenwichtheatre.org.uk

☎ (Box office) 020-8858 7755 (Stage door) 020-8858 4447

🖳 020-8858 8042

🖂 boxoffice@greenwichtheatre.org.uk

↑ Located on the edge of Greenwich Park, a five-minute walk from Greenwich station

🚇 Greenwich (from Charing Cross or London Bridge); or via Docklands Light Railway to Cutty Sark or Greenwich Stations

⊖ Jubilee Line – change at Canary Wharf for DLR services to Lewisham, or con-

tinue to North Greenwich and catch a bus to complete your journey

P Pay and display car park in Park Row (off Romney Road); or limited street parking in area

♿ There is full access to the Bar & Cafe via a new wheelchair lift and there is a wheelchair-accessible toilet on the ground floor. Only two wheelchairs can be accommodated per performance, so early booking is advised; transfer seats are available if preferred

🎧 Sennheiser Infrared Audio system – collect equipment from the cloakroom staff

👁 A limited number of seats are kept at

the front for people who are visually impaired – please ask when booking Guide dogs are welcome and brochures are available in large print.

★ Excellent bar and café beyond the box office

ⓘ Greenwich Park and Observatory (with the Greenwich Meridian passing through it); Royal Maritime Museum; Cutty Sark; foot tunnel to the Isle of Dogs

The first theatre on this site, established in 1855, was The Rose and Crown Music Hall – a name that now lives on in the pub next door to the theatre – and survived through various ownership and name changes until the Second World War, when an incendiary bomb crashed through the roof. Thereafter, it remained empty until plans were drawn up for its demolition in 1962; but a local campaign was launched to restore it. Plans to retain parts of the old building had to be shelved, however, when the removal of the fly tower caused the walls to begin to split, and instead, a completely new theatre was planned in its place. The building that resulted opened in 1969, and the theatre soon became established as a major London producing theatre that attracted stars from Mia Farrow to Glenda Jackson, Felicity Kendal and Max Wall, and from where productions like *Another Country*, starring the then-unknown Rupert Everett and Kenneth Branagh, were launched before transferring to the West End. But in 1997, its run of success ended when local funding was withdrawn and the theatre was forced to close. Happily, this was not permanent, and since it re-opened in 1999, it has become mainly a local receiving house, though director Hilary Strong has ambitious plans to focus it as a centre for developing new musicals through an annual 'Musical Futures' season of developmental work and full-scale productions.

Best seat in the house:

The 421 seats are laid out in three steeply raked sections on one level. The centre block or side aisle seats afford the best views.

Guildford: Yvonne Arnaud Theatre

✉ Millbrook, Guildford, Surrey GU1 3UX

🖱 www.yvonne-arnaud.co.uk

☎ (Box office) 01483 440000 (Stage door) 01483 440077

🖳 01483 440792

📧 box office@yvonne-arnaud.co.uk

↑ The theatre is on the A281 Horsham Road and is a 15-minute walk from Guildford station

🚇 Guildford

P Town centre car parks close to theatre

♿ Lift to the Circle and space for one wheelchair in the Stalls. A wheelchair may be borrowed free of charge. There is an adapted toilet on the ground floor

🎧 Infrared induction loop

🍴 Harlequin Restaurant (best to pre-book), Riverbank Café, Foyer and Circle bars

It's a sure bet that if you asked them, most Guildfordians couldn't name one single play starring French-born actress Yvonne Arnaud, who was a West End star living near Guilford and who died in 1958. But anyone will be able to direct you to the Yvonne Arnaud Theatre, pleasantly located on an island on the River Way close to the hilly town centre. A local landmark, this welcoming amphitheatre, with a raked auditorium providing universally good sightlines, was built by public subscription in 1965 and now presents a wide variety of shows and plays, often starrily cast and en route for the West End, plus films and music events. The 590-seat theatre also boasts an excellent restaurant and an 80-seat studio theatre, The Mill, located next door in the former 18th century Old Town Mill where the Youth Theatre meets and a programme of small-scale plays provides an alternative to the main house's mostly Home Counties fare.

Hammersmith: Carling Apollo Hammersmith

✉ Queen Caroline Street, W6 9QH

⌐ www.cclive.co.uk

☎ (Box office) 0870 606 3400

🖶 020-8846 9320

↑ Located right on the massive traffic roundabout, just under the flyover that takes cars to the M4. The District and Piccadilly line tube brings you straight into the Broadway centre, from where an underground pedestrian subway connects directly to the Apollo; from the Metropolitan branch of the Hammersmith & City line, you need to cross first to the Broadway centre and then proceed through it to the underground subway.

⊖ Hammersmith

P Free parking on local streets after 6.30pm. Car park on Glenthorne Road.

&. Wheelchair access through side exit door. Space for two wheelchairs plus two helpers at rear of Stalls. No guide dogs allowed in auditorium but staff will dog sit.

⌒ No facilities at present for the hard of hearing

◨ Three large licensed bars, two in the entrance foyer and one in the Circle foyer. All drinks served in plastic glasses so that customers can take them into the auditorium. Also serves a range of hot and cold snacks, ice cream and confectionary.

What's in name? It's vast streamlined frontage is mostly obscured by Hammersmith Flyover, but the Carling Apollo Hammersmith is still like a 1930s super cinema both inside and out, even though the last film was screened here in 1984. But it's never really been sure if it's the Labbatt's Apollo (1990s), the Hammersmith Odeon (1962), the Hammersmith Gaumont (1946) or the Gaumont Palace, as it was called when it opened on Easter Monday 1932 with a film programme preceded by cine-variety backed by the Gaumont Palace Symphony Orchestra and augmented by the Compton organ. Architect Robert Cromie, who was in charge of the 1922 re-build of the Theatre Royal Drury Lane and also designed the Prince of Wales Theatre, has left behind a 3,485-seat leviathan, best suited for pop concerts (the Beatles famously packed it for Christmas 1964), large-scale musicals and big name comedy turns, like French and Saunders.

Best seat in the house:

Always sit in the front blocks, otherwise you might as well be watching from Barnes. You are also less likely to be distracted by the constant stream of boozers popping out to the bars for another plastic glass of foaming Carling.

Hayes: The Beck Theatre

- ✉ Grange Road, Hayes, 2UE UB3
- ✆ www.cclive.co.uk/becktheatre or www.tickets-direct.co.uk
- ☎ (Box office) 020-8561 8371
- ↑ The theatre is set back from Grange Road, which is a turning off Uxbridge Road
- 🚉 Hayes & Harlington
- ⊖ Hillingdon

- P Car parking next to theatre
- ♿ The Beck once won Hillingdon Council's Access Award for its excellent resources for disabled and elderly people. Call box office for access details.
- ∩ Infrared induction loop
- 🌟 Licensed bar, restaurant and function rooms

After the deluge of cars on the Uxbridge Road you turn off for the Beck and suddenly the ozone vanishes, there's no traffic and you are in parkland territory with a pond, a fountain and the Beck. This intimate 600-seat multi-functional theatre is 25 years old and under the management of Clear Channel Entertainment UK presents one night concerts, drama, comedy, dance, musicals, children's shows, films, pantomimes, am-dram productions, is home to The Beck Youth Theatre and remains a popular conference venue with a fully licensed bar, restaurant and function rooms, the large foyer doubling as an additional performance space. It might be sequestered in quiet woodland, but everyone who is anyone has played the Beck – from Noddy to Eartha Kitt.

Hornchurch: The Queen's Theatre Hornchurch

- ✉ Billet Lane, Hornchurch, RM11 1QT
- ✆ www.queens-theatre.co.uk
- ☎ (Box office) 01708 443333
- 📧 info@queens-theatre.co.uk
- ↑ The theatre is next to Sainsbury's in Billet Lane. Catch a bus or a taxi from Emerson Park, Upminster or Romford Stations
- 🚉 Emerson Park/Romford
- ⊖ Upminster
- P Free car park adjacent to the theatre.

- ♿ Limited spaces for four wheelchair users. Reserved parking spaces for Orange and Blue Badge holders at the front of the building with a ramp giving wheelchair access from street level to the Box Office and auditorium
- ∩ Infrared induction loop
- 𝔇 One sign language performance for each repertory production.
- 🌟 Café and Green Room bar

Hornchurch without a theatre would be like the Queen without a crown. This 500-seat purpose-built theatre located in the heart of Essex-London border country was opened in 1975 by Sir Peter Hall, continuing a theatre tradition which began in 1953 with a weekly rep company based in a former cinema turned furniture store. A glorious 50-year history has been marked by West End transfers and closure threats, but under the artistic direction of Bob Carlton the Queen's has returned to its rep roots and is now home to the vibrant Cut to the Chase – the UK's only resident company of actor-musicians who present a popular programme of plays and musicals in a people-friendly theatre with an open stage auditorium that is always worth the effort to reach, even if it's near the end of the dawdling District Line.

Richmond: Richmond Theatre

✉ The Green, Richmond, Surrey, TW9 1QJ

🖰 www.richmondtheatre.net

☎ (Box office) 020-8940 0088, (Information desk) 020-8939 9277

🖷 020-8948 3601

📧 richmondboxoffice@theambassadors.com

↑ Located on a quiet corner of Richmond Green, it is a three minute walk from Richmond railway and tube station.

🚇 Richmond (20 minutes from Waterloo)

⊖ Richmond

P Free parking on Richmond Green and the Old Deer Park after 6.30pm

♿ Stalls, stalls bar and an adapted toilet are accessible to wheelchair users

🎧 Infrared hearing system, headsets available from the cloakroom in the foyer on payment of returnable deposit

👁 Guide dogs are welcome in the theatre

🍸 Bars on all levels of the theatre

It's something of a surprise that one of London's most beautiful, and beautifully restored, Victorian theatres isn't to be found in the West End at all but further afield, at the end of the District Line at Richmond in Surrey. It also operates a touring programme of visiting productions of shows that arrive for week-long runs that you might see on their way to or from the West End, which makes it a useful place to either catch something first ahead of the rest of London, or the touring cast of something you might have missed when it was in town (or want to see again). Either way, there is hardly anywhere nicer in London to see a show. One of a handful of surviving London theatres designed by the great Victorian theatre architect Frank Matcham (his other London buildings include the London Palladium and Coliseum, the Victoria Palace and the Hackney Empire), it opened in 1899, as the Theatre Royal and Opera House. It was built originally for drama and music – hence the decoration of scenes from Shakespeare plays in the theatre's ornate plasterwork ceiling – though it would later become a variety house. The theatre had been in more or less constant use since it opened, except for a £4.5million refurbishment in 1991 that restored it comprehensively and means that it will continue to delight current and new generations of theatregoers.

Best seat in the house:
The elegant but cramped dress circle seems to be the favoured top price place to sit here, but for a bargain and more legroom, the second-price side stalls bring you surprisingly close to the action.

Stratford-Upon-Avon: The Royal Shakespeare Theatre and Swan Theatre

✉ Waterside, Stratford-upon-Avon, CV37 6BB

🖰 www.rsc.org.uk

☎ (Box office) 0870 609 1110, (Information desk) 01789 403444

🖶 01789 403413

↑ Located in the Warwickshire town of Stratford-upon-Avon – where William Shakespeare was born and died – the base of the Royal Shakespeare Company has three theatres, the 1,412-seater Royal Shakespeare Theatre, the 432-seater Swan Theatre, and a flexible studio theatre, The Other Place (currently not open for public performances).

🚃 From Paddington, via Oxford. Call 08457 484950 for details of all national rail services to Stratford.

P There are a limited number of spaces outside the RST, but numerous spaces in the pay and display Recreation Car Park on South Side of the River Avon and Church St. Car Park

♿ Contact 020-7256 7504 or e-mail access@rsc.org.uk for details

🎧 Sign language interpreted and open captioned performances offered for most productions

🍽 First floor restaurant, Quarto's, overlooks the Avon; modern café bar, 1564, is a self-service restaurant

ⓘ Shakespeare's birthplace, grave, school and other landmarks

The Shakespeare Memorial Theatre – Stratford's first permanent theatre dedicated to performing Shakespeare – was built in 1879, but destroyed by fire in 1926; the current imposing redbrick theatre, designed by Elisabeth Scott, was erected in 1932. Beautifully situated alongside the river Avon, it became the Royal Shakespeare Theatre after Peter Hall founded the Royal Shakespeare Company in 1960 here. In 1974, the Other Place was created in a tin hut and later replaced, in 1991, by a purpose-built studio theatre, though it is not currently being used for public performances. In 1986, the site of the original Memorial Theatre was converted into the Swan Theatre.

Former RSC artistic director Adrian Noble announced controversial plans to demolish and replace the Royal Shakespeare Theatre, but these plans have now been put on hold with the arrival of new artistic director Michael Boyd.

Though Shakespeare is a bit of a tourist industry in Stratford-upon-Avon, the RSC remains a central, serious focus for the production of his plays with a worldwide influence and reputation. Serious criticisms have been levied against the main theatre, it remains a thrilling place to see the plays with a real sense of occasion, while the Swan provides a wonderfully intimate place to see the plays of Shakespeare and his contemporaries on a thrust stage that comes right to the audience.

Best seat in the house:

The RSC sell 'Superseats' in the main Royal Shakespeare Theatre that cost £10 more than top price seats, but it's not strictly speaking necessary to lay out the extra if you can get the seats immediately around them. Watch out for restricted views in the Balcony. In the Swan, the sides of the Galleries can have distorted views.

Watford: Palace Theatre

✉ Clarendon Road, Watford, Herts, WD17 1JZ

🖱 www.watfordtheatre.co.uk

☎ (Box office) 01923 225671

📧 enquiries@watfordtheatre.co.uk

↑ Located in Watford town centre just off the High Street and a ten minute walk from Watford Junction station along Clarendon Road

🚉 Watford Junction

P Several town centre car parks close to theatre

♿ Phone for details

🎧 Infrared induction loop

𝔇 Sign language performances

👁 Audio described performances

★ Green Room Bar and Cafe

The Palace Theatre was restored in 1984 to reveal its original Edwardian opulence, and a new Green Room Bar and bistro wing added. But after the discovery of two hitherto hidden Victorian underground culverts at the rear of the building during the latest £7.5 million refurb, a grand reopening planned for Christmas 2003 was put back to the summer of 2004, by which time (funding permitting) the Palace should be getting back to what it does so well – producing its own shows in a delightful 663-seat theatre for audiences reaching from Watford's one-way system to Hertfordshire's leafy lanes and beyond, some of which transfer to the West End or tour nationally. Meanwhile, the Palace has gone back to basics and is working with other theatre companies in regional schools, arts centres and even village halls.

Regional Theatres

Despite the disproportionate press attention that is lazily lavished on London since that's where the national press is largely based, the British theatre doesn't begin and end in the capital.

There's a whole separate book to be compiled of Britain's extensive network of regional theatres and arts centres that also play a crucial developmental role in developing the careers of writers, directors, actors and crafts people as well as producing important work in their own right.

But any guide to London's Theatreland has to at least acknowledge the vibrant theatrical culture that co-exists with what's happening in the capital – and often feeds London stages with some of its liveliest work.

There are variously important producing theatres (ie venues that produce their own work to an artistic policy), as opposed to receiving houses (ie. venues that merely act as temporary homes for touring productions that have begun their lives elsewhere) all around the country.

Below is a list, not intended to be comprehensive, of some of the best of these that are consistently worth checking out.

Belfast: Lyric Theatre

✉ 55 Ridgeway Street, Belfast, BT9 5FB   ☎ (Box office) 028 9038 1081
🖰 www.lyrictheatre.co.uk

Birmingham: Repertory Theatre

✉ Broad Street, Centenary Square,   ☎ (Box office) 0121 236 4455
Birmingham, B1 2EP
🖰 www.birmingham-rep.co.uk

Bolton: Octagon Theatre

✉ Howell Croft South, Bolton, BL1 1SB   ☎ (Box office) 01204 520661
🖰 www.octagonbolton.co.uk

Bristol: Old Vic

✉ King Street, Bristol, BS1 4ED   ☎ (Box office) 0117 987 7877
🖰 www.bristol-old-vic.co.uk

Colchester: Mercury Theatre

✉ Balkerne Gate, Colchester, CO1 1PT　☎ (Box office) 01206 573948
🖰 www.mercurytheatre.co.uk

Coventry: Belgrade Theatre

✉ Belgrade Square, Coventry, CV1 1GS　☎ (Box office) 024 7655 3055
🖰 www.belgrade.co.uk

Dublin: Abbey Theatre

✉ 26 Lower Abbey Street, Dublin, 1　☎ (Box office) +353 1 878 7222
🖰 www.abbeytheatre.ie

Dublin: Gate Theatre

✉ 1 Cavendish Row, Dublin, 1　☎ (Box office) +353 1 874 4045/874 5042
🖰 www.gate-theatre.ie

Edinburgh: Royal Lyceum Theatre

✉ Grindlay Street, Edinburgh, EH3 9AX　☎ (Box office) 0131 248 4848
🖰 www.lyceum.org.uk

Edinburgh: Traverse Theatre

✉ 10 Cambridge Street,, Edinburgh, EH1　☎ (Box office) 0131 228 1404
　2ED
🖰 www.traverse.co.uk

Glasgow: Citizens' Theatre

✉ Gorbals Street, Glasgow, G5 9DS　☎ (Box office) 0141 429 0022
🖰 www.citz.co.uk

Glasgow: Tron Theatre

✉ 63 Trongate, Glasgow, G1 5HB ☎ (Box office) 0141 552 4267
🖱 www.tron.co.uk

Ipswich: New Wolsey Theatre

✉ Civic Drive, Ipswich, IP1 2AS ☎ (Box office) 01473 295900
🖱 www.wolseytheatre.co.uk

Leeds: West Yorkshire Playhouse

✉ Quarry Hill, Leeds, LS2 7UP ☎ (Box office) 0113 213 7700
🖱 www.wyplayhouse.com

Leicester: Haymarket Theatre

✉ Belgrave Gate, Leicester, LE1 3YQ ☎ (Box office) 0116 253 9797
🖱 www.leicesterhaymarkettheatre.org

Manchester: Library Theatre

✉ St Peter's Square, Manchester, M2 5PD ☎ (Box office) 0161 236 7110
🖱 www.librarytheatre.com

Manchester: Royal Exchange Theatre

✉ St Ann's Square, Manchester, M2 7DH ☎ (Box office) 0161 833 9833
🖱 www.royalexchange.co.uk

Mold: Clwyd Theatre Cymru

✉ Civic Centre, Mold, CH7 1YA ☎ (Box office) 0845 330 3565
🖱 www.clwyd-theatr-cymru.co.uk

Newbury: Watermill Theatre

✉ Bagnor, Newbury, RG20 8AE   ☎ (Box office) 01635 46044
🖰 www.watermill.org.uk

Northampton: Royal Theatre

✉ Guildhall Road, Northampton, NN1 1DP   🖰 www.northamptontheatres.com
☎ (Box office) 01604 624811

Nottingham: Playhouse

✉ Wellington Circus, Nottingham, NG1 5AF   🖰 www.nottinghamplayhouse.co.uk
☎ (Box office) 0115 941 9419

Plymouth: Theatre Royal

✉ Royal Parade South, Plymouth, PL1 2TR   ☎ (Box office) 01752 267222
🖰 www.theroyal.com

Salisbury: Playhouse

✉ Malthouse Lane, Salisbury, SP2 7RA   ☎ (Box office) 01722 320333
🖰 www.salisburyplayhouse.com

Sheffield: Crucible Theatre

✉ 55 Norfolk Street, Sheffield, S1 1DA   ☎ (Box office) 0114 249 6000
🖰 www.sheffieldtheatres.co.uk

West End Map

MAP – WEST END

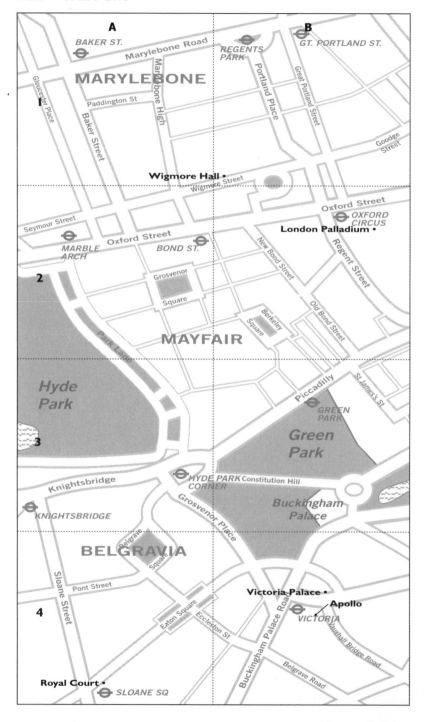

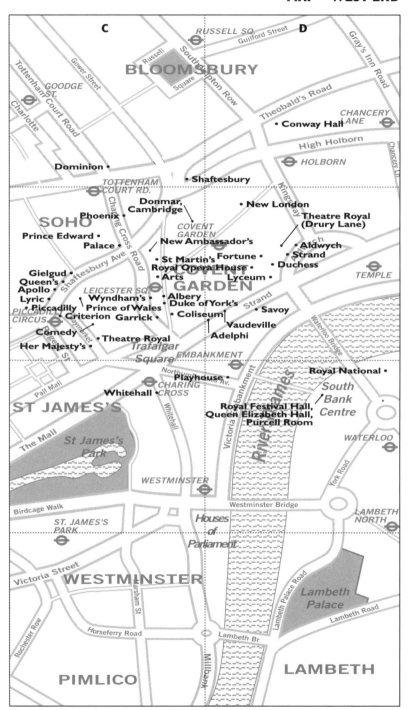

Glossary

GLOSSARY

Air Cooling/Air Conditioning
Most theatres have the former – a method of recycling and chilling warm air from the auditorium. The latter is a rarity in the West End

Auditorium
The area where the audience pays to sit and watch the show

Agent
Middleman or woman who represents the actors' interests, for a percentage of their earnings. Literary agents do the same job for playwrights. Ticket agents add their percentage to the face value of the ticket

Backstage
The unglamorous behind-the-scenes regions, including the wings, the dressing rooms, a Green Room and the stage door area

Balcony
The cheap seats, or the Gallery 'Gods', usually the top tier in the auditorium and often reached via a separate entrance

Binoculars
Release them from a coin-slot holder on the back of the seat in front of you. Depending where you are sitting, the magnification is often next to useless, so take your own opera glasses

Box Office
Usually small and cramped, this is the kiosk in the foyer where you go to book your seat

Critics
Opinionated journalist, sometimes recognisable from their shabby appearance and/or vigorous note-taking during a performance, who write about plays on press nights, and who rush off as soon as the curtain comes down to file copy for the next morning's papers, or just to get out before everyone else

Company Manager
In charge of the overall running of the production, from arranging the rehearsal space and actor's holidays to paying the wages

Comps
Free 'complimentary' tickets, sometimes issued by theatre managements and producers on first nights or previews to bump the numbers up

Director
The key creative person employed by the producer to work with the actors and the lighting, set and sound designers to transfer the play from the page to the stage

Dress Circle
Next tier up from the Stalls – and usually just as expensive. Sometimes called the Royal Circle

Dressing Room
The actors' home-from-home during a long run, where they get made up and prepare for the show. Number One dressing room nearest the stage is usually reserved for the star, though not always

Fire or Safety Curtain
Sometimes called the 'Iron', this huge fireproof curtain cuts off the auditorium from the backstage area. By law, it must be lowered and raised at least once in the presence of the audience, usually during an interval

Flies
The area above the acting area where scenery is suspended before it is lowered onto the stage

Front of House
The foyer, bars, management offices and public areas at the front of the theatre

Gallery
Another term for Balcony

Gods
The cheap seats in the Balcony or Gallery, so-called because they are so high up they almost touch the heavens

Green Room
Communal backstage room where the performers put their feet up during the performance and sometimes receive guests

House Manager
Responsible for running the theatre, the House Manager checks everything, from the usherettes and the Box Office returns to the state of the loos

House Seats
Best seats in the house kept aside for special guests, like royalty or VIPs. Sometimes sold to the public at the last minute if no-one "important" wants them

Impresario
Think 'Mr Producer', think Cameron Mackintosh, think the guy who puts up the money, takes the risk - and rakes in the profits

Infrared Audio System
Sound amplification of on-stage dialogue through headsets for the hearing impaired. The Sennheiser system is installed in many West End theatres

Legroom
The distance between the edge of your seat and the back of the seat in front is how much, or little, space there's left for your legs, and can be a major factor in how comfortable you are

Listings
Magazines like What's On In London, Time Out and the free Guardian Guide list theatres or productions in alphabetical order

Luvvie
Another word for Sir Richard Attenborough, or a synonym for Christopher Biggins

Matinee
Day time performance, usually in the mid to late afternoon

Proscenium
From the Greek: means 'before the scene'. Now used to describe the high arch separating the acting area from the auditorium and hiding the wings. In-the-round theatres are proscenium-less

Producer
The person – or nowadays, more likely group of people, or corporate organization

– who not only provide the bucks, but where the buck also stops, to put on a show

Programme
Flimsy magazine containing the cast list and biographies of everyone connected to putting the show on that you'll have to shell out up to £3 to buy (or £6 at the Royal Opera House). If you're lucky, there may be something to actually read. On Broadway, they're called Playbills and they're free

Prompt Corner
Traditionally, the place where actors who forget their lines are prompted from, but nowadays, the place where the stage manager cues everyone, from actors to sound, lighting and crew, into action – or sometimes, still, to help them to remember their lines

Rake
The surface of the stage is usually angled on a rake, or slant, to afford better views of it

Returns
When a performance is sold out, you might strike lucky by joining the 'returns queue' – awaiting the return of previously purchased tickets that their buyers no longer need

Review
The hopefully considered, but possibly unreliable, opinion of a journalist paid to see a show, stay awake and report on it afterwards

Revue
A variety or musical show constructed out of disparate sources to make a new whole

Sightlines
The term of reference used to illustrate how well you'll be able to see from where you're sitting

Stage Door
The point of access to the backstage area of the theatre, and where 'stage door Johnnies' and other fans congregate to meet the actors afterwards

Stalls
Known in the US as 'orchestra stalls', at the front of which may or may not be an orchestra pit, this is the lowest level of the auditorium, closest to the stage and usually level with it

Surtitles
For foreign-language operas or plays, a screen may be offered over the stage or on the sides offering a simultaneous text translation of what is being sung or said

Ticket
The bit of paper, usually computer-printed, that lists the exact seat location you have purchased the right to occupy tonight, and will gain you access to the auditorium to do so with

Ticket Agency
A licensed 'ticket broker' who sells tickets, usually for a greater price than the face-value of the ticket that you could have bought direct from the theatre but are sometimes unavoidable

Tabs
Originally called 'tableaux curtains' (hence the abbreviation tabs) which drew outwards and upwards, the word now applies to any stage curtain separating the auditorium from the stage

Tout
Sometimes also known as 'scalpers', touts offer difficult-to-get tickets for sold out shows at inflated prices – as much as the gap between supply and demand will bear

Understudy
Replacement actor for the person who usually plays the part, hopefully properly trained to be ready to take over at a moment's notice

Upper Circle
Third level up, sometimes known as the Grand Circle, where the air starts thinning.

Usher
The person who tears your ticket and shows you to your seat – though more often than not you'll probably have to find it yourself

Wings
Areas on each side of the stage, not visible to the audience, from where actors (and maybe some of the sets) make their entrances